MY NEW YORK

Mabel Osgood Wright

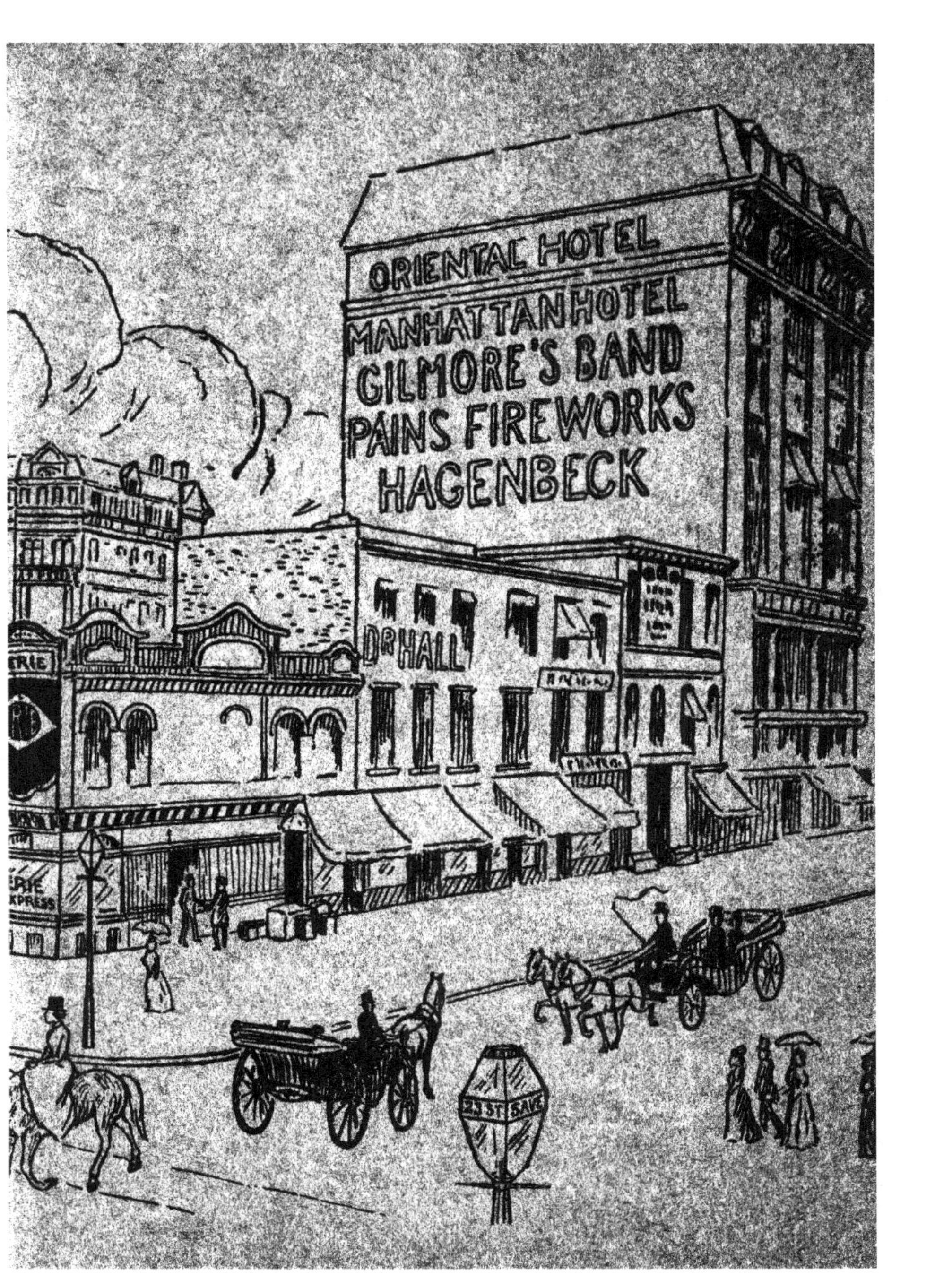
ORIENTAL HOTEL
MANHATTAN HOTEL
GILMORE'S BAND
PAINS FIREWORKS
HAGENBECK
Dr HALL
ERIE
ERIE
23 ST 5 AVE

MY NEW YORK

THE MACMILLAN COMPANY
NEW YORK · BOSTON · CHICAGO · DALLAS
ATLANTA · SAN FRANCISCO

MACMILLAN & CO., LIMITED
LONDON · BOMBAY · CALCUTTA
MELBOURNE

THE MACMILLAN COMPANY
OF CANADA, LIMITED
TORONTO

MY NEW YORK

By MABEL OSGOOD WRIGHT

Illustrated by Ivin Sickels, 2d

THE MACMILLAN COMPANY

PUBLISHERS NEW YORK

1930

SET UP AND ELECTROTYPED. PUBLISHED MAR., 1926
REISSUED MAY, 1930

PRINTED IN THE UNITED STATES OF AMERICA
BY BERWICK & SMITH CO., NORWOOD, MASS.

TO J. O. W. (EVAN)
WHO HAS GONE ON A JOURNEY IN WHICH
I SHALL PRESENTLY JOIN HIM.

M. O. W.

"If you should say,
'Who goes there?'
Then I would say,
'You go there—'
It's your hand at the door,
And your foot on the stair
Of my heart every day
And everywhere."

CONTENTS

MY NEW YORK

My New York

I

THE REASON WHY

I SAT before the hearth fire huddled deep in a well-worn divan, a souvenir that had once supported beauty, wit, and courtship, in Peter Marie's salon. Books of many sizes were wedged between the pillows, books written in many moods and chiefly about New York, the city where I was born. Solid gifts from friends were these, sent to a dweller in the real country fifty miles from town, to fortify me against loneliness of winter nights. I had been searching among the many pages for my New York, of intimate if unimportant happenings—the city that I had looked at brightly, a dominie's daughter with a seat behind the pillar, quite glad of even that sitting, for to see and not be seen gives one an independent outlook.

Names of streets and people rang true, but I often lost my way, for the little pleasant byways I had trod were missing, as were the everyday folks who trod them. No one had seemed to have known the foolish hurdy-gurdy man whose coming to the west side streets above Washington Square was as sure a sign of spring as the marbles, hoops, tops, or the tangling of our kite lines in the branches of the ailanthus trees in West Eleventh Street. Not one of them all mentioned the terrifying boom at night of the great bell in the Jefferson Market watchtower that called the firemen out on the run, at the same time that it caused me to hide my head in the bedclothes, even as thunder does to this day.

One volume among these books, smaller than the rest and less new, I had pushed away with a resentful kick. For it belied the cheerful, jumbled, after-the-Civil-War city that was, and cramped it into corsets even tighter than those of the then prevailing fashion. This book fell face upwards and the fitful flames picked out its title, *The Age of Artifice*, while the sleeping dog whimpered, growled, and started at its fall, quite in fright, as if a joyous dream of rabbit hunting had come to naught. The oldest beagle yawned and curled closer between the fire and my feet, making an uneasy footstool.

Then I forgot the printed books. Memory pictures came distinct as if in a portfolio resting on my knee, and greeted me whichever way my eyes turned. Pictures clear and lifelike as the old daguerreotypes that challenge newer art. The close walls opened, the paintings on them became people or landscapes, according to their kind. I travelled fast back to that first score of years where were the roots of life. Events stood in high relief as only such detached happenings can when the brain plate is new, clear, and unrecorded. Trifles scarce comprehended at the moment, yet ineffaceable, had been developed fully by riper interpretation.

"Make haste! Soon it will be too late and all will be forgotten or as if it had not been. Even now your friends scarcely believe that this was my really-truly-go-to-church dress, and yet it was only in 1830 that I wore it."

It was the voice of little Mother, aged nine, that spoke, little Mother in her chinchilla bonnet, sable-trimmed coat, and crimson gown, looking down from over the mantelshelf with a smile half caressing, half mischievous.

"Do you remember?" said two deeper voices from

the ivory miniatures of Mother and Father painted when they were betrothed. They faced each other, joined by a bowknot frame, a little apart from the portrait. Pleasant thoughts yet serious withal smiled from their eyes and lips.

"We were born in Boston, but we moved to New York because the climate was warmer in every way. We lived and loved and saw and heard," they explained courteously to an old colored print of Luther and his friends quite in the corner. "Oh, yes, we lived in New York in the homespun fifties, sixties, and seventies, before the listing of society began or the sheep of the Golden Fleece had crowded all the pastures."

Out in the hall the tall clock chuckled after its habit when nearly run down, and struck eleven, then went on drawling constantly, "I know, I know!" The clock would not be stilled. Yes, surely it did know many things, the most timely being that it was Saturday night, the time for winding it. This had always been a man's job until now. First Father's father in his farm housekeeping at Andover in 1792. Next Uncle Isaac, the bachelor bookworm, who baffled his maiden sisters by keeping an elaborate diary in French which completely sealed it to them. Next the clock came to live with us here in the country in the stately old home, where I loved to lean on Father's shoulder as he wound it and follow with my finger the ship, atop the pendulum, that sailed unceasingly above the dial toward the lighthouse that it never passed. Last man of all, Evan turned the crank with rapid, vigorous sweeps, making the weights knock heads as they sped upward grumbling to each other: "Who can he be who tries to hurry Time?"

I mended the fire, not heeding the clock's hint of midnight, loath to leave the pleasant company that was beginning to gather. The first score years of memory viewed from a waning threescore,—too long a bridge, do you say? Perhaps. But, no! the two are the same to those who have known love in all its phases even from the dawn of life. To these age is but a second youth of clearer vision, with those things that were of no import in the betweentime sleazed away. Happy memories are hopes that have been lived and, refusing to die, become so vital a part of a future that we know we are immortal.

Do you care to see my pictures? Look over my shoulder, then, as I finger the random pages. But pray be mellow-hearted in judgment, and above all things do not seek to prison me between dates, or try to prove that it rained on a particular day when I said the sun was shining. It might have done both—for so comes the rainbow!

II

COMPASS POINTS

STEP back a space to gain perspective. When Father, Mother, Agatha, and Beatrice were yet in Providence, where Father was pastor of the Westminster Church, before I joined the family, New York was to them a vision, a mysterious *somewhere* at the foot of the rainbow. Then came the positive call to go, the consideration and the acceptance. They were Unitarians then—Channing Unitarians, a denomination that was the rebound from the unchristian bitterness of Puritanism, illuminating with its beauty of belief (not born of dogma) and liberal culture New England's greatest minds. Its keynote was Faith—Love—Work—, the legend of Father's primitive and crudely drawn bookplate. A once vital if much misinterpreted sect this, not to be confused with the dilute and irresponsible ethical culture complex of today that branched from it.

The length, breadth, and depth the new life promised, the expansion of salary offered, seemed to be so great that all pressure, save that of acceptable work, must surely be kept at a comfortable distance. Yet when they had made the change and were temporarily settled in an odd little house in Amity Place, a by-street of Washington Square, and convenient to the Church of the Messiah on Broadway opposite Waverly Place, a fact as old as the very dawn of Protestantism was soon to be written in ineffaceable letters across their horizon. This condition, which still obtains with a few rare exceptions, is that a minister's salary is based upon a half or at most two thirds of the sum necessary to support even a family of moderate size, in accordance with the dignity required of his cloth. Can it be that this habit had its origin in a fanatical desire to keep before the cleric the Master's words, "The poor ye have always with you," thereby inculcating the most subtle form of sacrifice, scrimping those most loved, thus quite outdoing the requirements of celibacy and fasting of the Roman clergy? This deficit must be bridged by outside work, or the timely kindness and gifts from good-hearted parishioners. Dole thus takes the place of wage. Evidently another of the Master's sayings has been overlooked, "The laborer is worthy of his hire." Also to be quite acceptable to the minds that usually form the parish majority, the dominie must walk a very narrow way. Barefoot, as it were, on a knife blade, yet without visibly cutting his feet, for such a spectacle as that would be distressing to their sensibilities.

Mother evidently did not grasp the situation for many months. At this time she was a very beautiful woman, turning thirty, of graceful carriage, slender, yet curved and in no wise angular. Her eyes were large, deep set and expressive, her color brightly brunette. She was musical by temperament and voice. She had, Heaven be praised, a perfectly shaped Roman nose and a spirit to match. Without this nose she must have faltered and turned during those first few years of changed environment. With it, and a keen sense of humor, she survived and a good bit more. The church greeted her at once as a welcome novelty, while it made up its mind.

As the members of the parish were scattered all the

way from Great Jones Street to the far-away thirties, Amity Place was quite within the middle boundaries. Washington Parade Ground was a welcome open space, where one accustomed to the light and air of the Rhode Island hill city might draw a long breath. It was used variously as a park, playground, and later as training camp for the militia. About the north and west sides of the Square a colony of substantial people were gathered in ample, cheerful brick houses, and among these might be found strains of New England blood. These latter were esteemed rather newcomers by those of strictly Dutch origin whose homes, starting at the Bowling Green, had gradually backed up the Broad-way, then broken away to scatter in the cross streets. It was not more than twenty-five years before that this Square was so far out of town that it was the Potter's Field of the city, and the road leading from it to the northwest crossed marshy soil and went to Greenwich Village, quite a country resort.

Conservative in many ways, New York was yet cosmopolitan in spots and many doors opened, nay flew open, to the newcomers who were found to be genuine and free from pretense. Such a city Father and Mother found it. Then Mother especially began to pick her way among new customs. At the west side of the Square, in adjoining houses, lived the Alsops, Mr. and Mrs. H. W. Gray, and Mr. and Mrs. J. W. Haven, the ladies being sisters, of the Griswold family of solid merchants. On the northeast section lived Mrs. J. C. Green, their half-sister. In these households, except for great functions, dinner was not later than two o'clock, the men coming uptown for it and returning afterward. As late as 1873 an invitation to a formal dinner at the W. C. Bryants' reads, "at six o'clock," and at about the same time Donald G. Mitchell in giving a dinner invitation to Edgewood writes: "The hour will be two and I will call for you at one-twenty and drive you up." Which, considering that Mosswood was twenty miles from Edgewood, proves that there were other writers of the day besides the publisher Robert Bonner of *Ledger* fame who liked to drive a good horse.

Tea was a substantial evening meal, that we should now call supper, not in any wise akin to the afternoon cup. It was to these high teas that the dominie and his wife were bidden the autumn of their arrival. Such parties were also the habit in New England and all went well.

Came New Year's Day, 1850. "The year greeted us with a smile, June done in crystal . . . also a full measure of good company," Father wrote in his journal from which I now draw the happenings before my time. I do not know how far the making of New Year's calls obtained either in Boston or Providence, as Father had never mentioned it. But as a custom of Dutch origin its stronghold was naturally in New Amsterdam, and its manifestation was a complete surprise to the newly arrived minister and his wife, when over one hundred men from various walks of life, and by no means of the parish, came to the little by-street to give greeting, friends made by pen and voice, friends of old intimacy and friends to be. In a list set down in Mother's flowing writing (the distinctive hand of many of the pupils of Madam Rowson's school and their descendants, and quite apart from the colorless copper-plate style of many young ladies' seminaries), I read, among others, these names: Henry Tuckerman, Franklin and Warren Delano, David Lane, Winthrop Ray, George William Curtis, George Bancroft, William Cullen Bryant, Edward Everett, George Ripley, George P. Putnam (the elder), Thomas Tileston, Gustavus Kissel, John Paine, J. Woodward Haven, Dr. George O. Stone, Frederick De Peyster, and Evert A. Duyckinck, representing the Dutch stock.

Mrs. Gray and Mrs. Haven, who became the intimate Madam Gray and Aunt Kinnie of my youth, hoping to save Mother embarrassment, sent and helped to arrange an adequate collation in the back parlor; Aunt Eliza, Mother's younger sister, in a blue cape and knitted hood, making many trips across the Parade Ground to Numbers 31 and 32 West, for supplies that needed careful handling, finally upsetting a basket of the square New Year's cakes, for which Madam Gray was famous, down the front steps. They were successfully retrieved, however, and no one was known to have been poisoned by the accident, probably because germs had not been discovered and anything that looked well ate well.

Aunt Eliza was Mother's only sister, under thirty and unmarried. Everyone wondered why, for she was lovely to look at, blue-eyed and as fair as Mother was dark. She was warm-hearted and so generous that she would give away anything that she had, but there was a little twist in her makeup. If the merest puff of wind blew the wrong way it sent her flying up in the air. Though she was sure to come down again sooner or later, the place from which she had started oftentimes had moved, or the people, tired of waiting, had changed their minds, and—so she was unmarried. Father, always an optimist, said an unmarried sister was needed in every family. "Yes, to be like Cinderella," Aunt Eliza had replied, almost flying up the chimney, but this time she came down again in the same place and stayed there for some years. So in fun she was called Aunt Cinderella, which was shortened to Cinder. "Hum," she said. "Cinders smoulder along for a great while without going out," and so she did until she was almost ninety. But that part does not belong here.

What did Mother wear on her first New York New

Year's Day? Without the telling of this there would be no picture in the frame. She wore her blue and white gown, her choice being between two only. It was made of a Chinese silk fabric called pina or pineapple, sheer as organdy but not crushable; an almost invisible white line gave it the sheen of moonlight. It was a pattern dress, that is, not sold by the yard, with a border of wider groups of stripes running lengthwise of the goods to make the trimming. It had come from over-seas and Aunt Abbey's husband, Thomas Mandell, of New Bedford, had sent it to Mother the year before. He was in both the China and whaling trades and many lovely fabrics and rare curios fell into his hands. I kept a bit of the stuff for years after it had gone through its final transformation.

The skirt was made quite full, and was banded in tiers with the wider stripes, and circled sufficiently without the aid of hoops. The bodice, cut half low, with half-sleeves frilled at the elbow, was sharply pointed back and front. An adaptation of the fichu draped the shoulders and was held by Mother's cherished pin, an oval cameo of Diana, Father's betrothal gift. Short white kid gloves with but a single fastening were finished by two closely fitting band bracelets. A primly arranged wicker basket of flowers had been sent to Mother early in the morning and from it Father had selected two blush-white, fringed camellias with their leaves, for each side of Mother's hair. She no longer wore it in curls, as in her miniature, but in bandeaux that puffed out a bit over the ears. Back of these the camellias were tucked. Truly a thin gown for the season when all New York matrons wore velvet, satin, and rich brocades. Yes, but there was an open fireplace in the front parlor bedded with glowing coals; not a real hearth fire, but the high, hard-coal grate of the middle century, resting clear of ashpan and fender. A lyre-shaped blower stand flanked the hearth on one side, and a cut-steel frame for poker, tongs, and shovel on the other. These were a gift from someone who knew of Mother's half pagan fire worship, that craved the sight of the flames that warmed her, even though the vogue of the stove, air-tight and otherwise, was heavy upon the land, and many a pair of gracefully turned andirons of Colonial days were biding their time in attics, ready to come into their own again when the ugliest period in furnishings that civilization has known should be eclipsed by the twentieth century renaissance.

I said that Mother wore her blue gown; aside from some wear for strict utility, she had but one other. This was esteemed her very best, with low neck, puffed sleeves, a deep bertha of the material, edged with silk moss fringe, acting as a lining to an overcape of Honiton lace that had belonged to Great-aunt Susanna Rowson, actress and novelist. Fringe-edged flounces climbed up the skirt quite above the knee. The material of the gown was of a pale green, rosebud-strewn *mousseline de laine*, a fabric long since gone by, but most nearly comparable to a fine French *challis*. This in thrifty Providence town had been Mother's state garment. If it was out of keeping now she did not realize it, for it suited the known limits of Father's purse and, to her mind, anything better would have given cause for criticism.

New Year's Day being over, the John Paines were moved to give a formal six o'clock dinner party, in order that the minister's wife might meet some of the women of the parish who had remained late in the country. Without the least misgiving Mother put on her *mousseline de laine*, her open-work wedding silk stockings and slippers, oh, so slim and dainty—I have them yet. Her one-button gloves were this time fastened by watered ribbon bands held by mother-of-pearl clasps. Over her shoulder she wore, scarf fashion, a creamy tinted Oriental shawl woven of silk and camel's hair, a narrow side border in color matching the palm leaf pattern at the end. Great-grandfather Robert Haswell had brought it home to his sister Mary on his last voyage. To be sure, her outside wrap was of woolen and not the fur garment of wide sweep worn by other women of Mother's class, but its collar was banded by the same warm-hued sable that had trimmed little Ellen's coat when she was nine. People were careful then and furs were treasured like jewels, not dyed and plucked and snipped into bits to suit any passing fashion.

Aunt Cinder was to stay with Bea and Agatha that evening, for Mother might be out late, possibly until eleven! And Jane Dugan the helper—Mother never called the houseworkers servants and the term maid came in much later—was not exactly reliable, especially after dark. She was one of the series of warm-hearted, loyal, Irish immigrant girls whom Mother had the gift of training, but as yet she was so new to the country and its houses that when excited she sometimes backed downstairs on her hands and knees.

The dinner party was both large in numbers and sumptuous as to food. Menu cards, decorated by Mrs. Paine, who had a pretty taste in painting, and were then a novelty in private houses, were placed at intervals along the flower-trimmed table that was covered with rich damask and glittered with silver and glass. The napkins themselves were so large that they covered the widest crinoline and would well serve as small tablecloths. Very stiff and prim that card looks today, and the offering of food is quite appalling,—beginning with large, fat Chesapeake Bay oysters it meandered through nine courses until it reached a solid wall of plum pudding.

Other guests came in after dinner. The party being for a clergyman, the middle-aged people did not sit down to cards as usual, for there were still those in the parish who regarded cards as "the devil's picture books," and a minister who countenanced them might have lost caste. In spite of this the party waxed quite brilliant, and good conversation and some music, partly professional, evidently offset the weight of the food. Mrs. H. played the harp, and Anna Lynch from Boston, afterward the wife of Vincenzo Botta, the student of Dante, recited one of her own poems. Then Mother was asked to sing, for it was known to the hostess that her clear soprano voice had led the choir in the Westminster Church in Providence, when Farther had preached there as a candidate. Also that after the benediction, when looking across the church to the choir loft, where the rays of the morning sunlight fell across her face, his eyes meeting hers had paused so long that the organist had fairly to play him out of the pulpit. Indeed her beauty and charm, coupled with the understanding that grasped the most difficult situations, was a perpetual revelation to him of the possibilities of perfect womanhood, hence to frame the picture of this time I must quote from a letter written to him on his betrothal by Dr. James Walker, then president of Harvard, showing that his prediction came true, and also the intimate relation that existed between the Chief and an alumnus, expressed with an appreciation of humanity worth recording.

Cambridge, Aug. 9, 1842.

Ah, you rogue! so you thought to steal a march on us at last. But not so. We had some inkling of what was coming. And now you have my blessing and I wish that it was worth a great deal more than it is.

You must know that the lady is the daughter

of a much valued friend of my wife's. The mother I understand is an excellent woman *in grain.* This is a great point; for I believe more and more in the *breed;* almost as much as I do in the *breeding.*

I am glad on your account, and on every account, that you have not sought out "a money ambitious match," as it is called; which often consists in marrying a girl who will bring you, if you live long enough, some twenty thousand, spend from the first, the interest on half as much more. And then there is the patronage to be expected from the great family;—save the mark! . . . And now that you have been such a philosopher in the matter of being engaged, I suppose that you mean to realize the wonder of a philosopher in courtship. You are aware that the outgoings and incomings of a minister are fair game for the gypsies; and the vision of a thousand busybody tongues, flying at both ends like watchmen's rattles, is enough to give any man a fit of the proprieties. . . . But enough of this. Courtship is an anomalous state; a dispensation, not of law, but of grace. From the bottom of my heart I wish you all happiness, and advantage from the new connection. I look forward with pleasure to the time when you will become a whole man by taking to yourself the better half! . . . As for Professor F. I do not know what will become of him. While on a short journey in western New York last winter he fell in with me in company with the Misses L. He seemed to be very attentive to the younger of the two. If he does not make a match of it I shall give him up. He has spent too much time in indecision and I begin to suspect that the needle of his affections has lost its magnetic virtues by much use, and 'twill now travel around without becoming fixed anywhere.

We are happy to learn that Miss Murdock proposes to pass commencement week with us in Cambridge and we shall not fail to make her known at every opportunity.

Most truly yours—

James Walker.

Was Mother embarrassed at singing before strangers? Yes and no. In Providence she had always been asked to sing and in her Boston girlhood she had been under good masters, Foster, and Dempster who had taught her his own songs. So laying her gloves and little ivory fan upon the grand piano, the first she had ever touched, she took her seat without either hesitation or self-consciousness, Father said, her only nervous gesture being the rolling of her handkerchief into a little ball between her palms. Her color deepened as she paused a moment before making her choice from memory, for she sang and accompanied herself without notes: She Wore a Wreath of Roses, Wha Shall be King but Charlie, Jock O'Hazeldene, The Bell at Sea, Roy's Wife of Aldevalloch, We Are Coming, Sister Mary, followed each other in quick succession. Then when she had spoken to Anna Lynch who stood behind her, they sang the duet "I Know a Bank Where the Wild Thyme Blows," Miss Lynch taking the alto. Reassured by much genuine applause she went easily on through her simple repertoire. Mrs. Paine told me of this evening years later, when I was a woman grown and just betrothed, so that everything concerning Mother's youth and romance was like a precious gift. This much Mrs. Paine knew but not the inwardness of what followed.

When the Paines' ample carriage, with horses to match, bore their guests back to Amity Place, midnight was striking! "We must remember that we are in New

York," was Father's answer to Aunt Cinder's surprised greeting at the lateness of the hour as she opened the door.

A week later a large package was left at the house, having come from the depths of the same carriage. The package was accompanied by a note, which Mother read twice, giving a little gasp as she put it back into its envelope, without saying a word to Aunt Cinder who stood beside her, all eagerness. Then Mother untied the outside paper, which held two boxes, one large and deep, the other small and quite flat. From the larger came a sumptuous mink cape, more than knee length, with a large flat collar trimmed with tails of the fur. The smaller box held a dress pattern of rich watered silk with embossed velvet bands for the trimming and velvet to match for the bodice, the color being a deep golden brown that would blend with the lighter shade of the fur. Still without speaking, Mother replaced the things carefully in the boxes, then handed the note to Aunt Cinder. It was kindly, generous, and tactful, both in word and spirit. Mrs. Paine took it for granted that Mother would be very popular in the parish and to hold her own must have a rich and dignified calling costume at the very least. So she had sent her little offering, giving the name of her dressmaker whom she had directed to make the gown to Mother's measure.

Meanwhile Mother was rewrapping the package, the rose of her cheeks deepening to vivid crimson. "Surely you are not going to return the gift," expostulated Aunt Cinder. "You know you have many calls to return, and your old coat does not look as well as it did in Providence."

"I well know that, yet I cannot dress so far beyond our means, for every one must know that the cape alone is worth a half year's salary. Not return it? How could you ask such a question, Eliza?"

Father came in from his study at the moment, lured by the curiosity that all men have but conceal rather more adroitly than women. He read the expression of Mother's face, then the note, understood at once, yet quailed before the situation.

"Do not act hastily. Better wait a few days, wife, and think it over. Who knows but such gifts may be the custom in New York. Of course New England is much more—more"—he hesitated for a word—"restrained!"

"Madam Gray would know," ventured Aunt Cinder.

"Yes, Ellen, better consult her before doing anything so final as rejecting this gift. You know that we are navigating strange waters and our compass may not point truly."

Madam Gray on being consulted sat for a moment deep in thought. She saw Mother's viewpoint and what the necessary and continuous taking of dole would mean to her.

"Dame," she said (she always addressed Mother so), "it is your part of the sacrifice of your husband's calling. When your little girls grow up let us hope that they may find conditions altered."

Then the sense of humor, that always lay behind her serene face, breaking through, she added, "Don't think of the fur as a cape only, but remember, when its best days are over, that it will make capes, muffs, and collars for Bea and Gatha!" So it did, for even I, who did not arrive until nine years later, had my coat sleeves lengthened with a bit of the fur, and when I was a girl of fourteen I took immense pride in a skating cap adorned with two of the tails.

So Mother kept this gift, but ever after she tactfully avoided smart parties. Music might be listened to without social effort or circumstance, and friends in the home could be entertained on the same plane. Then came, that same year, Jenny Lind to sing at Castle Garden, and Mr. Barnum, her manager, who sometimes went to Father's church, was generous with his tickets. Father always said that it was hearing the Swedish Nightingale that buoyed Mother over the shoals and away from the rocks of that first crucial year in New York. Mother herself told me this quite in her old age and that she had only to close her eyes to hear that voice ring forth the aria from Handel's Messiah, "I *know* that my Redeemer liveth," to have all doubt forever fade away.

Yes, Mother was happy again, though the struggle and the victory were known to but few. The Roman nose still kept its place, like the gnomon of the sundial, and there was daily need for it. What was all this to do with me, who had not yet arrived? It was as the setting of the compass that was to point the way for my first score years of memory, and though the circle of city streets soon widened to an ellipse and shot out ever lengthening rays, our North Star remained fixed.

III

THE DAY I WAS BORN

FATHER said that I was born laughing. Friend Gibbons said that it was merely hiccoughs and gave me a smart slap on the back to ease them. Be this as it may, Love o' Laughter was one of the fairy conclave that gathered at my coming to wish me well, or ill, and has survived all the others, excepting Love o' Nature, who was of my blood and flesh.

It was on a keen, snowless January day in the year 1859, a rather stagnant time nationwise—slack water before the tide began to swell for our country's second deluge, the Civil War.

Our house was on West Eleventh Street, about the northern boundary of Greenwich Village, a section then known as the Ninth Ward. The crisscross streets and little pent lanes that still mark its village origin (causing Waverly Place to collide with West Eleventh Street and bend it backward, after it had played leapfrog with Greenwich Avenue) did not run straight from east to west until Fourteenth Street was reached. Eleventh Street, blocked at Broadway by Grace Church, because the balky Brevoorts would not sell right-of-way through their farm, angling sharply at Greenwich Avenue, was thus cut off from the noise of through traffic and has even now a seclusion all its own. Then too the block of seven brick houses wherein was ours, was set well back from the street itself; all had ample front yards with trees and three-story wrought iron balconies draped with wistaria vines. Old Tom O'Connell, who did our chores for us, coming up from MacDougal Alley, told lovely tales of his boyhood when the tract was called the Ailanthus Garden and there was a frog pond hard by and a brook called Minetta Water that never ran dry. The ground upon which these houses stood was part of a farm, and the row of dwellings was the special pride of William C. Rhinelander, the first, who might be seen almost any pleasant spring day inspecting his property in person, giving directions for trimming the vines or bettering the well-turfed lawns.

The Amity Place house was but a temporary lodging, and as Father refused to have his family live in a parsonage, and so have Mother become a part of the church equipment, a rent allowance was added to his salary. Home life was very dear to him and it must be free. This is the reason that I was born in the middle house of the Rhinelander block.

The house itself was one of the most comfortable of the middle-class type of the fifties, wide and with long French front windows for each of the three stories. The stoop was wide with easy treads. Two large parlors with sliding doors between and a small room, having running water and a fireplace at the end of the hall made the first story. Above, the two stories had each two square bedrooms, joined by ample dressing closets and the so-called hall bedrooms, two to a floor. One bathroom sufficed for the two living floors, yet we were considered to be quite clean and were unusually healthy.

Below stairs, at the front, was the inexcusable basement dining room with pantry and china closets leading to the kitchen and washroom. I never heard this room called a laundry until it was rebuilt in the late seventies. Kitchen and washroom opened pleasantly on a large, turfed yard, but except the sink and tubs there was no inside plumbing for this floor. The flagged cellar was cavernous and had bins for everything, a ventilated closet for hanging meat or poultry, a butter-box with lock and key, and a large hot-air furnace.

The dining room was dreary. The mantel and shelf were of black marble. The ornamental iron window-bars were too suggestive of a prison. The view from the windows as we sat at table showed only the feet of the passers-by, somewhat distorted by looking over the grass plot through the fence paling. I think that this early meal-time perspective must have given me the habit of identifying people by the expression of their feet as well as by their faces!

Mother's was the front bedroom, very plain, yet no wise grim. Gray painted walls with a heavy plaster cornice, an elaborate white mantel and shelf framing a high set grate, wherein coke or English cannel coal was burned under special stress of weather when an open fire was always a must-be in our house. The bed had half-length posts topped by urns, and a high chest of drawers was on the window side. Between the long windows curtsied a homemade dressing table; the petticoat of buff nankeen was edged with a blue stripe, curtains of the same material were draped about an oval mirror, held at the top by a great gilt rosette, then falling away on either side to blend with the table's ruffled petticoat. A side-wing easy chair and a few others, straight of back, made up the total. Set corner-wise and near the bed was a small, chubby bureau. In the contents of its drawers sister Bea took daily interest, handling the neatly piled garments there arranged, lovingly. Atop this bureau stood Bea's silver mug, now used for a flower holder and this day graced by white rosebuds, some stiff bouvardia and a white jasmine spray, these having been a part of some flowers sent Mother by Mrs. Green from her hothouse in Staten Island and begged by Bea for her shrine to the unknown. A single engraving in an oval topped gold frame hung above the mantelshelf. In it two children, supposedly boys, though the slightly sidewise parting of the hair was the only hint of sex, were leaning on a carved table upon which was an open book. On this the hands of the elder were clasped reverently. "Reading the Psalms" was the title, the Knoedler imprint and date in very small letters below.

A son I was to be else the name would lapse, a veritable child Samuel, and this picture was so placed that Mother's first morning glance would fall upon it. Blessed Father! He always had the night-before-Christmas faith of a child, but I have often wondered, for I have the print still, if the impersonality of the children pictured had not discounted the intended effect! So much for the setting.

Friend Lucy Gibbons the Quakeress, a daughter of John Hopper the Abolitionist, had come to take the midday meal with Mother. As it was a school holiday, Beatrice and Agatha were spending it at Madam Gray's over at Washington Square. A little airing had been planned for Mother but I thought differently. Suddenly feeling tired, Friend Gibbons dissuaded Mother from going out, saying, "Suppose that thee and I go up into the good man's study and visit for a while. I've a message that I wish he should carry for me."

When told the errand Father walked quickly; the tinkling horse cars went with brisk precision at infrequent intervals and in few directions. A carriage? Such a thing was only for emergencies. This might be one. Anxiety and expectation mingling caught his breath and decided for him. Dr. Robert Watts? Not in the city, impossible to locate him. Dr. Willard Parker was at home but ill of quinsy throat. "Draper, my new assistant, will be in shortly and I will send him. Young? Yes, but thoroughly skillful. He charms everyone. I thought you had met him. Brace up, Sam! are you going foundered?"

Dr. Parker had coached Father for Harvard and in exchange shared his home where his elder sisters, the Aunties, had mothered both young men when mothering was real, so that the binding tie was more than friendship. Those were the primitive days when board at commons was twenty-two dollars a term and when, if a bit of fowl was left over, the lucky possessor would spike it under the table with his two-tined steel fork for the next meal! Home went Father soon to be followed by young Dr. Draper.

Along the street wandered a little German band, five pieces in all. Quite out of season in January, but the ground was dry and the temptation to gather a few dollars in better air than the back room of a saloon must have been alluring. It halted across the street, and doubtless spying Father, who was breaking his nervous pacing through the lower rooms by pausing frequently before the long front windows, the musicians not only came over to our side of the street but quite into the front yard. Father shook his head gravely at them, but intent upon draining the moisture from their instruments they gave no heed, and suddenly broke into the *Carnival of Venice* with great vigor, Father's continued gestures only seeming to stimulate them.

Friend Gibbons called a few words over the stair-rail. Father seized his gray long-shawl from the hall-rack, yes, men wore shawls as extra evening wraps and oftentimes by day, together with high hats, in the late fifties. Pulling some money from his pocket as he went out, he had some difficulty in making the musicians understand him, for though he was a student of German thought he did not speak the tongue fluently. Suddenly his meaning dawned upon them, the puckered lips widened into smiles. They looked up at the partly curtained windows, raised their hats and paused in consultation. Then as Father turned to go up the steps the music began again. Softly, reverently, the notes of *Stille Nacht* floated up, and Father, full of sentiment and symbolism, paused at the open door to thank them by a gesture, his eyes filled with grateful tears.

It was growing dark, a breath of air freshened the room and scattered the jasmine odor. The fire glowed steadily and at the bed-foot stood the young doctor, with his exquisite spiritual profile outlined by the flames. A bit pale he was and evidently steadied himself by an urn-topped post.

"Samuel," said Mother's musical voice, clear but without strength, "will you get that poor young man a glass of wine? — he is very tired."

Downstairs Father and the doctor went together speaking earnestly, forever after fast friends. Presently when they went to the door night was creeping over the low housetops. Zigzagging across the street the lamplighter man with ladder swung on his back stopped abruptly, hooked the ladder to the crossbar of the post, struck a match as he pushed up the trap under the lamp. It failed. He struck another, lighted the gas, and so on to the next post. So do trifles make impressions.

The fairies had all gathered at last, together with music gay and grave, fragrance of flowers, hearth fire of home and love to enclose me with its many walls— so I was born, but I was not a boy! One belated fairy (there is always one such) being peeved, yet unable to change my sex, gave me the doubtful gift, that I should always see the man's viewpoint more clearly than the woman's, and from it sit in judgment upon myself. Moreover, that I should never be able to practice or understand the accepted indirect social or domestic tactics of women.

How do I know all these happenings? From the source books, so that the pattern is woven true and I treasure the intimate details of the telling even now when I am old.

IV

DOWN TOWN AND UP

THE streets that I knew best in the homespun sixties were those that ran evenly across town east and west above Washington Square, together with the avenues that also ran straight, and the fascinating, wandering Broadway, that north of Twenty-third Street, took a slantwise, westerly course as if searching for the Hudson River and an exit to the country, which was quite open and wild after Bloomingdale was reached. Below Washington Square the streets had many crooks and turns that spelled confusion. Fifth Avenue was a serious place wherein to walk decorously in one's best clothes. A very long walk (for city women were not as much at home on their feet in those days of skimpy shoes and bulky skirts as now) would be as far up as Forty-second Street where was the grim, stone reservoir, of Egyptian type, that gave us sufficient power to force the water up to the third story of downtown houses so that every member of a family might have a bath the same day, instead of the beforetime hot water rations carried up from the kitchen in polished brass cans.

Even with this water supply there were many of the older houses without inside plumbing or even sewer connections. In fact our family had moved from Amity Place to upper West Eleventh Street and thence to the Rhinelander block in search of healthier conditions. For Mother was always ahead of her time in sanitation as in other matters, and in both the earlier homes there were neighboring houses where the wash-water was dumped into the gutter to find its own way to the corner sewer opening where street met avenue, while back-yard toilets bred and broadcasted flies without let or hindrance. This was the age when youth was taught that to kill flies was an equal sin with stealing a pin—

"It is a sin to steal a pin,
To kill a fly as bad."

Be it also remembered there were no sanitary laws in the city until General Vielé organized the first Board of Health in 1865.

Sometimes, as a great adventure, Father or Aunt Cinder would take me around the top of the reservoir, on a walk that made two hollow squares dividing the water, which was open to view and seemed to me deeper and more terrible than the ocean itself.

Sixth Avenue was always a very friendly way, for it ran by our street and straight up into the arms of Central Park, the most desirable end of all journeys, for long before the park was reached the city noises had quite died away and the scattered buildings and little squatter truck farms made it seem almost like the real country. Except for the park the most interesting part of Sixth Avenue was below Fourteenth Street where there were many small shops. Two types of horse cars traversed the avenue, Central Park being the north terminal of both. Long cars having a front and rear platform with both a driver and conductor were drawn by two horses. These, starting at Broadway and the Astor House, threaded their way upward by way of Vesey and Carmine streets until they reached the straight avenue at Eighth Street. The short cars, with only a rear platform and a single horse, were manned by a driver, who in addition made change, and released the strap that held the flap door when a passenger got on or off. This process made one very alert lest he be trapped by the feet. "Bobshear cars," after the meadow mouse, they were called by a country parson who once came to exchange with Father, and we adopted the name at once as quite comprehensive. The Bobshears ran to Canal Street and Broadway only, but even that was quite a ride and not one to be taken lightly, or more than twice or thrice a year when Mother, Aunt Cinder and sometimes Bea and Gatha went down to Arnold & Constable's to buy a dress length or possibly a coat.

Be it said here that people in those days chose their tradesmen with discrimination and stood by them with the same loyalty that they showed to their physician or church, and many a heated discussion there was between the relative merits of Arnold & Constable, and Lord & Taylor, while A. T. Stewart was always regarded by the most conservative shoppers as a parvenu. Sometimes if the weather was fine we would divide in groups and walk home via Broadway, stopping at Lord & Taylor's at Grand Street, a block above Arnold's. We were Arnold & Constable-ites, but when some of the Boston kin came for a visit we would occasionally go with them to the rival shops. Personally Mother never *shopped*—by that I mean she did not have the habit of going from place to place examining and handling articles that she did not intend to buy. Snooping, sister Bea called it, this having roll upon roll of heavy woolens or delicate silks taken down and displayed simply for a morning's amusement. At this time all materials of light color or delicate fabric when stored upon the shelves were usually wrapped in cloths, so there was little or none of the permanent display of goods as in later years.

There were trials as well as pleasures connected with these shopping trips. Often when the visitors had made a purchase and the goods been taken to Boston or Providence, they would come back by way of Mother for exchange. Up to a certain point she was very patient even though she had no sympathy with indecision. All the martyrs did not die in the Roman arena. Our budget always being an eel-skin fit, buying, with Mother, was the art of harnessing need and desire as evenly as possible, so every purchase was final. There were no mail-order departments in the shops then to relieve city dwellers of this responsibility of exchange shopping. The day came, however, when Mother shut down upon any and all exchange making. This was when a friend of a second cousin in Boston, having in May bought a cut-off dress length of summer silk, the same being of an extremely splashy pattern, returned it the next December to be "exchanged for something more seasonable."

Sometimes in spring there was a far downtown trip that was a veritable excursion, down below the Astor House terminal of the two-horse cars. The hotel itself was a landmark of romance, the centre of a popular go-to-bed story, for it was there that Mother and Father had spent three days on the return from their Niagara wedding trip in 1843, this journey having in part been accomplished by canal boat. This long trip was taken in a Broadway stage, the choosing of which was a matter of some moment to me, for the high-swung stages showed elaborate pictures painted on their sides and of these I had my favorites so that I would coax Father to allow several to pass until the desired picture came by. So real were these paintings to me that when once seated in the stage I felt myself a part of the landscape or scene depicted. The Broadway stages ran past Trinity Church quite down to the Bowling Green, a neat little park enclosed by a high fence. Beyond this was land's end, not no man's land but every man's land—Castle Garden, the gate thrown open to welcome all strangers, where a clearing house for immigrants had followed the Concert Hall of Jenny Lind's fame.

In the open space about the building there was a strange mixture of romance and geography, strange faces and strange costumes. From what countries had they come, and why? Father's answers and putting them together made a game for me to play, half reality, half make-believe, for one day I was quite sure that I saw Hansel and Gretel walking hand in hand. I loved these trips, for Father was always my companion. We usually stopped at Trinity Church, if there was a service or choir practice, or if not there was always a chance that the bells might peal the hour and these bells spoke a tongue that I understood beyond the power of words.

Even the usual walks up Broadway from Canal Street were also Wonderland to me if Mother was my companion. Besides the broad-fronted houses of many people who belonged to the parish, all of whom Mother knew, there was Barnum's Museum and the Olympic Theatre, where I was always allowed to stop and read the display bill of the play. Next we passed Ball & Black's, the silversmiths, and Tiffany's from which last came the christening cup that Madam Gray gave me because her last name was put in the middle of mine.

Then came the bookshops, Scribner's and David Francis', who, not being a publisher but a general dealer, spread forth many delectable meals, so that it was almost a club gathering place where Father was sure to meet friends, both amateur collectors and the real grubbing bookworms. Mr. Francis knew Mother's

Boston kin and also the two shared a fine sense of humor. Chances were that, as we passed, Father himself might be coming out the door with a package in his hand and a bump in each side-pocket of his coat. By this time Bea and Gatha, being grown-up young ladies who were mindful of the fashions, had coaxed Father to give up his heavy gray long-shawl which had done noble service as an extra winter wrap, so that now in addition to the straight black overcoat worn of Sundays and for funerals he had an ample and quite modish mixed gray coat called a raglan, with shoulder capes covering the arms. This was much more efficient for smuggling books home than the shawl, which, if suddenly and heedlessly loosened, would dump its contents with a thud and a slide-off as startling as when a two-wheeled coal cart lets down its load.

Of all these places the best came last, the picture shop, that was called an Art Gallery because it had an exhibition room with top light. This was not far from Father's church and on the opposite side of Broadway. In the front of this shop were counters and drawers full of prints. In the rear the walls of the gallery were hung about with paintings and prints both black and white and in colors. It was in this room that the proprietor Wilhelm Schaus could be found. He might have traced his lineage back to Santa Claus, so big a heart had he and so well could he read and understand the mind of a child. A child who vaguely but intensely loved color and beauty of form, but whose art sense and love, at this period, was centered upon a series of kitten pictures in which snow-white kittens with blue eyes were doing all the possible tricks of the pets beloved by childhood. I would stand quietly for a long time dividing my attention between the kittens and what must have been awful and very robust still-life studies, the combination of a dish of cherries, a white napkin, a yellow rose, a pomegranate and a decanter.

Meanwhile Father would be seated before a portfolio of steel engravings, some friend having asked Mr. Schaus to ascertain his likings prior to the next Christmas or perhaps Easter, having a gift in view. While in what seemed to me a dismal rotation he would be shown prints of *The Christian Martyr*, *Rock of Ages*, *The Night Before St. Bartholomew*, *The Prayer Before Battle*, *John Calvin*,—yes, and they gave them to us, for we had these and many more on our walls in the course of time, all framed in heavy black walnut with sad gray-tinted mats. It is but a short time ago that I have shaken myself free from the last of them and not wholly free even now, for *John Calvin* has elusively slid down behind the rafters in the country attic and may again see light when the roof is reshingled. Mother meanwhile would flit gracefully about in her black velvet bonnet, plain cloth gown, and the bright India shawl, chosen by Father be it said, looking among the dark frames very like a scarlet tanager in the country woods. She never paused long until she reached the corner where were kept the colored prints of hunting scenes, stage coaches and prancing horses and such like, for Mother dearly loved good horses and the pictures of them. As a very young girl she had possessed a riding horse of her own and Grandfather Murdock let her pin up the skirt of her long habit well above her boots when she was quite out of Boston town and together they explored the wild, unpathed fen country in a freedom almost of today.

The time came when one of the kitten pictures preceded me home. It was with difficulty that I was kept from taking it to bed for a pillow. Most of us have had a kitten period in our lives, from which, circumstances permitting and if we are wholesome out-of-door folk, we graduate to dogs, not lap pets but gentlemanly dogs. Yet not to have known at least one kitten intimately is to have been cheated out of one's rights, just as a child who has never had a wide-branched, climbable apple tree in its life, with whispered secrets of birds' nests above and a strong branch to hold a swing, has missed a lasting thrill and a good bit of education as well.

Dear Wilhelm Schaus! He was of the type of whole-souled Germans that will be cherished long after the taint of Prussianism is washed from the race. In course of time he led me from blue-eyed cats to nobler animals, though of course there were a few of Prang's chromos, in between; and I vividly remember the day when with a smile he said, "*Meine herz blumen*, now thou shalt see true art," and he took from a newly arrived packing case the engraving after Landseer's *The Twins*, —sheep and two collies; *Two Nut Crackers and a Piper*, gray squirrels and a bullfinch, the latter being a combination of line, stipple and mezzotint giving the squirrels' fur such an effect of reality that I tried to stroke it with my hand, also a brownish print of Moreland's *Rural Pleasures*. Many years after Evan gave me proof copies of these prints, but the memory of that smile and his pleasure in my first delight has never faded.

After this we would walk up Broadway until we reached Eleventh Street and turned west. This street, unlike other crosstown thoroughfares, was then numbered from Broadway instead of from Fifth Avenue, as the refusal of the Brevoorts to sell a right-of-way through the original farm cut off the street. The architecture of two churches broke the monotony of rows of very uninteresting houses, Grace Church at the head of the street and the First Presbyterian at Fifth Avenue. This latter to myself I called the "wicked church," and I stood in great awe of the building and the graveyard surrounding it. Once I had been taken to a service there by Norah Goodnuf, a very nonconformable Scottish second-girl. Instead of the singing being led by organ music, a tall, thin man stood up and tweaked something that looked like a twig and when it hummed the hymn began. Norah called it a "tuning fork" and said that the man was setting the key, also that "organs were ill-favored, unseemly instruments of Baal and wicked to have in a kirk, not being mentioned for such use in the Scripture." In my young mind, however, it could not be the organ that was wicked, as Father had one in his church, that rolled out deep music like the sea in a storm, hence it must be that the church was too wicked to have an organ, but the people did not like to tell of it!

Soon after this one day when I was walking with Aunt Cinder we saw a group of people dressed in black standing in the grassed yard at the north of the church close to the edge of a deep hole. Aunt Cinder said it was a funeral and wished to hurry on. I understood funerals as I knew them in the country, but here there were no name stones and no flowers. Thinking she was mistaken and being balky, I clung to the bars of the high fence and watched. Presently some men came up a ladder out of the hole; a tomb I found was the name of it. They covered the hole with earth, put back the sods, and went away, leaving nothing behind, not even one flower—only loneliness. Then I felt sure that it was indeed a wicked church whose yard swallowed people and left no sign.

V

JEFFERSON MARKET AND EVERYDAY STREETS

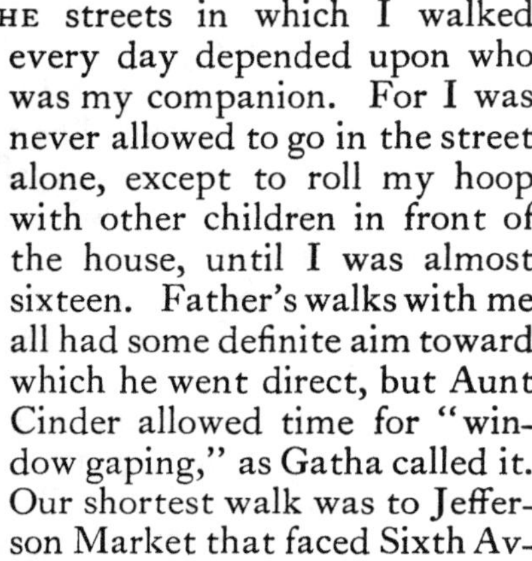

THE streets in which I walked every day depended upon who was my companion. For I was never allowed to go in the street alone, except to roll my hoop with other children in front of the house, until I was almost sixteen. Father's walks with me all had some definite aim toward which he went direct, but Aunt Cinder allowed time for "window gaping," as Gatha called it. Our shortest walk was to Jefferson Market that faced Sixth Avenue in the crooked angle between Eighth and Tenth streets under the shadow of the old fire-bell tower. Once or twice each week Mother asked Father to go to market, because, as I heard her tell Madam Gray, "it gives Samuel a reason for leaving his desk and taking a breath of morning air, it brings him in contact with many groups of people, and it keeps him in touch with the exact cost of our daily bread without any words of explanation from me. Oh, unnecessary talk about money is so bad for family life!"

"Dame," said Madam Gray, "you are a very wise woman. The Dominie must come out of the clouds to earth occasionally and in this way you do it without jarring him."

Then Mother would smile half to herself, her eyes growing tender. Two dimples played about the corners of her mouth and then disappeared as her lips took serious lines. Of course I did not then understand Madam Gray's exact meaning, but in later times it became as a distinct message. Mother loved her mate in so complete and protective a way that she would never jar his sensitive nature by letting material needs become a personal matter. Thus through a life of much strain, many dark corners and heart-rending sacrifices, the veil of romance was never rent in twain by her and she turned the silver lining toward Father from many a sable cloud. . . . . .

Jefferson Market was a delightful place to go. Everyone knew us and said good morning even though we did not buy at their stalls. The first stand as you entered the middle door belonged to the pork butcher, who also sold butter, eggs and cheese. This stand was kept by a middle-aged man and his old mother. His real name has gone from me. I called him the Pink Man and so it is written in memory, for his skin was the color of the meat of a rosy ham and his hair the hue of the pale yellow rind of fat. Back of this stall, with its cleanly scraped white wood counter, was a sort of closet with a half door. Within this little pen was a small stove holding a tea kettle that seemed to be always purring and anxious to boil.

The Pink Man's mother used to take refuge in this coop on cold mornings or when trade was slack. She was a buxom little English woman also of very warm coloring, through which her age was told by its deeply veined quality. She wore a clean white apron over her black gown, and a tartan shawl folded diagonally was crossed over the chest and tied back of the waist to keep the ends from dragging. Above her shining, well-oiled black hair (I did not realize then that it was the half wig called a frizzette), beginning almost between her shoulders there grew a bonnet of curious pattern. It was half sunbonnet, half coal-scuttle poke. Lace tabs fell over her ears. These I later discovered belonged to the typical lace cap worn by self-respect-ing British market women in provincial towns. The wide bonnet strings were usually untied and rolled up neatly and pinned into little bobs under the ears. She seemed always to be either drinking or brewing tea. An iron bracket was hooked on the side of the stove as a hob for the steeping, for if the teapot were set directly on the fire it might "over do," as she worded it. Back of the stove was a shelf holding half a dozen dark blue china cups and saucers, a tin box for bread, and some jars of jam. As soon as the old lady came to the door of her retreat, cup in hand, and the aroma of the freshly made tea floated out, it was a sign as sure as the hands of the market clock that it was nine, and quite time that early risers should have a cup and a snack, she said.

"Cup o' Tea" was my name for her, as in truth she was one of the first who gave me my lifelong love of the well-brewed cup that cheers. In the beginning she had sometimes asked me into her "bit coop" to warm myself, as often Father met friends also bent on marketing with whom he stopped to chat. There was Chief Justice Daly, who lived in Clinton Place, and so resembled Father that they might have been brothers; Mr. John Taylor Johnson, who owned the gallery of beautiful pictures up at Fifth Avenue; Mr. Samuel Ward also, who gave wonderful dinners, so delectable that they made Father eat too much, Mother said, and was so witty and had so many long stories to tell the other men that when I saw him I was glad to take refuge in the coop. Then one day Cup o' Tea brought out a funny little china mug with FOR A GOOD GIRL printed on it in gilt letters. This she said was for me, and I was to tell my mother that it was only calico tea she was giving me. I failed to see any calico in it, I only knew that it was hot and tasted something like when you chew a stalk of new hay, and it always had four big lumps of loaf sugar in it or else a big piece of rock candy.

Next beyond the pork stall on the opposite side of the aisle came Tyson with poultry and vegetables; next was Devoe with meats. Devoe was very pleasant and smiling; very good meat he had too, but I had heard Mother say the weight was very short. Then one morning when Father remembered to ask him if his scales were in good repair, he said that lately he himself had suspected them and had just ordered new ones. After that Mother said there was at least one more chop in the pound. At the end of the main aisle was Davis the fishmonger. Sometimes I found small shells, tiny fiddler crabs, sand-dollars and starfish in the seaweed packed among the oysters and clams. But after all it was the pork butcher's store that attracted me most, not his wares but Cup o' Tea, his comfortable mother, and in spring the bunches of fresh lilacs that garnished the stall long before the half starved bush in our yard opened a single bud, added to the lure.

Especially was I glad of Cup o' Tea's coop and company if the great fire bell above our head began to boom. For some years after the fire engines were drawn by horses, instead of, as in the early sixties, by the volunteers running afoot, this bell was sounded from the watchtower and it was by counting the strokes that we might locate the fire. The key to these numbers was in the form of a small book with a dull pink cover. This book cost six cents and could be bought, among other places, at Taffy John's Candy Shop near the brewery at the Greenwich Avenue corner of Eleventh Street. I always kept this little book in my apron or coat pocket, for going to fires was one of my greatest desires. In those days when my home name was Tommy and I could stand on my head without reproof, I usually had to take it out in wishing. I had seldom seen a really big fire, for neither Father nor Aunt Cinder cared to run after the engines. Mother usually had sewing to do, or callers when the fire bell rang, Gatha would be at her music lesson, and Bea her drawing class at the Cooper Institute.

One day, however, I did see a really satisfactory fire though in a very unexpected way. There had been a triple alarm, and people were running down the street westward toward the river. Clouds of heavy smoke rising above the brewery were goading me to desperation. O'Connell the chore man, who had a trade in rags, bottles and scrap-iron as a side issue, was coming out of the basement and found me hanging on the front gate in the hope of having an invitation to run to the fire. Melted by the sight of my tears, which were too profuse to be licked up, without asking a question or by-your-leave, he lifted me into his two-wheeled pushcart with its string of bells dangling merrily above and seated me on a bundle of papers. Looking up at the windows and seeing no one, he bumped me over the cobbles toward the North River pier where a great five-masted schooner laden with lumber was in flames. These had leaped over to the shore to feed on piles of lumber as well as many low rambling buildings.

When O'Connell got as near as he thought safe he lifted me on his shoulders so that, he being a tall, bulky man, I not only saw perfectly but sat comfortably. We stayed until the brilliancy of the fire had passed and O'Connell, fearing that I might be hungry, bought some oysters from a grimy-looking man who was peddling them from a large basket, opening them for the buyers who ate them out of the shells. O'Connell, who would have none of the strange man's handling, did the opening himself with a stout clasp knife. I had never eaten raw oysters before and these were very large and fat. I almost felt afraid of them, for the first seemed to wiggle its way down as if it did not like being swallowed. But these being my Tommy days I felt that I must live up to my name and so I managed five, one after the other rapidly, their intense saltiness coming to my aid. To attempt the sixth I felt would result in a calamity of which no child who wished to be a good sport would be guilty in the street. Six was the number that O'Connell felt suitable for me, so, as he shifted me from one shoulder to the other, I slipped the final oyster inside the neck of my frock where it slid coldly down until it was stopped by my belt.

Be it said that home was reached in safety and I was again swinging on the gate when Gatha returned from her music lesson. Of course I told Mother about it in the go-to-bed-time of confidences and conscience-easing confessions, and O'Connell squared himself in the kitchen with Mary Daly and she passed his apology on to Father who, judging by the way he took me about with him, had much the same ethics concerning my bringing-up. "You had orter give childer something grand to see, so as when they gets old they'll have some'at to remember and chin about besides gossip, like how—'Casey, they do be saying, walks straighter going to work than coming back'—and, 'if all there is to know about Mag McGuire was known, some folks wouldn't tumble over themselves to make much of her!'"

The other great fire I went to was one which, to use an Irish bull, I didn't see until after it was out and then I smelt it. This was the fire that destroyed Barnum's Museum down at Ann Street and Broadway. All the family went excepting Mother and me. Mother was too busy sewing, and as for poor little me, I "might take cold or get in the way," Gatha had explained, when Aunt Kinnie Haven's invitation came for as many of the family as wished to go to drive down in her carriage as near to the blaze as possible.

On their return the account of the thrilling scene was told and retold downstairs to Mary Daly, the most angelic, big-hearted Irish helper that we ever had. She listened and at first said nothing, but gave a little twitch to her left shoulder which I knew by experience meant that she was thinking out something, while I stood beside her wide-eyed and disconsolate.

"We'll be going down the morn's morning, you and me," she said comfortingly as soon as we were alone in the kitchen, a happy place where I might go freely except on washing day or just before mealtimes.

"I want to see the fire, and it will be all out tomorrow," I quavered.

"What matter'll that be, acushla?" she chirped soothingly. "When the place was afire, you could only see what was there, which you've seen many a time before. Tomorrow there'll be smoke and smoulder enough, I'll warrant ye, and we'll have the grand time seeing what isn't there any more." The promise was kept. There was enough confusion and smoke left to satisfy anyone and my curiosity was soon gratified, for I had not only seen what was not there, but the smell of the "smoulder" is yet a vivid memory.

VI

NABOB

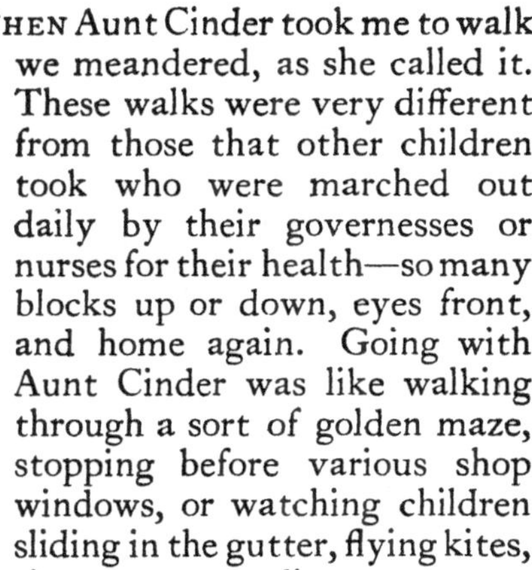

WHEN Aunt Cinder took me to walk we meandered, as she called it. These walks were very different from those that other children took who were marched out daily by their governesses or nurses for their health—so many blocks up or down, eyes front, and home again. Going with Aunt Cinder was like walking through a sort of golden maze, stopping before various shop windows, or watching children sliding in the gutter, flying kites, playing marbles or pegging tops according to season. Dear Aunt Cinder, I wonder that her right hand could hold either pen or needle, from the pulling it had from mine in these walks. For I always held her hand from choice, touch is so subtle and means so much; to be able to squeeze her hand expressed pleasure more quickly than words—a return squeeze meant approval.

As our circuit was limited, every detail in consequence became of importance. Below Jefferson Market, before Sixth Avenue melted into Carmine Street, was Burnton's Bookshop. It was here that school books, stationery and valentines could be bought. This was one of those very useful stationer's shops of the old era, in which books were treated with a respect which lent dignity to the salesman and impressed the buyer, a dignity that is lacking in these days of competition when literature and face powder or flesh-reducing rubber corsets are sold in adjacent sections of a department store.

The return from Burnton's was usually a detour

via Washington Place to the Square, where, the park being safely enclosed from the perils of runaway horses, I was left to play for a time while Aunt Cinder went to Number Thirty-one to chat with Madam Gray. If it was very cold or threatened rain I went in also to look at the Chinese curiosities that Nabob had brought home. Or perchance I might have the good luck to see Nabob himself. This was my name for Madam Gray's eldest son, who having been in the China trade was caught in one of the periodic uprisings against the English, in whose defence he had taken up arms. Having been shot by a poisoned bullet of cruel, triangular shape he had lost a leg well above the knee. This was replaced by one of cork, which he did not always use, but mostly sat in a deep chair with a wrap thrown over his knee and a small table beside him for his books, cigars, or whatnot.

To me Nabob was a cross between a potentate and a magician, who told wonderful tales of Oriental splendor, half folklore, half experience, and was always sure to produce something desirable, by what appeared to be sleight-of-hand, for me to take home. Sometimes when he felt very poorly and did not leave his chair, he would send Lewis Potter, his body servant (these men were not called valets in New York at that time), to bring some candied ginger or sweetmeats, or, if it was mid-morning or late afternoon, he would call for his tea service of egg-shell porcelain set on a lacquered tray with raised gold figures, a burnished metal kettle with spirit lamp, and a tea caddy of octagon shape decorated with dragons. On the tray were two bowl-shaped cups, without handles but covered, broad as they were deep; in fact the cups and covers looked the same. The cup partly rested in a little frame of exquisitely fine wicker that kept it from slipping in the saucer. The fact that tea was *oban* for young persons only gave Nabob an added mischievous pleasure in giving it to me, for he was quite ignorant of my initiation by means of the "calico tea" of the pork butcher's mother, but in truth the two beverages were not even remote kin.

I can see his thin nervous fingers now, as, after Lewis Potter (he was always addressed by his full name) had scalded the tea cups, he measured an even half caddy-spoonful into each, poured on the boiling water, and covered the cups for exactly three minutes. To impress upon me the importance of exact time in tea brewing he always made me hold his watch and count the seconds. This done, with a deft motion he poured the liquid into the cover which then became the cup, and the potion was ready. Nabob drank his tea clear, as he said one would never think of spoiling a finely flavored wine with sugar and cream. In my cup he dropped a few bits of rock candy as a concession to childhood.

It was in these halcyon days that Nabob gave me, besides a red lacquered cabinet, a desk and several chests of small boxes, and the figure of a porcelain mandarin done in bright colors, whose lack of clothing over the abdomen caused me to wrap it in a flannel garment on cold nights even though its home was on the mantelshelf above the fire. He also had made for me a complete sailor suit, bell-shaped trousers, wide-collared blouse, cap, bos'n's whistle and all, and taught me by directions executed by the horrified Lewis Potter, to dance a sailor's hornpipe, slap my thighs and say, "Shiver my timbers!" But remember this was in the days when I was a little boy.

My walks did not always lead to Washington Square. On the east side of Sixth Avenue a little above Eighth Street was the Shop of Severe Temptation—Minner's the confectioner, in whose window there was always a display of bride's cake sometimes three stories high, with trimming of silver lace and rosebuds, topped by a miniature bride and groom. Then there would be moulds of jellies and pyramids of ices of the monumental form so fashionable, probably made of glass, but appetizing when seen from the street. This was the hungry side of Sixth Avenue, for a block above was Walduck's bakery that lured both eyes and nose with cracker rabbits and sheets of crinkled gingerbread. Then came De La Vergne's chemist shop with glorious-colored glass jars in the windows, and one small counter holding rows of highly flavored lozenges and barley sticks that could be bought for a few pennies, as well as rock candy of several colors that one might make into a necklace by joining the strings about which it had crystallized. Rhubarb and senna were also bought at this shop, but one could forget that when looking in the window.

If Aunt Cinder steered successfully by these places, for she had a soft heart and always a little money in her purse, we walked more briskly. The Grapevine, the saloon at the corner of Eleventh Street that always smelled of beer from the kegs piled on the sidewalk, and Quimby's hardware store on the opposite corner, were easily passed except when displays of sleds or skates were in season.

At the English Goods Shop of Samuel Heath we often paused. Heath was one of the long-bodied, short-legged type of perfectly self-sufficient English tradesmen; he had straggling side-whiskers, parted his hair down the middle at the back, and shed a musty odor such as wasps gave to our attic in the country. Mrs. Heath was a timid, slender gentlewoman whose mismating was quite evident, even if silently borne. She had a little parlor back of the shop to which we sometimes went, where many bits of old china, figurines, candlesticks and such like interested both Mother and Aunt Cinder. One of her old country treasures, a candle-holder with three lilies painted on its porcelain screen, is on my table now. Samuel Heath was set against hoarding them. "'Sell 'em, Charlotte,' says

I, 'sell 'em, since there seems to be a walue on 'em, and buy some 'at new that won't ache ye at the thought of them breaking.'" Value in money was S. Heath's keynote. So Mother and Aunt Cinder, who understood, often dropped in for a chat and to admire the little woman's possessions which seemed to restore her pride, making, as a reason for these visits that S. Heath could understand, purchases of odds and ends, though most of the stock on sale was unseasonable.

J. Jones, stationery and notions, came next. Everything was desirable there; slates with a place in the frame to hold the string of a sponge, for we used slates then with stone pencils that scratched and squeaked until you had spent a deal of time working them soft between your lips. I can even now taste that slate-pencil flavor. Book slates were the last word of refinement. These were made of some light unbreakable black material on which a soft pencil could be used. Paper dolls were in a glass case, sharing it with colored picture books and picture books to color with boxes of crayons, and cardboard palettes on which were fastened half a dozen cakes of paints and a small brush. Beside these everyday things Mr. Jones kept a large assortment of decalcomanias, transferable pictures of many sizes and types, with which children were prone to decorate door handles and various articles of furniture to the horror of their parents. These were sold in sheets and only needed moisture for their transfer. One was supposed to dip them in water, but in a hurry licking would serve as well. Mr. Jones himself was tall, and always wore a top hat in the shop. He had a wry-neck which made it quite uncertain whether or not he was looking at you, but if by any chance you handled his wares too freely, you were sure to find that he could see round a corner.

Until Fourteenth Street was neared temptation waned. Near that corner was R. H. Macy's shop, where we often went for the many little things that Mother said she could not find anywhere else, but when the corner was rounded joy beckoned from the north side of the street, for there was the greenhouse of W. C. Wilson & Brothers. I suppose it must have been a rather small affair, but it was to me a sort of dreamland, and the rosy haze of it still clings, for my love of flowers has always been as instinctive as breathing. In the centre of the glass-covered portion of the house was a rockery. Pot plants were banked about this, pink and white bouvardias, fuchsias and heliotrope. Vines of passion flower were trained to the roof supports. An orange tree or two, fragrant white jasmine, and some camelia shrubs filled the long side benches. There were several small basins among the stones with goldfish in them, and as a great treat one of the men would turn a faucet and water would flow, very cautiously, over the larger of the rocks. In the rear of the shop where orders were taken there was a small display of cut flowers in jars. The tea roses being in tight buds and pungently fragrant were of two kinds only, yellow and pink, chiefly Safrano and Bon Silene, I should judge. Not sumptuous or long of stem, for there were no sturdy hybrid teas or forced hybrid perpetuals then, but very dainty and charming were these buds when made into what were called nosegays, the roses being set deep in heliotrope or double violets, edged with jasmine, bouvardia and the leaves of rose geranium. Flower seeds might also be bought here at five cents a package, the limited selection not being confusing to a shallow purse.

As spring came on five cents meant to me a package of seeds, the same holding their own in a tug-of-war with marbles, kites or hoops. Usually we merely walked about the rockery and looked at the flowers, but once a year there came a veritable orgy for me, the day when Father went to pay for the Easter flowers used at the church, for though friends sent flowers from private conservatories they were supplemented and arranged by the Wilson Brothers. Then I was always given a small tight bouquet for Mother and five packets of flower seeds for myself. A package of early radish seed was usually my first choice. These I planted in the back yard, but the place being shady and the soil like brick, they were never edible before we went up to Mosswood, yet as spring came I always hoped against experience. I do this sort of hoping still, for when experience succeeds in downing hope, then one is indeed emotionally dead.

The greenhouse visited, then came the Van Beuren house and its piece of garden, part of the original farm that reached up to Fifth Avenue. Here, nipping at the frosted grass, browsed two placid cows, that hurried eagerly to the fence to get such bits of green stuff, a carrot or apple, as Mary Daly had crowded into my small Shaker basket. Sometimes a few hens and a gallant rooster followed the cows. Then we might continue on to the Peacock House at Broadway and Nineteenth Street, where the Cruger ladies lived, and gorgeously plumed peacocks preened and strutted in the garden, enclosed with a high iron picket-fence.

One longer walk there was, but I never enjoyed its ending. It ran eastward on Fourteenth Street across town past Union Square, up Irving Place by the Academy of Music, where the Bancrofts, Madam Penniman, or the Havens sometimes took Mother and Father to hear the opera. Irving Place stopped at Gramercy Park, a private enclosure set in the midst of wide comfortable houses somewhat like those surrounding Washington Square but on a smaller scale. The park itself was guarded by a high fence and locked gates. The children of the surrounding householders, who held keys, might play in the park and be safe from street accidents, but when they went in *the gate was locked behind them!*

I was sometimes asked by family friends living near to take a "nursery dinner" and go for afternoon play in this park, but there was something about the exclusive privilege, combined with the locking-in, that froze the spirit of play in me. There were well-kept walks without interruption of traffic, to be sure, but it was always the same round and round, no delightful excitement of having one's hoop skid into the gutter or all of a sudden cross the street in peril of being crushed by one of the swiftly moving, dare-devil, two-wheeled butcher's carts dreaded by all staid pedestrians. Outside the fence there were always some "beggar children" looking in at us who sometimes jeered, and I always craved the very exclusion that caused their envy—the liberty of action, the most desirable thing of all. It was not in the least akin to lawlessness, but the very shadow of restraining bars was dreadful to me. Thus I always resented the enclosing feet of the flannel night gear that Mother made with such careful stitches. I preferred to be able to kick my feet under the covers and wiggle my toes at will, insisting that it made me feel much warmer than being bagged, until finally she quite understood. Our own front yard, small as it was, was so much better than this park. A fence and gate it had, but the gate was only closed to keep out stray dogs and never locked, while the Red Lion of our favorite game, who lived in the den under the openwork iron steps, was chosen from among my playmates who could growl the best, irrespective of caste or place of residence. The foolish hurdy-gurdy man who often served as orchestra for our plays, enjoying them as much as we did, sat enthroned on the top step of the area-way with the door-mat under him, lest his twisted back should grow worse from taking cold. There is no child's play unless Make-Believe is there, and Make-Believe refuses absolutely to be deprived of liberty.

VII

THE DAY WHEN NEW YORK STOPPED

NEW YORK had found itself after the first shock of the Civil War, and every one settled down to work. New ways began to creep into every set. The "We are and that is sufficient" inner social circle began to fray at the edges. New terms, one of which was shoddy, crept into the language.

How do I know this, being one of the other people? From the after-interpretation of talk by way of the Cookie Jar Sewing Society that foregathered twice a week in the temporary work-room in Father's upstairs study. Long after the peace, work went on daily at the New England Relief Rooms and at the headquarters of the Sanitary Commission, but this little betweentime gathering at our house, consisting of Madam Gray, her daughter Elizabeth, Aunt Kinnie Haven, Mother and Aunt Cinder, was luminous in many ways. Came ten o'clock in the morning, marketing and day-planning all done. Tom-dog, Madam Gray's very independent Skye terrier, would appear around the corner of the street, push open the gate and give a few sharp barks at the door, to be followed more slowly by his mistress who progressed rather than walked. Madam Gray usually came afoot from Washington Square to these meetings but Aunt Kinnie always rode. Sometimes her pet dogs, two very small black-and-tan toy terriers, with bulging eyes, needle-point barks and dispositions sharpened by lack of real dog liberty, would come with her. She always had several of these dogs and in her back yard at the Square were several little marble headstones to mark those that had been, "Tiny" seeming to have been a favorite name in a clan which needs no further description. If the black-and-tans came, considerable diplomacy was a prelude to the sewing, for Tom-dog was of the actions-that-speak-before-words type, while Tiny and Teeny were all words. Usually, however, Aunt Kinnie's Ann, the ever-smiling and much enduring maid, remained in the coupé and took the dogs for an airing.

The work being arranged, the cookie jar was placed on a stool within easy reach of every one. Our house was, it seemed, quite famed for the contents of this jar, and the Washington Square folk were convinced that no other cookies equalled these, not excepting Madam Gray's famed New Year's cakes. The cookies were of three kinds: sugar, cut in oak-leaf shape and sent on monthly from Boston by the Aunties; Grandmother Murdock's hard gingerbread, made by Mother, rich and spicy, spread with a crinkled rolling pin and cut in squares to prevent having to reroll between bits; the third and prettiest kind, Aunt Cinder's lemon jumbles, not cut out but made into rings by a deft motion of the spoon. All my days I nibbled the hard gingerbread with great respect, for this and a Christmas pudding were Mother's only cooking achievements. Anything and everything else she would and could do, everything but cook. A family date from which things were reckoned forward and backward was "the day when Mother burned the omelet." (This, though an interpolation, has its place in picturing Mother.)

At Mosswood, the home of summer rest, in the early days when living was very primitive and informal, it was arranged that some member of the family should assemble, on Mondays, the midday meal that we called a tea dinner. In New England Monday was the day sacred to the wash-tub. Two or three Mondays passed comfortably that summer before Mother's turn came. This day, there being on hand fruit, a cold custard, and a salad, only an omelet was to be beaten up and the tea drawn. Cousin Mary from Boston was staying with us and she, Mother and Aunt Cinder were reading aloud of afternoons *Jane Eyre*, which had just reached America. At Mother's suggestion each one was pledged not to open the book between whiles and so gain on the others. No! Mother said emphatically, she didn't wish any help with dinner, she surely could be trusted to make an omelet. Cousin Mary and Aunt Cinder therefore were to go out in the orchard and stay until called.

They went, but when a reasonable time of silence had passed, after the egg-beating stopped, they wondered. Presently Aunt Cinder, having, like myself, a hunting-dog nose, sniffed. "It's nothing but smoke coming from the railroad," said Cousin Mary. Aunt Cinder's nose, however, reported differently. Slipping into the kitchen by the back door she not only smelt, but saw the smell—the ten-egg omelet in its pan was the foundation of a column of black smoke, and the tea kettle had boiled over into the stove so efficiently that the fire was failing. Outside, seated on the wide step in the shade of the well-house, sat Mother reading the last page of *Jane Eyre*, in complete oblivion of her surroundings. The family quite agreed with her that cooking was bad for her morale. Then, too, her fingers were shaped for taking fine stitches and smoothing tired foreheads with the divine gift of touch that was hers, rather than for being blistered by egg-beating and handling hot pans.

I was allowed to come to the Cookie Jar Sewing Society provided I did not ask unnecessary questions

I threaded needles, picked lint, and—listened! To this day a comment heard then will flash through my memory bearing a new meaning.

"A child does not understand what we are talking about," said Aunt Kinnie one day in response to Mother's raised eyebrows. No, children may not understand but they remember, and by and by when they are able to interpret happenings they never forget their source. There was an unhappy marriage under discussion followed by something they called divorce. It seemed from their attitude that this thing was much worse than death. Then the talk turned to a wedding so intimate that the affair came almost within family lines. It had evidently been marked by untoward frivolity on the part of the young couple.

"What can you expect of a couple, the girl married at seventeen to a spoiled-child sort of man, who both came out of church laughing and almost romping as if playing a game of tag?" said Aunt Cinder.

I listened, and when a dozen years later the sequel followed, I remembered, as I do still, sister Bea's pitying attitude toward the tragedy. Divorce had come. The children were to be separated, and only one, who seemed to be in some way undesirable, was left to the mother, herself not yet thirty. Then there was a duel and the father shot and lamed the other man, who was a friend of his and much older and who had, it seemed to me, been very kind to the lady when her husband was away on journeys.

"Perhaps if she'd seen the older man first and married him, she would not have laughed and romped but stayed married," said sister Bea. "How could she know? If she played tag and tagged the wrong man in a hurry—it makes me sad and sorry."

Mother switched the subject as usual, but it laid a foundation stone of knowledge of which I was unconscious, and Bea's words built pity into it. Years later the understanding followed. She had in truth tagged the wrong man, which comes of taking marriage as a play. But the right one scored at last, and when she was gray and worn, and it was possible, he married her and nursed her through the cruelest of all illnesses until she died.

The term "Shoddies" came from one of the greatest manufacturing evils of the Civil War, the making of cloth for uniforms and blankets that sleazed out and was not properly woven. The bad stuff was so concealed by a little real wool as to appear to be durable material of the required standard. This cloth that melted and gave scant service was called shoddy, and it soon became a term also for people not up to form or standard. The profiteer of today was in Civil War times called a Shoddy, a class who bought their way where personality or previous standing would not admit them. The climb via the golden ladder is nothing new, and people have used the same methods to get money since the days when the robber barons lay in wait for the pack-trains at the fords. Gradually the Shoddies have prevailed, been accepted, and become a part of New York life. Nobody cares except a few of the "other people" with traditions. Yet in the sixties to be termed a Shoddy was a serious matter, and it was said the term was first used for a class by Brown, the celebrated sexton of Grace Church, the predecessor of Ward McAllister as a social herdsman. Be this as it may, there were some doors unopened to them. Late in the last year of the war George Bancroft, the historian and later our Ambassador to Germany, gave a masterly reception to Professor Goldwin Smith of Oxford, then visiting New York.

"It was a most unusual gathering," Father wrote in his journal, "as the guests were chosen to show

England what material America can now produce in the third generation of its native-born."

In going to the carriage (there was one, because Mother had gone to the party and in consequence it was a red-letter day for Father), Brown, in helping them down the steps, said, "Doctor, an elegant affair; all the best people of the city and not a Shoddy among them."

Today we think that our cities carried on their amusements heartlessly during the World War, which after all was geographically apart from us, and we imagine those men and women of the sixties with death always near the door sat with tear-stained faces and downcast eyes. They did not. Theatres and the opera flourished, Brignoli, Strakosch, Clara Louise Kellogg and Annie Louise Cary were constant entertainers at musicales in private houses. The cotillion or German had grasped the youth of the city. One dance late in 1864, at Edmund Miller's great house in West Fourteenth Street, to which Gatha was bidden as the dominie's daughter, lasted so long that there were two suppers. The ballroom, done in yellow satin and gold, was lighted by splendid candelabra of glittering crystal, and when Gatha had to leave at one o'clock (a very late hour for one of our family), though the twentieth figure of the cotillion had been reached there were as many more and the second supper ahead. A popular dancing man was always chosen as the leader of the elaborate figures, in this case a Mr. Peabody from Boston; and the late Jules Vatable was long a favorite cotillion leader. So important was the function that in describing the various attributes of a man when his engagement was announced, this grace held a conspicuous place, closely following his pedigree and the list of his clubs.

Many social and civic organizations flourished amazingly in the late days of the war and immediately after it. A notable group of New Yorkers founded the

Harvard Club in 1865, choosing Father for its president. The club's first home was at 835 Broadway, upstairs, as reads a circular printed on vellum, now in my possession, and the times of meeting were monthly, eight a year, the gap being from May to October. It was in this same year that Faganni did a very introspective portrait of Father in oils, which afterward fell to my share, so that when Evert Wendell, the staunch and enthusiastic son of Harvard, was some years ago seeking to assemble the portraits of the presidents for the clubhouse in West Forty-fourth Street and lacked two only—Father's and that of Joseph H. Choate, which was duly painted—I gave him this portrait, which now hangs in the great hall in dignified architectural surroundings. By strange chance the first of the two portraits sought was of the minister who officiated at Mr. Choate's wedding in 1860, and in referring to the fact a few years before his death Mr. Choate said to me "Your father did an excellent job, sound from cellar to attic. Even though the shingles on one part of the roof are a trifle thin, they are still water-tight." The Harvard Club began with a membership of one hundred, the organizing officers being president, Samuel Osgood, D.D.; vice-presidents, John O. Stone, M.D., Frederick A. Lane, and George Baty Blake; treasurer, Charles Emerson, and secretary, A. C. Hazeltine; while in the list of members are names of families that represented the city at its best—Henry W. Bellows, D.D., Samuel Blagden, George Bliss, Jr., Joseph H. Choate, James T. Carter, Willard Parker, M.D., Francis Howland, Thomas Kinnicut, H. W. Poor, John O. Sargent, George Cabot Ward, E. A. Washburne, D.D.

Yet during the war years the minister had a weary time of it. The day on which the Seventh Regiment marched down Broadway on its way to Washington,

Father took his stand under the Stars and Stripes displayed from the small balcony above the door of the Church of the Messiah. The next Sunday some of the main props of the parish had stepped out, leaving empty pews, their patriotism being first of all a matter of trade, with which the call to arms had interfered. Others that remained grew restless and said the city was moving up town, and the Church must follow. So the old Church of the Messiah was sold, and a landmark not only of Christian culture but of the appreciation of symbols disappeared, for it was the first Protestant church, after Trinity, not only to use flowers at Easter, but to weave them in the form of the Cross. Why did the Puritans shrink from this symbol and avoid its use? It often seemed to make them as uncomfortable as it did the stage Mephisto of *Faust*.

When the war was technically ended by the surrender of Lee, New York drew a long breath. Reconstruction must follow. Marvellous prosperity and dire disaster were both predicted. Which would it be? Spring came on, the spring of 1865. In early April it was mild enough for children to play out again. The little tufts of round-leaved blue violets, that huddled in our back yard in the exact spot that the sun touched first, were showing buds. The long windows were opened each day in the late morning, "to blow the winter out of the house," Mother said, for she was a pioneer of ventilation and therefore rather dreaded by her friends, who sought to preserve their health in winter by huddling behind double windows, three sets of curtains, and felt-covered, inside vestibule doors.

Father had begun his morning walks. He dressed ahead of Mother and went for a glass of Kissingen to Hanbury Smith's Spa in Union Place, where mineral waters were sold. Here he usually met a few friends who had come out for the same reason—either they all had sluggish livers or it was a fashion. Greetings and bits of news were exchanged and when Father returned, bringing the morning paper, breakfast was always ready.

On this particular April morning Mother was quite dressed and I was sitting on my small bed that was alcoved into Mother and Father's room. I had taken my bath and was being very slow in putting on a new pair of blue and white striped stockings, presently discovering that the difficulty came from invisible metal tags that held them together. How clearly those stripes were to be impressed upon me!

The front door opened and closed sharply. "Samuel, is that you?" said Mother from the bedroom doorway, adding to herself, "No, it cannot be, for he has been gone only a few minutes." Steps on the stairs; very slowly Father came into the room, stopped by the fireplace, steadying himself with one hand on the mantel shelf, the other clutching a newspaper to his breast. His face was white and drawn, dry sobs tore at his throat.

I can never forget how he looked, also how I could neither wholly put on those striped stockings nor get them off. I almost fell from my bed and stumbled over to get closer to Mother.

"What is it, Father?" she whispered. "Do speak," she implored, putting an arm about me and going toward him.

"Lincoln has been assassinated!—Ford's Theatre, Washington—last night," he managed to say, and the tears rained down his cheeks.

It is strange how in tense moments trifles impress themselves. As I think of this time it seems as if the new striped stockings kept coming between myself and Father's face like bars, until I ceased struggling with them, took another pair, and finished dressing without help. The words that passed between Father and Mother sounded as if they came through deep water and did not bear a meaning until long after.

"Who did it, Samuel?" asked Mother as soon as she could control her voice.

"Wilkes Booth the actor, the brother of our gentle friend Edwin—Laura Keene, who was on the stage, saw him as he made his escape."

"Then he has not been taken?"

"No."

"Was this the brother who was a witness at Edwin's wedding when you married him to Mary Devlin in your downstairs study nearly four years ago? Has the assassin been in *our house?*"

"Yes, it was Wilkes Booth, and the other witness was General Adam Badeau."

Then Gatha and Bea came in and Bea led me downstairs and gave me my breakfast, trying to make me talk about other things but she soon gave it up. I had been daily taught, and by what I knew that others felt, to love "Father Abraham" as someone wedged tightly in between my own father and God, in importance and power. A framed picture of him, in which he sits with his arm about his little son Tad, hung in my room.

"Will the poor little black children have to be sold away from their mothers again, now that he is dead?" I quavered, the tears salting the milk in my mug.

"Never!" said Bea. I was comforted, for sister Bea always told the truth.

Father said afterward that New York stopped that day, was dead to all other thoughts. The next days, until the funeral procession should pass through the city, were confused and strange. I scarcely saw

Mother, or Father who was busy at the temporary church arranging for the memorial service, and there were many meetings that he must attend. Gatha sat all day sewing long strips of black that were to be hung from the top piazza of our house on either side of the flag. Bea took me over to the Grays' for a walk but I did not like to be in the streets, the closed blinds and so much black everywhere frightened me. I wanted to get home again, for our blinds were left open, Father would not have them closed. "God's sunlight is the best cure for ills of body or spirit, we should not shut it out now, least of all times," he said, when Gatha, whose habit was, Nabob said, to "tie a black bow on trouble lest it should be mislaid," had begun to close them.

The funeral procession was to come up Broadway to Fourteenth Street, through to Fifth Avenue, then to Thirty-fourth Street and continue up Broadway to the Hudson River Railway Depot. Father and all our family were invited to the house of Mr. U. J. Smith, who lived on the corner of Union Place and the Square, to see it go by. From this house a wide view could be had toward Broadway and the procession would pass the very door. There was a balcony outside the parlor windows and wide front steps, while the railing about the yard would keep the great crowd from pressing in on us. Mother was fearful least I should become tired at the hours of waiting that might be necessary, but I promised not to complain, and as there would be no one to keep the house at home but O'Connell and the Frog, his dog, I was allowed to go. We had a hasty lunch before leaving, but owing to my excitement my stomach soon forgot it, and as the day wore on I grew painfully hungry. Middle afternoon came, division after division passed and it grew monotonous, the novelty wore off. At this moment some light refreshments were served to the guests indoors, those outside not caring to miss any of the procession.

How good the hot cocoa tasted, and the buttered biscuits spread with honey! Then came a filigree silver basket of the small, round, pink, frosted cakes that only Mrs. Carleton, the society cake-maker of the time, turned out. Very dear to my heart were these cakes, only to be had by us for the New Year's table or some great festivity. I took two. They didn't last very long. The basket made a second trip. I took two more and put them in the pockets of my much prized gray beaver cloth coat, the first coat that I had ever owned that was neither made over nor cut down, but came straight from Mrs. Paddon's over in Thirtieth Street and was a birthday gift from the Aunties,—as was also the round velvet hat from Honeywell with a lovely white ostrich plume to complete it. I had feared that the sugar frosting might stick to the coat lining, but there was no time to hesitate and immediately afterward one of the gentlemen said that we would all better come to the windows. Picking me up, as being so small that I should be lost in the crowd, he carried me down to the steps and gave me a fine place on a broad-topped fencepost of wrought iron.

It proved to be a false alarm but I was quite happy, even though when I tried to eat my cakes the icing stuck fast to the pockets. Suddenly I spied the basket, refilled and alluring, being passed to those outside. Would it reach the fence? It did, and was thrust quite under my nose. I took another pair! At this moment some one next me called, "Here comes the guard of honor, General Dix and his staff!" and every one pressed forward. I couldn't eat the cakes and I must use both hands to keep my place on the post, so slipping the elastic of my hat from under my chin I stuffed them into the crown.

Then the crowd became silent, not a murmur. The tramp of the officers of the Army and Navy who were on foot resounded from the cobbled pavement. Then horses' hoofs—a break—more horses' hoofs. Slowly, making a wide curve, the great car supporting the catafalque swung from Broadway into Fourteenth Street, an escort of the Seventh Regiment on either side. It was my first sight of this noble regiment, which afterward had not a little part in the days that backgrounded my life in early womanhood.

The car came on slowly, the various trappings of silver and black relieved by many flags. In spite of its solid structure the whole framework trembled from the unevenness of the pavement. It seemed to me as if something unearthly *must* happen. I should not have been surprised to see the pall fall away and Father Abraham come forth, like Lazarus at the command of Jesus, as pictured by Doré in his illustrations of the New Testament. The horses, almost hidden from sight by black drapery, were led, a man at the bit of each. As the car came nearer every head that I could see was hatless so I quickly pulled off my own hat. Out fell the two pink cakes, and rolling between many pairs of legs, disappeared in the gutter!

After the car had passed we soon went home, Father alone remaining, to join the group over in the Square for the memorial service, to be held near a bust of Lincoln that was surrounded by flags and flowers. George Bancroft was to give the oration, and Father was to read the poem that William Cullen Bryant had written for the service, he being selected for his clear ringing voice.

I told sister Bea about the cakes sticking to my

pockets and she promised to make them quite clean again, but I did *not* tell her about the other cakes in the gutter. That night when I was going to bed Mother, seeing that I was wrought up and tearful, said that I might sleep with her and that she would go to bed with me then, for she was so very tired. So when my head was all comfortable and quiet on her soft shoulder I whispered in her ear about the cakes and that I hoped a nice hungry dog had found them. She said she hoped so too, and did not scold me at all, only her shoulder shook just a little. We were both awake when Father came home looking very white and worn. He stood at the foot of the bed looking down at us and then he smiled and said, "Mab, sister Bea tells me that you are worried now that Father Abraham has gone lest the little colored children may be sold again. Listen to what your friend Mr. Bryant has written and I read to the people in the Square this afternoon:

'Thy task is done—the bond are free;
We bear thee to an honored grave,
Whose proudest monument shall be
The broken fetters of the slave.'

"In death he has made all secure."

I was comforted. Father had come home. I was by Mother's side and therefore safe. Drowsiness waved its truce flag to the excitement of the day. Then the balky striped stockings and the pink cakes danced happily together across my vision followed by a playful dog, hiding all the black draperies, and so I fell asleep.

VIII

KITCHEN DAYS IN THE SIXTIES

Though the war had long ended as a matter of action, factions and consequences still were rife. New York was very gay, there were all sorts of parties given by all sorts of people, for many had great profits of war to spend while just as many struggled to make both ends meet. I heard Madam Gray tell Aunt Cinder about some one who had set up an elaborate establishment, a carriage, coachman and footman, on a fortune that was made from the metal trimmings of coffins.

Bea had finished school and I had regular lessons with her in the morning. I had learned to read almost by myself in the midst of the general tumult. The beloved Mary Daly, kitchen commandante, had received an old-country, convent-school training and not only read aloud distinctly with a delightful brogue but wrote a good hand. She would seat me at the white table between the kitchen windows and show me how, by cutting words from the headlines of the newspapers, short sentences might be pieced together. Then all of a sudden, how to read came to me over night, as it were. Immediately I waded knee deep through the *Rutherford Children* and a series of probably inane and very detailed but to me delightful books called *Susie's Six Birthdays*, thereby saving the family the misery that the reading and rereading would have caused them.

Through the war days and long after, Mother and Aunt Cinder had so much that was extra to do, aside from parish work, that it became a habit for me to spend a couple of hours every afternoon with Mary Daly in the big sunny kitchen, to which the willow-ware and pewter plates on the dresser gave the brightness of a living room. I never had a nurse at any time in my life, the second girl, as she was then called, with the exception of Norah Goodnuf being usually quite young and of a less responsible type than the cook. Besides, she was too busy to care for me, for she must answer the door bell, take messages to Father, and do the bit of fine ironing that fell to her share. I fully realize, as I close my eyes now and the whole scene takes vivid form, that there was nothing about the home kitchen that was anything but healthful and wholesome for childhood. It was a clearly defined and respected part of the house. Those who came to it stayed for years, as they do with me now even in this time of upheavals.

There were many people among our friends who had comfortable and lovable colored help. There were some who had waiter-men such as Hopkinson Smith loved to portray; others who had ladies' maids, who did up the fine muslins and laces and renovated ball gowns; these latter were always supposed to be French. Help, was the term used, at least by people of New England ancestry, and the number for a family such as ours, of educated New Yorkers of middle-average purse, was at most two women and a chore man. Of course at times we had what Bea called fit-ins and Gatha, supernumeraries, flotsam and jetsam who were as much employed for their need as our own: a French girl from Martinique who coached my sisters, but was found to have an exceedingly bad pronunciation; a widow out of work and home, who had come to the Employment Society of the Church for help and did plain sewing and other branches of "accommodating."

Mrs. Curry was the certainly uncertain seamstress of

our little world. She weighed two hundred and fifty pounds but did miraculous things with her needle, plied with her left hand. She was in constant demand when little or nothing of underwear for either male or female could be bought ready-made. The sewing machine had been quite recently introduced and in conservative homes was considered, except for coarse work, a lazy woman's makeshift. Mrs. Curry not only systematically overlapped engagements, but there were periods when she simply *was not.* She said her absence was because her son Peter was subject to spells and at such times she must stay with him. But it was known that she drank, and it was whispered that she had been seen taking a trip in the Black Maria (then as now the name of the police court van), but the man who saw her go by was very careful not to assume the responsibility of telling his wife.

I think at this time that the usual viewpoint toward the misdeeds of what was called the working class, and especially toward the rights of the poor, was very hard and narrow in many ways, and the division fence high. The love of beauty and its expression was a right quite denied them, and I well remember Mother's account of Friend Gibbons' strongly expressed feelings on the subject, when a case that had come before the Employment Society of the Church was under discussion.

It was concerning the widow Logan, who had applied to the Church for aid and was given sewing to do at home; she also came to us as a fit-in and to help Mother when Peter Curry was having a poor spell. Mrs. Logan had a craving for pretty things and a color-sensitive eye. If given a chance to talk she would always tell about how in the old country (she was Channel Island born) she had been apprenticed to a dressmaker who worked for the quality; how, before her hands became hard from scrubbing, with closed eyes she could well-nigh tell the color of a bit of velvet by the touch; also about the over-seas China her mother had on the dresser. The coarse gray flannel and unbleached muslin of the garments she made for the Employment Society sometimes seemed really more than she could bear. She once said this openly and rather unwisely. Such sentiments were of course sniffed down with raised eyebrows by some of the management. Such presumption! Poverty was poverty and well matched with gray flannel. It had no right of opinion about color or material.

Friend Gibbons and Mother, however, defended Mrs. Logan. There was something in the outlines of her face and head, in the gestures of her small, twisted, thin hands that told of a strain of blood in her veins other than that her condition indicated. She made graceful gestures, and had a way of making a curtsy full of dignity quite unlike the usual bob. So between them they cheered her along with some children's aprons of plaid gingham and petticoats made of red flannel, a piece of which Nabob had contributed to the Society for the especial benefit of this misfit.

One day, however, the crash came. Her daughter Jeanie, who was chair-bound with rheumatism, had been very poorly and Mrs. Logan had asked for a dollar in advance on her work to give the girl a change of food.

"That will buy enough salt pork and potatoes to last a week, it being spring and the old crop getting soft," quoth Mrs. Oldam, who was treasurer at the time and held the purse; as she spoke counting out grudgingly four dirty twenty-five cent bills—we were then in the throes of paper currency of small denominations, big copper pennies, and very losable silver threepenny bits.

Two days later Mrs. Oldam and Mrs. Wick, affinities in uncharitable charity, called upon Mother so early that the breakfast silver was unwashed. Mother, Aunt Cinder or one of my sisters always washed the flat silver every morning in a small wooden tub filled with boiling water. This little tub was brought into the pantry and set upon a trestle-supported wooden tray. Soft soap of home make of which, city or country, there was always a barrel in the cellar, was used and the silver in this way was always kept bright without other handling. There was no Tiffany powder in handy little packages or any of the many silver creams; the only silver cleaner that I remember to have seen was a powder called whiting that was first moistened with alcohol, being very difficult to apply evenly and requiring much elbow grease to remove.

Mother did not encourage morning calls from the parish and at once saw that this visit boded no good, so she was very deliberate in going upstairs, but before she had more than untied her apron the ladies bore down upon her and began a somewhat incoherent patter song of indignation, the gist of it being this; the day before, Mrs. Oldam being in Jefferson Market—*Jefferson*, mind you, an expensive place to which she herself went but seldom—whom should she see but Mrs. Logan, at Tyson's, the very *best* stall for fruit and vegetables, where she had just selected a fine bunch of asparagus and a pottle of fresh strawberries! On being asked for whom she was marketing, she replied, without the least sense of shame, "For my girl, my Jeanie. I'm not buying for just the meal that's in the things, but the thought of them, the sight of their freshness, that is what will be doing her the good. And do you know, ma'am, when I told the man at the stall about my girl, he threw me in a knot of radishes and a pull o' lilacs for good luck to her?"

"Strawberries and asparagus early in May!" cried Mrs. Wick. "Not the left-overs of a street peddler, either, but from Jefferson Market! She must be either crazy or an impostor."

"Both!" shrilled Mrs. Oldam. "She must be dropped from our books. I will see to that tomorrow."

"She is surely not an impostor," Mother replied very slowly. Bea, who had come into the room, said that Mother's Roman nose was at its best, while her full lips straightened and grew so tight that they swallowed the dimples at the corners. "She asked for money that she has since earned, to buy a change of food for her daughter. She has bought this food and given you a good reason for its quality, if I understand you rightly."

Bea said that the ladies suddenly wizzled up, making little noises with their twisted lips, unformed words, that sounded like crullers dropped into fat that was too hot.

So it came to pass that Friend Gibbons and Mother took the widow Logan into their own hands, and she came to us to be tried out as a home dressmaker. Her first garment, for Gatha, was rather unfortunate, as Mrs. Logan "disremembered" how to lay a pattern on goods that had an up and down, as well as a right and wrong side, and cut the pair of sleeves running after each other. As the material was a remnant not to be matched, contrasting sleeves had to be used which were not in the mode. However, patience and understanding finally conquered and opened a way. Mother and daughter came to keep the house in summer when we went to Mosswood, caring for Father as well on Sundays when he must be in town. To Jeanie the long back yard was like going into the country; it had two grass plots and for shade a sweet gum and two ailanthus trees, fortunately not of the ill-smelling sex. A flower border gave room, between two rose bushes and a grapevine, for a few geraniums and some cheerful nasturtiums, while the overhang of the back porch made a shelter that could be used even in rainy weather, as the ground beneath was paved with flagstones.

As soon as they came to us, both Mrs. Logan and Jeanie began to find themselves, and by the end of the season Jeanie was quite herself. Then by the aid of Nabob and Aunt Kinnie Haven—dear Madam Gray having passed on within that year—a little needlework shop was financed for them, with living rooms in Patchen Place hard by. Jeanie, too, was developing the gift of design both in embroidery and crocheting.

"The star-marks of the sweet-gum leaves when they fall on the wet pave in the yard gave me the first thought of patterning from things that grow for my work," she told Mother, in gratefully giving her a bit of fine crochet lace with the star-pointed motive of these leaves as its inspiration.

This led to Jeanie's taking lessons in design given at the Cooper Institute over in Clinton Place. So the longing for color and beauty was satisfied, and a decent living made possible for two lives, by the way of a single dollar spent for strawberries and asparagus in May—coupled with a summer in a city back yard, and understanding.

I have strayed from the kitchen, but the many issues leading either to or from it make this inevitable. At Christmas time the kitchen wore a festive air somewhat akin to what one reads about in the stories of Old England. Gifts came from many places to plenish the store room and pantry, or to be hung in the grated cold closet in the cellar. The Aunties always sent a barrel, as carefully packed as if the contents had been of priceless porcelain. In the bottom, well slatted down to prevent crumbling, came an array of mince pies and two plum puddings, one rich and very fruity, one less so, supposedly for my benefit. Then a box of Aunt Mary's very best oak-leaf cookies, that only at Christmas time had caraway comfits dressed in colored sugar on top. Next, packages of nuts, raisins, homemade peppermint drops and molasses candy, pulled until it was almost white and quite brittle. On several occasions the padding necessary at the top was made up of a dozen damask napkins exquisitely hemmed, or a pair of linen pillow shams (as they were called) with an elaborate border and center initial done in beautifully exact knot stitch. One year Mr. Balcom of the Spingler House on Union Place sent, beside a baron of beef, a turkey, a pair of capons, and a brace of partridges; and Nabob, four sugar-cured Virginia hams!

That Mary Daly was unusual even in the middle Victorian days will tell itself. But then we have always had unusual helpers with whom we have seemed to share a common viewpoint. Mary was a rather pale woman of a type otherwise that should have been blooming; large blue eyes set wide apart, and features such as Meyer von Bremen has often used for his Madonnas. Mother noticing this pallor and that she sometimes had a stitch in her side, as she called it, sent her to Dr. Draper. He said that Mary should go out every day for a walk in the fresh air. No, not at night, in the morning, and moreover have a motive for the walk.

Then a council was held the next time that Madam Gray came over. How could the cook be given an airing with a motive, every day before noon? The family gave it up. Father was appealed to. He never interfered in domestic matters unless pressed, though he had established an inflexible household law, in four sections.—No disagreeable topics were to be discussed at meal times. No one, not even Mother, must touch anything on his desk. The gas was not to be left burning when no one was in a room, and pins, the usual aftermath of dressmaking, must never be found on the floor of his study or bedroom! Dressmakers are porcupines for shedding pins, and Father had as great a dread of them as my otherwise fearless Mother had of mice.

As the present matter did not come under either of these heads he paused, and then asked why Mary herself might not be asked for suggestions. Mary appeared, curtsying low, and excusing herself for coming upstairs in her working gown.

"There is always trouble about that milk can" (a gallon can of milk was sent down from Mosswood daily). "The coming and going of it is bothersome and many a time I am put about with my noon meal for lack of it. There is no trustability in chancey young lads such as do the fetching. Now do you let me fetch and carry it, and put the money you paid the boy to the doing of my heavy sheet ironing."

Madam Gray upon being told the suggestion paused in a long gesture of astonishment, leaving the cookie jar uncovered to Tom-dog's great joy.

"But how will she manage, Dame?" she finally asked.

"She proposes to walk up to the railroad depot at Twenty-sixth Street and Fourth Avenue, the can being empty, and ride down in the Sixth Avenue cars with the full can. This can has a wooden guard on the bale, and in addition I will make her a small padded holder."

So it came to pass each morning that a little woman wearing a knitted hood and warm plaid shawl, that quite covered her can, might be seen going up the street, except in storms when O'Connell replaced her. Sometimes I went to the depot with her, sitting in the carpeted, parlor-like waiting room while Mary went for the can. Standing then on the northern boundary of the present Madison Square Garden this depot was a place of great interest to me. When we went to Fairfield, the cars were pulled out of the shed by six horses and sped up Fourth Avenue and through the tunnel into a wide open space above Forty-second Street, at what seemed to me a breakneck pace. Here the engine, after a deal of fussing with a turntable, picked us up, gave a long hoot, and we were really on our way. But if we arrived quite ahead of train time I would stand in the doorway of the depot and watch the crating of street cars in the famous Stevenson shops across the way. They seemed to have made these cars not only for the United States but South America as well, so I amused myself by finding where they were going and imagining that I was travelling in them—a wholly new game of make-believe.

The kitchen furnished much amusement for me when lint-picking grew monotonous and finally ceased altogether. For this occupation I had a cleanly scrubbed pastry board and a rather dull knife. The old linen which every household collected, first using everything that was possible for bandages, was torn into squares of various sizes and then shredded, thread by thread, into soft pad-like masses for dressing wounds, there being then no such article as absorbent cotton or any form of sterilized gauze. It was a tedious process, for if the threads were too short the dressings would be crumby and useless. Small fingers could do it nicely and I revelled in my task to a certain point, and then I took refuge in more exciting things, such as were to be found in the Dutch oven and the top drawer of the kitchen dresser.

The dresser was a sort of museum in itself. The top shelf was flanked by pitchers of all sizes, shapes and colors, for Uncle Isaac, who lived in Boston, took great delight in haunting auction sales and frequently sent Mother a barrel of odds and ends of china and earthenware. He was especially fond of bowls, pie plates and other dishes of a deep yellow color mottled with brown like imitation tortoise shell. One pitcher that was my delight was a white syrup jug with a pewter lid and was so exactly in shape like the lighthouse on Fairweather's Island opposite our beach at Fairfield, that I used it as such in the make-believe scenery built on the washroom tubs, and it has been called the "lighthouse jug" ever since.

The kitchen ware of daily use filled the next two shelves, this being the remains of Grandmother Murdock's blue willow set with its drooping trees, bridge and pagoda design, then scorned and moved down in the world. This had been forced below stairs by a new white porcelain set with glittering gold bands and a red line, a parish gift, and the very last word in elegance. Please remember that this was the ugly American period, plush furniture, albums, wax flowers which I adored, or Rogers groups for the centre table (ours was less awful than some others, being Ichabod Crane and Katherine Van Tassel), and homemade plaques, all of which lasted well into the eighties until the year of the Centennial Exhibition had made people realize how new we were as a people, and, awakened and looking back to find their roots, they began to realize the beauty and simplicity of the put-away furniture of Colonial days. But even then I preferred the willow ware with its dramatic scenery. And presently, though the pieces were few in number, the set crept up stairs again into its own, now ranking with the respectable antiques.

On a lower shelf the pudding dishes lived, great and small, also a revolving stand that held twelve cups for soft custard, eleven being in a circle, the twelfth the king cup, raised a little above the others; the handles of the covers were shaped like flames, somewhat after the classic emblem of the soul. The whole structure was an object of awe and was regarded chiefly from the decorative point, except when the cups were filled with Aunt Cinder's arrow-root custard, lemon-flavored, ice-cold, smooth as cream and topped by a little flurry of grated nutmeg. It was so nice that this custard was thought good for colds and sore throat. So few pleasant things in those days were thought good for the young when they were sick. As I look back I think the reasons were from an economic standpoint, not a medical. Dainties and butter were expensive, so butter was not considered good for childhood, and gruel was cheap. But as Mother did not believe in sloppy food, I revelled in crisp buttered toast ahead of my time.

On the farthest corner of the dresser's lower shelf was an equipment belonging, if not to the times, at least to the economy of our house, the jars and covered dishes in which left-over food was prepared and kept for the poor. There seem to have been no organized food charities, no soup kitchens, no bread lines, such as Fleischmann of the Vienna Bakery near Grace Church started many years later in a stressful time of panic. So the worthy poor and the professional beggars with baskets prowled from house to house and were a recognized part of New York street life. The women carried deep double-handled baskets under shawls that completely concealed them, these being sometimes large enough to cover the wearer's head also. Together with this form of female begging the males of the same tribe, called ash-pickers, came with bags slung on the back and bent pokers in hand with which they raked and rummaged in the ash barrels for coal or garbage, making unwholesome dust and adding to the litter of the never clean streets. There was no organized street cleaning department until late in the sixties, mind you.

That the door-to-door begging was a nuisance all agreed. But what to do about it? There were, during and after the war, many really hungry people who must be fed. So Friend Gibbons with Mother and some other women of the parish looked up a number of cases of real need, and divided them amongst themselves. Whatever left-over food was suitable was put away neatly in jars or dishes, the tea leaves were drained and saved in small earthenware pots, and the coffee grounds also. This saving of tea leaves may sound strange, but as a family we were specialists in tea, for Nabob sent Mother a large lead-lined chest direct from China every Christmas, Mr. A. A. Low of Brooklyn doing likewise. Hence the family really swam in fine tea, morning, noon and night, which was always brewed quickly in Chinese fashion, therefore the leaves had plenty of flavor for those old-country folk to whom tea that was not boiled ranked as dish-water. Each woman receiving food had her regular day for coming, and was required to return the dishes and pitchers. For such families as had children great puddings were made of bread or rice with currants and a dash of spice, the tops being well sprinkled with cinnamon. Having country milk we could make these things at little cost, and Mary Daly would often bake an extra loaf for some poor body who, craving a bite of homemade bread, yet lacked the strength to knead or the coals to bake it.

So much for the outside of the dresser, but the lure of the top left-hand drawer was concealed. In it were kept paper-covered books of both poetry and adventure! Beadle's *Dime Song Book*, Beadle's *Dream Book*, and several volumes of Beadle's *Boy's Library*, all of which O'Connell had bestowed upon Mary Daly in return for her putting up with the Frog and letting him take the air in the back yard. The Frog was a pet bull dog that belonged to one of O'Connell's sons, who was sometimes away on business up the river: The Frog according to O'Connell was worth "big money." He held a record, his fighting name was Hennessy's Mike, but I called him the Frog from the way in which he squatted when he sat and looked up over his head as if he wanted to catch flies. O'Connell liked to bring him, as he said, "to get the air where he couldn't get into trouble but just sniff about and blink at the cats on the fence top." Mary used to give me odds and ends of meat to cut up for the poor dog, for he had such an upside-down face that he could not really enjoy a bone. At first I was afraid of him and then we became good friends, for he had so much character under his ugly features that I ceased to care for the pink-eyed white poodle puppies such as were sold in Fourteenth Street. Aunt Cinder had bought me such a puppy for two successive springs, one having turned into something wholly different by autumn and the other having weak eyes and fits. O'Connell also sang the *Wearing of the Green*, and *Paddy Duffy's Cart* beautifully, and could dance a real jig when his rheumatism was not too bad.

Of the story books the *Pampas Hunters* was one of my favorites, the *Dream Book* stood my hair on end with its prophecies, and the rhymes of the *Song Book* lingered long in my head, especially one about Mrs. Lofty, which I can only quote imperfectly from memory:

> Mr. Lofty has a carriage,
> I have not.
> He can give his bride a palace,
> Mine a cot.
>
> Mrs. Lofty has a husband;
> Naught cares she.
> Mine comes home a dewy evening—
> Kisses me.

The moral of these primitive songs tended to prove that if one married a rich man he wouldn't kiss you when he came home at night. Father always kissed Mother when he came home, even in the daytime, hence I argued that we must be very poor, to which I was quite resigned, which was well!

The Dutch oven, which had beforetime been used

for roasting, by pushing it up in front of the open grate, was no longer needed, since the Rhinelander house had a Knickerbocker range with an oven in which the meat was cooked: baked, Mother said, but not roasted. Mary Daly had used the Dutch oven as a treasure house for papers also brought her by O'Connell, the *Police Gazette*, the New York *Ledger*, and several really lurid "penny dreadfuls." "Those are only for grown folk," chided Mary, and packed them away after I had little more than looked at the ornamental headlines. There came a time much later on when I found a copy of the *Fireside Companion* tucked under the basement door. I seized it and read a thrilling story of virtuous poverty triumphing over wicked wealth. It might have been written by Laura Jean Libby. As I became deeply interested, the sentence ended abruptly with "Continued in next week's issue." This might be bought at any news stand for six cents so I must have six cents immediately—five was possible but the extra penny was the sticking point. My financial resources were not only limited but uncertain. Gatha, whose work it was to dust the parlor daily, gave me three cents a week for dusting the fluted legs of the Worcester square rosewood piano. Gatha had a lovely small, round, eighteen-inch tight waist and stooping bent the bones of her stays, so I sometimes dusted the curly legs of the big sofa out of sympathy.

The money from the sale of colored rags belonged to me, that from the white rags and papers belonged to Bea, but owing to everything having been made into something during and since the war, the collection of rags of any kind was a slow process. The Aunties from Boston when they came to visit sometimes brought me a roll of fifty pennies done up like a stick of candy. They made up these rolls very carefully but now you can get them at any bank. These pennies I could keep to spend for myself, but if they gave me five dollars it had to go into the savings bank towards music or dancing lessons. Oh, those music lessons! When my whole desire was to draw and paint—to create something beautiful. I had been very unlucky lately, for the two visits of that winter had been of the five dollar kind, so, as far as the *Fireside Companion* was concerned, I was financially destitute.

Something happened about that time to make me forget the six cents, so that I never knew what became of Annabelle's lover. Father came home from an afternoon walk one day with a book for me in his pocket. His friend Mr. Appleton the publisher had sent it to me. The leaves were gilt edged, the cover was of red linen with three gilt lines around the border, and in the centre was a circle framing a little girl with long hair who was holding a small pig in her arms as if it was a doll. The name of the book was *Alice's Adventures in Wonderland;* inside it said, "By Lewis Carroll, with forty-two illustrations by John Tenniel," and the date, 1866. I looked at the pictures and began to read it before supper but I could not read very fast. Mother and Father were going to Professor Botta's to meet Mr. Longfellow, so sister Bea said if I would go to bed early she would read *Alice* to me. But when the time came for putting out the light, the Duchess had just thrown the sneezing baby at Alice and it was beginning to turn into a pig—and I simply *had* to know what happened next.

Bea said, "Try to go to sleep and if you can't I will peep in a little later." I tried but I simply could not. Who could settle down, with the Lizard Bill stuck in the hotbed sash, and the Hatter quite near the end of the clean tea cups? After a while Bea came back and when she saw my eyes wide open and shining through the dark she brought in Mother's candlestick with the screen, the one that Mrs. Heath gave her, and read

Alice through to the end, and what do you think, it was after eleven o'clock! After this Bea tucked the book under my pillow, for I was afraid that it too might vanish or prove to be like the Duchess, only a pack of cards.

Then she cuddled me to sleep—yes, I suppose that it was wrong to do this. Lovely sister Bea! I have only to close my eyes and see her exquisite face and feel the sympathy and warmth of her arms. Of course children should go to sleep stark and alone in the dark, it is doubtless the right training, but then there can be no beautiful bedtime home memories. Are we not thus cheating them of more than we give?

Next day I took *Alice* to the kitchen and read it to Mary Daly; she liked it, but it vexed me because she was not a bit surprised. She said that Father William in the poem "You are old, Father William," lived in the next village to them, and that her father always went over to help him at pig killing, and as for people's changing their size there were many things that any one might eat or drink that would make them swell up or shrink. O'Connell came in just before the end of the story and said, "The outcome of a pack of cards has given many a one quare dreams," and that his father had caught a Mock Turtle his very self in Bantry Bay, and when they had made soup of the calf's head part they kept the shell for a porridge bowl, adding that he wished he could give the Frog just one chew at that Duchess, for titled folk were all of a piece, in stories and out.

Alice lived under my pillow for months, I nearly loved her to death. I also made the mistake of coloring the dainty pictures clumsily with crayons. Yet was it a mistake? They say, lacking the color, that this first American edition of *Alice* is now a collector's book with a price on its head. Praised be the crayons, for it is pitiful to have a money price set on the head of aught one loves, either book or dog.

Besides reading aloud so convincingly that you could imagine that the book people were really in the room, sister Bea was a wonderful teller of tales, both adapted and original, but she absolutely balked at reading the *Rollo Books* and *Harry and Lucey*. One of her serials about a little girl called Lily Maitland, taking her from birth to marriage, lasted two years. *The London Doll*, *Esperanza, or the Home of the Wanderers*, *Leila on the Island* and its sequel, and Lillian's *Golden Hours*, bridged the time until the publication of *Little Women* came when I preferred to read to myself. One time for story telling was in the morning when I was having my hair curled. It was fairly long and a bit curly, and Bea's job was to keep the upper and lower tiers separate, brush the curls over a stick and loop the top row back with a ribbon. Bea knew all the fairy stories by heart, Grimm, LaBouillet and Hans Christian Andersen, and adapted many more never seen in print. Most fairy stories end with a wonderful Prince, a wedding, and "they lived happy ever after." Sister Bea fully realized that children are primitive and direct, and grasp life first as a whole, not in sections; a father, mother and children are must-be's and belong to every day. Birds are in pairs and have nests and young. The house cat has perhaps caused a sensation by nesting her kittens in a drawer of the guest room bureau! It never occurred to Bea to tell me a stork put them there, and it was the same with babies. They were happy normal arrivals much better than kittens. Also they never had to be given away because "six were too many." Consequently vague neuter stories of the merely narrative type deemed proper for children, however cleverly planned, never held my interest.

With *Alice* from over-seas for a luck piece began my

own book shelf, and with *Little Women* for a really truly story a joyous if somewhat "human various" group soon gathered. *The Girlhood of Shakespeare's Heroines*, *The Memoirs of a London Doll*, *The Wide, Wide World*, Napier's *Tommy Try and What he did in Science*, *The English Orphans*, Lillian's *Golden Hours*, *Lamb's Tales from Shakespeare*, *The Wilds of Africa*, *Leatherstocking Tales*, and finally Marion Harland's first *Cook Book*, Longfellow's poems, Miss Yonge's *Dove in the Eagle's Nest*, and so on, and these still foregather side by side. If only Mary Daly had not taken Beadle's *Song Book* and *Dream Book* and all the stories of adventure, when at last she went to California for its milder climate, the sequence would be complete, yet the kitchen days are far more than a memory—I'm sorry for the child, when grown up, who has never known them.

IX

WINDOWS AND STREET CRIES

"Glass Put'een!"

In winter many phases of life come in to one through the windows. This was very true of our house, the outlook being wide through the long windows in front, where one might step out on the porch for either sight or sounds, for the street cries were as varied as the street sights and quite as interesting.

The first balcony, called the front stoop (stoep), led to the long yard and street. This was the place to run at the always exciting cry of "Extry, Extry! Great disaster—br—br. . .!" Two men worked the street at the same time, one on each side, alternating their calls until excitement was well whipped up. All through the war the lower hall was drafty from constant door opening. The Eleventh Street block being bluntly wedge-shaped on the Tenth Street side, a very large garden at the front and east fell to the first house from Sixth Avenue. In it were many walks and a grass plot large enough to be used for the new game of croquet, and Frank Schenk, the solitary boy who lived there, had a Shetland pony, stabled in the side yard, upon which he rode about the walks. As he was not allowed to come out or to ask any children to play with him, making faces through the fence was the only exchange of compliments. But as the borders were planted with pansies and daisies at the first sign of spring, the garden yielded something that every passerby might enjoy. Running between this yard and the back of the shops on Sixth Avenue was a narrow paved lane, it could not be called a street, upon which four or five small wooden houses faced. Garden Row it was called, thereby often causing it to be confused with the larger block. In earlier times it might well have been a rambling outlet to Milligan Place running in from Sixth Avenue, as the ends of the two almost met.

These houses, though rather picturesque and cottage-like, were so located that neither sun nor air could reach them, and many funerals, especially the small white ones, came down the narrow way. Once O'Connell in the late sixties reported that a man had died from smallpox in the middle house. Presently, late in the afternoon, a quantity of soiled bedding and a mattress were heaped upon two wooden ash barrels at the curb, it evidently being expected that the ash collector would remove them on his next but rather uncertain call.

Mother was agitated, Father prepared to complain to the as yet feebly functioning Health Board going at once to his study to write the letter. "A written complaint when the whole neighborhood meanwhile is being infected," said Mother, the Roman nose being particularly in evidence. "There are more direct methods."

She went quickly down the basement stairs, we could hear her steps go to the kitchen and return. Then the basement door closed emphatically. Father paused, his pen poised over the paper, awaiting results, for results and Mother usually travelled together.

Shortly she returned, a little out of breath, giving a quizzical smile to Father and saying, "A live coal can light other things than O'Connell's pipe." She told me to look out of the front parlor window. Lo and behold! there was a lovely, lively bonfire blazing in the gutter near Sixth Avenue. Moreover it lasted a long time, for after the rags and straw mattress burned, the two barrels were more lasting. How happy the street boys were as they pranced about it! When it was over two policemen came; one stamped on a few perfectly dead ashes while the other wrote something in a pocket book. Then they shook their night sticks at the dancing boys and went away.

The most unique front-window view of this time was the cart and the woman who came to get the swill. This material does not seem to have been called "garbage" in the sixties—just plain swill, and about its disposition and the care of the pails Mother was most particular. Squatter farms flourished in many places from Forty-second Street north and westward. The squatter farmers, many of whom were from Holland and Belgium, were thrifty and very eager to collect anything that could be fed to poultry or pigs or used for fertilizer, asking for the same among the householders to whom they peddled vegetables. Our swill was considered very desirable, because, in return for its prompt removal, Mother forbade anything like broken glass, tins or wires to be put in the pail. Mrs. Bom was the woman who came for it. She was a Hollander, of a broad, lean shape, with a weather-beaten face and no front teeth. But she had a very pleasant smile, and in spite of her messy business, the oddly shaped cap that she wore under her hood was always starched and spotlessly clean. A daughter came with her sometimes. Her husband never came as he, she said, saved her from real toil and let her do this light work. The cart was strongly made, had two wheels and held four large pails. The straight shafts were joined at the top by a band of leather, and outside of each shaft a large dog was harnessed. When the load was ready to move, Mrs. Bom took her place between the shafts, and placing her hands on the straps she pushed and steered at the same time.

Of what breed were these dogs? Having the memory of many distinct races in mind, I judge them a breed of themselves. Huskies, with St. Bernard traits and the intelligence of the difficult-to-raise police dogs; hardy, patient and kind if you did not lay hand on their cart or freight. I loved them at first afar off from the parlor windows, then one happy day I was introduced to them. Mary Daly, seeing my longing, saved me bones and scraps, then, wrapping me up in her thick plaid shawl, took me out to feed them, their owner warming herself in the kitchen while she enjoyed a bowl of black coffee without sugar. One very snowy day Mrs. Bom came, her feet, wearing two pairs of heavy knit stockings, thrust into a pair of wooden shoes. These had spikes in the soles to prevent slipping. I never again saw any outfit such as hers, until nearly a score of years later when on my honeymoon I met the same combination in the market place at Antwerp. There the cart did not hold swill pails but spotless, shining copper cans with narrow necks from which milk was being peddled.

On the opposite side of the street the houses were chiefly three-story plain brick buildings, with the exception of Mr. George Wetmore's, which was of extra width and had an ornamental iron-work veranda draped with wistaria and other vines. There were three Wetmore boys, Charles, George and Howard; they were too grown up to associate with our group of youngsters, still we could look at them across the street, which was some comfort, for there was not one real boy on our side of the way. Bobbie Spence lived directly opposite by the lamp post, and was much cultivated as he always had the latest thing in sleds, roller skates, and a velocipede that ran smoothly, and was worked in a leisurely manner by the feet. My velocipede was of the type that had two back wheels and one in front, with pegs running from the hub upon which you put your feet to steer. The bar that divided your legs and braced the seat supported a wooden horse's head. The machine was worked by two upright bars connected with the rear wheels, beyond question a chest-developing article, but one that was prone to squeak if you went at all fast, or without warning to balk or take a sudden lurch into the gutter.

Next above the Spence house was the Donaldsons'. Harry, the only child there, was quite grown up and only crossed to our side of the street to talk to Blanche Groesbeck over the fence. Blanche was entirely out of our world, for her big brother Billie kept a horse and phaeton with a little seat behind called a rumble in which sat a colored boy in livery. This boy came into the house as soon as Billie took the reins, brought out the whip and lap-robe, tucked in his master and whoever he took with him, jumped into the rumble after the horses had started and sat immovable with folded arms. Sometimes Blanche went with her brother, and sometimes no one. Then the older girls, who did not jump rope but walked up and down arm in arm, began to gossip about who might be going with him, but Bobbie and I thought it would be great sport to sit alone in the middle of the seat snapping the whip all the time with no one to say "Don't, it makes me nervous."

The Donaldson house furnished some amusement even after dark, for the light of the street lamp fell full upon it. We could always tell when Mr. and Mrs. Donaldson were going to a party, for the door would fly open and the colored waiter man would roll a bundle of red carpet down the steps, carefully placing weights on it to hold it in place. Soon Mrs. Donaldson would come down to the carriage, sometimes wearing slippers that shone like gold, carefully escorted by the serving man. Mr. Donaldson followed, wearing a cape coat and shining high hat. When the carriage had driven away the carpet was rolled up and taken into the basement. Bea and Gatha were always interested in this performance, and even Mother, who was not usually what Madam Gray called socially curious, watched one night to see what happened when they came back. Mr. Donaldson tapped on the basement window, then came the same process, only reversed. The man rolled the carpet up the steps and followed the couple into the house by the front door.

Between the Wetmores' house and the Spences', set between houses where the tenants never changed, was one where the people never stayed long. The white-paneled inside shutters, such as almost all houses had at this time, were kept closed night and day, except the middle section of each, and one side of the double door to the vestibule was always closed even in pleasant weather. I should never have noticed the house, it was so dull and dreary, except that I sometimes saw two ladies and a very pretty young girl dressed in pink and green gauzy-looking evening gowns, though it was only afternoon, peeping out between the shutters. They seemed to have a good many friends who called, men alone and men and women together, but the strange part was that the callers did not wait on the steps but dodged quickly inside the partly closed vestibule. I called it the House of the Pink and Green. One day I heard Aunt Cinder and Mother speaking about it, and I asked why she never called on the pretty ladies as she did on other neighbors. She said that they were not well-behaved people and did a great deal of harm in the world so that those who visited them were ashamed of being seen there. I wondered why and how, then forgot about them.

A little later one night there was a noise in the street and presently Mother came up from the study and sat by me, thinking that I might be awake and frightened. There was a great crowd across the way, and she said that a man had been drugged and robbed in the House of the Pink and Green, also that the police had taken all the people away. Other people came to live in this house who had children that came over to play Red Lion with us, but the incident of the Pink and Green stayed in the back of my head and later threw into relief one of the shadows of the life of the city.

Midway between Sixth and Seventh avenues was a gray stone church, the Owl Church I called it because of the owl-eyed effect of its Ionic columns. Though protected by an iron fence and gate, a loose latch let us open it and the more daring among us, who were allowed to cross the street, played Sunday school on the steps almost every seasonable afternoon. The ingrained Puritan influence of the time suggested this as the only suitable game. But when the same group came to play on our steps it was either plain school, or one-foot-hop-up, the winner being the child who could take the flight on one foot without either losing balance or touching the hand rail.

Fire engines often dashed by after the horse apparatus replaced the volunteer firemen, as there was an engine house in Tenth Street back of us, and now and then an excited and jeering crowd would follow a pushcart propelled and guarded by a couple of policemen, the passenger being a drunken man or quite as often a woman, too stupid to walk, but able to scream or sing, there being at my first remembrance no police patrol wagon for this purpose. The Black Maria, which took prisoners from the police court to the Tombs, then as now was not used for a single passenger. By these happenings came the knowledge of the evil of the streets that is the penalty of growing up, but as it came gradually it was not so much a matter for curiosity, but rather one of the inevitable shadows of life.

This easy-going old-fashioned street always had a personality of its own and keeps it still in spite of shabbiness. Well do I remember our excitement late in the century when one of the houses on the side of the Owl Church (even then replaced by another, until finally religion was crowded out by an apartment house) was bought by Daniel Chester French, but lately come to New York. In due time the building was inwardly transformed, the middle being opened for two stories into a working studio, where this gentlest and least self-conscious of our great artists not only welcomed his friends but allowed them at times to see him work. Specially do I remember the figure of the angel of his monument to Milman, the strength and sweep of its furled wings, the only wings that I have ever seen either painted or modeled that seemed capable of lifting a human being. "Oh, yes," he said, "most wings are futile even as symbols. This was the model that I magnified"—and he took from the screen the wonderful muscular wing of a wild goose. Later Elwell remodeled an adjoining house, and for a brief time Kate Douglas Wiggin, then Mrs. Riggs, gathered her cheerful group of admirers about her, while there are but few of these old houses that have not at least temporarily housed artists of pen, brush or chisel.

There were some street cries and street sights that were seasonal. In spring, when we heard a marching band that drowned the tinkling bells of the street-car horses, we looked out, usually from the second story, to see a passing target excursion. Sometimes it would come eastward and turn down Sixth Avenue, sometimes the reverse. The members of the rifle club usually wore some attempt at a uniform. An ornamental, streamer-trimmed target was carried on a pole side by side with the prize. This last was frequently a wonderful silver-plated ice-water pitcher, or a three-story fruit dish of the same metal. Bringing up the rear was a colored boy with a water pail, in the contents of which a dipper rolled to and fro, with no individual paper drinking cups near to cry out at the sight.

On Thanksgiving Day the streets were alive with young people, dressed in the old clothes of their elders, or as Indians, or in every fantastic combination that could be imagined. They blew tin horns or swung watchmen's rattles and travelled in groups that finally joined in a go-as-you-please procession. Ragamuffins they were called, or sometimes fantastics, and we always went out to watch them. I, who have always wished to know the reason why of things, have never yet been able to trace the precise origin of the custom. Here in New England the young folks go about in costume and masks on Hallowe'en. In Old England, in Evan's youth, they did the same thing on Guy Fawkes Day, November 5th, singing the rhyme about "gunpowder, treason and plot" from door to door after the manner of the carol singers on Christmas Eve. Perhaps it may have been an unconscious blending of the two customs, for it is rather too frivolous to have a wholly Dutch origin.

The third story front windows looked out over the roofs of the lower houses opposite and gave a chance to watch fires to the northward. The upper rear windows gave an entirely different viewpoint. For many years the masts of vessels on the Hudson might be seen here and there between the buildings, and there was always the hope of a picture in the sky at sunset, or of seeing, in early spring, Orion marching slowly down to the west.

A couple of trees in our back yard partly concealed a very old tumble-down brick house. At the corner window of it, morning, noon and night by the light of an oil lamp, a Hebrew shoemaker kept up an endless tap-tapping on the sole leather, his profile, beaked nose and beard being of the racial type pictured in Doré's illustrations to *The Wandering Jew,* one of the books over which I loved to pore because the pictures were suggestive rather than final, and left elbow room for imagination.

To the left of this house a little court called Patchen Place, with houses on either side, pushed in from West Tenth Street. Our fence so nearly bounded it on the end that it was topped by heavy spikes to keep out thieves, for sometimes men chased by the police had tried to escape by running up this alley and crossing the yards of the Rhinelander block. These spikes were much disliked by Bobbie Spence and me because they so often caught our kites that, lacking proper tail balance, plunged suddenly when we were trying to work them skyward.

Patchen Place, as well as the more cramped Milligan Place round the Tenth Street corner, had plainly been a byway to the fields not so many years ago, and even at this time seemed to have an attraction for artistic people as being somewhat apart from traffic. Mr. Booth, in coming to see Father, was sometimes on his way to Patchen Place where some members of his company, I think named Pateman, lived.

Over the low roofs of this court I loved to look at the bell tower below the market, whose booming was the loudest of all street sounds before the "still alarm" replaced it, and the building, which was like a sturdy, over-grown Dutch windmill, vanished. In the late seventies the graceful clock tower of the New Jefferson Market police court added beauty to the skyline.

The Greenwich Avenue public school lent a sort of rhythm to the street sounds when the windows were open and the primary class shrilly chanted the multiplication table—"Twice one's two, twice two's four" . . . Sometimes it rasped one's nerves by its incessancy like the scraping of katydids, and even once stopped the Cookie Jar Club's conversation because Madam Gray and Aunt Cinder found themselves repeating "Twice two's four" in chorus.

One view, or rather sport, that the back yard furnished which was not a view in the strict sense, but you had to see it out of the window before the game could be played, we called Catch-Foam. On the southwest corner of Eleventh Street and Greenwich Avenue was Tracey & Russell's brewery. In some process of beermaking clouds of foam from the vats flew skyward, or else, if the foam was very heavy and sudsy, the wind being from the right quarter, some of the foam came our way and dropped into the back yard. The game that Bobbie Spence and I played, was to go out, each armed with a plate, and catch the foam before it fell, the one who caught the most of course being the winner. The excitement of the chase lay in the chance that when a beautiful meringue was almost on the plate it might collapse like an exhausted soap bubble.

A day came when, having become tired of merely catching the foam, we tasted it! It was bitter-sweet and not exactly delectable, but quite novel. Hence the next time we played we tried putting a thin slice of bread on the plate and finally ate it plus the top dressing. Mary Daly did not see this feat, but Norah Goodnuf did after a time. She, of course, being horrified at the thought of a minister's bairn eating beer sandwiches, immediately reported us, and as a food the sport languished.

There were so many street cries in New York in the sixties and seventies that I wonder they have not been recorded as have the street cries of London. There must have been many more than those that reached my ears in the days when peddling was constant and almost unlicensed, and housewives were glad to fill their needs at their own doors. Going to Mosswood as we did well before the summer odors escaped from the gutters, and staying until frost chained them again, I missed the strictly summer cries, chief of which was "Hot corn: Here's your hot corn."

"Sweepho! Sweepho!" with a man and a boy, one for each end of the rope that worked the brush, was a cry of spring and autumn, but one that early passed away as chimneys became more complicated and flues narrower, compelling furnace and stove makers to do their own sweeping. Even then there were no chimneys near us sufficiently large to hold the child of the well-known pitiful story, who was driven by a cruel master into a chimney from which he could not escape. The little Italian bootblacks once imported under the padrone system that flourished for years came nearest to this type of white slavery.

"Glass put'een! Glass put'een!" was a daily call at all seasons. The crier was usually a bearded Hebrew clad in a long linen or frieze gabardine, a slat box holding panes of glass of assorted sizes fastened pack-wise to his back, a straight yardstick carried in his hand.

The cry, "Oranges—sweet oranges!" might come from either a horse-drawn cart or a barrow. The fruit was usually of the tart variety from either Sicily or Messina, small in size and very juicy, also cheap, if the cost of much sugar was not added, twenty for a quarter being the usual price, and oftentimes twenty-five. Havana oranges were sometimes sold from carts, usually being the thick-skinned yield of old groves. The really juicy thin-skinned fruit, the real sweet orange of the time, had to be sought in the fruit shops. The travelling fishmonger blew upon a tin horn of a particularly braying tone, one long and three short blasts. Strangely enough no other peddler imitated him. In the spring the blasts were followed by the cry "Fresh sha-ad,—fresh sha-aad," a long drawling sound being given to the *a*,—and then one really could buy shad fresh from the Hudson.

The rag buyers had three ways of travelling. The man in the very small line of business carried a bag and a pair of scales. With hand to side of mouth to throw the sound he merely called "Rags—rags—any rags?" Next came the pushcart man with his over-head string of jangling bells who added "Bottles!" to his cry. Grandest of all, but least to be trusted to wait in the area, and never to be let indoors, was the man with the horse-drawn cart, string of bells, and small boy to fetch and carry, also to pick up any odds and ends as treasure-trove.

The knife grinder always rang a hand-bell of the boarding-house dinner bell type, or like that seen in old pictures of the town crier. The first grinder that I knew bore the machine upon his back, but before long it was carried on a barrow-like affair on wheels and pushed, the bell being a fixture. The man who peddled and ground horseradish to order, at your door, had a somewhat similar barrow.

In autumn and early winter came the pigeon man in a cart. The driver, who sat above a great heap of the now extinct passenger pigeon, grouse or prairie hens, was silent, but his partner, who went from house to house with a brace of grouse and a few pigeons swung across his shoulder, blew a bo's'n's whistle as a signal, after which he knocked or rang. Buying these wild birds was largely a matter of luck unless one knew something about plumage, etc. Mary Daly, however, seemed to have a second sight in the matter. How delicious her potted pigeons were, done according to Aunt Cinder's directions. So tender were they that a fork could almost sever them. A strip of bacon was skewered to the breast, and the covering was rich brown gravy without a suspicion of grease. Small wonder that they are no more, for we Americans of the middle of the nineteenth century in our dealings with Nature, behaved like mere cave men and women, sheer barbarians. We did not realize that there could be an end to natural production, any more than did one of the dear Aunties in regard to the milk-giving ability of a single cow. She sent Father the money to buy a cow for our wild acres, writing, "They tell me that a cow lives eighteen years and yields twenty quarts of milk a day, so that now the family will have a continuous supply and be nicely provided for." She was quite overcome to learn that calves were a must-be of milk, and that a cow could not be expected to give milk in equal volume every day in the year during the course of an unnaturally long life.

Pigeons were considered expensive if over a dollar a dozen, or prairie hens at more than seventy-five cents a brace; four of the latter roasted on a skewer and served with currant jelly made a dish that the Bancrofts, the Paines, or Nabob himself might be fitly invited to sup upon. Of course we could not give dinners, so called, and this was not then expected of a minister, but Mother saved her sense of hospitality by the meal called tea, a really delicious supper of well-cooked food that had the intensive, New England Thanksgiving flavor, without its unwholesome bulk.

"Umbrellas to mend!" was an all-the-year cry. Though really a trade, those who plied it were more of the vagrant tribe than any of the other peddlers. They seemed to have the wandering foot like the tinkers, and in some cases were quite travelled.

"Pots and pans!" cried the tinker, beating upon one of the latter. "Mend your pots and pans!" He carried a kit of tools on his shoulder, his charcoal furnace swung from his hand. The milkman, his long-handled dipper slopping about in the open can, cried *Yoick!* as he jumped from his cart.

"Strawberries, any strawbe-e-erees!" This to me was the most delectable of street cries, when in late May women, not unlike Mrs. Bom in figure, with arms akimbo, hands on hips, swinging easily along balanced a flat basket or board upon the head on which were arranged the pint pottles of ripe Jersey berries, packed in even rows like so many pointed emery cushions, green leaves protecting them from the roughness of the wicker. Oh, color and fragrance of the strawberries! The beauty in the barrows filled with potted plants! Spring in the air! My heart flew out of the window ahead of my body. What were hoops and tops and all the lures of Bobbie Spence's velocipede and Taffy John's wares? There were no street cries like a chickadee's spring note that I would hear as soon as the train left us at Fairfield station. What was there in shop windows like the young grass blown by the wind and the red columbines swinging their silent bells from the cedar-crowned rocks at Mosswood? What were the gay silks at Arnold's when I could see miles of sunset every night and the sky held together by diamond star buttons, as I imagined, so that the earth couldn't fall through and get away? There is surely a Pan born of a real spring madness as upsetting as that of the Mad March Hare, only mine outlasted the season and merely lay dormant in the dead of winter.

Pan came through the city streets, too, and piped and called. The little alley boys kicked off their shoes to dig their toes into the turf in our front yard, where undisturbed they often rolled or played the game of mumble-peg or stick-knife. Here after a rain the earth-worms heard the call and, coming out, sprawled across the sidewalks, though there was no one near to gather them up for bait and go afishing. Ah, yes, Pan walked the street in many guises, when the horse-chestnut leaves unfurled. The pinwheel men, who also sold balloons, appeared in Washington and Union squares and even waved their wares at the children inside the exclusive railings at Gramercy Park. Outside Taffy John's shop, soaking in pans of water awaiting young buyers, were pieces of cocoanut, and the awful but delightful "blubber rubbers"—flexible squares at a penny each that you worked soft in your mouth until they made little balloon-like balls.

In late spring young girls of good breeding sat on the house steps of an evening and visited to and fro, while beaux brought funny chubby bouquets in silver paper holders, or, if *amis-de-famille*, perhaps ice cream from Minner's opposite Jefferson Market. The street bands blossomed out, and the red-coated monkey once more rode on the hand organ to delight children and frighten old ladies by climbing the gutter pipe and appearing at upstairs windows. Daily the cry of strawberries or fresh "radishees" grew more insistent, and lo and behold, one day I saw the market man give Norah Goodnuf a rather shabby bunch of violets. I expected that she would throw them at him or in the ash can at the very least. She didn't. She put them in a little pitcher on her dresser and kept them quite a week. Ah! Pan walks through the city streets in spring and pipes and calls—another street cry that people hear but do not understand. They call him something different in the city and really he was never quite at ease in my New York.

X

BY-PRODUCTS—WEDDING CAKE AND FUNERAL LINEN

WHEN I was very young I could not be made to realize the difference between Father and God, so they gave up trying to explain until my mental evolution should clarify the matter. When Father was too busy to come upstairs for the good-night kiss, I would kneel by the hot-air register, through which I could hear the murmur of his voice below in his study, and say my prayers down. Our Father in Heaven seemed so far away of a cold winter night, while my father in the study was comfortingly close. Then too when a child is told that "God is always near," is it not natural for it to feel that the flesh-and-blood father whose hand it can hold and who buys the daily food is at least a part of God?

Dream as they may, children are logical and much goes on in those sensitive brains that cannot be interpreted in words, but the blighting or jarring of which may mar the whole life. I was never jarred, never told unnecessary, fabled impossibilities—never taught that the world was made in six twenty-four-hour days, but that God made a wonderful plan for the earth that was developed little by little throughout long spaces of time, called days in the usual Oriental imagery, and that one had only to dig deep into the earth itself to prove this true—the same interpretation of the creative plan that is used by Bishop Lawrence today and was voiced by Phillips Brooks.

When Father came to say good night it seemed to me like God coming upstairs. He taught me to put my hands upon his head and say, "Bless you, Father." Then he had a little heart-shaped locket made which he always wore upon his watch chain, with these words upon one side and my name upon the other. This was the symbol between us, and thus faith and love became my heritage.

Mother did everything material for me and understood some of the things that though real to me I could not voice, but Father always knew and interpreted truly. For this reason I think he never sent me to Sunday school, a strange thing, seemingly, for a pastor whose Bible class was one of his best efforts. But in those days the teachers of the classes for little children were too often untrained volunteers of the maudlin, sentimental type, in whose care it would be as perilous to place the spiritual side of a temperamental child as to trust its body to a street peddler of quack medicines. Sunday school was one of Father's great problems, as his journals well attest, it being almost impossible to reject the well-intentioned but inefficient women who wished to teach. Now a great light is breaking upon this subject, after a long period of storm that has largely swept the soggy Sairy Gamps out of the Sunday schools, as out of the nursing profession, doctors of divinity and doctors of medicine alike demanding intelligent trained workers.

From the doxology of three personalities I soon reasoned out a solution to my liking that seemed adequate and fitted in with life as I saw it,—God the father, mother Mary, and the baby Christ, a visible family. Again I was left with my fancy.

Also without verbal instruction I gradually sensed the normal life as it unfolded about me, without shock—bud, leaf and flower, as with a tree in spring—mother, father and child. Father was Mother's husband, therefore a husband was a most desirable person. In early childhood I had wished to be a boy, never afterward; no happy woman would be other than she is. Also in this way the balance of sex came before me. Mother was a receptive motive power, did things planned, made them go. Father created, accomplished very quietly, explaining so that you could see everything he said. There were times when the things that Mother started sleazed away and when she had to back up against Father's fixedness for support, he was always there. So gradually I came to think that after all Mother was the moon and Father the sun.

In the sixties, early and later there were a great many by-products of pastoral life that fell outside the church itself. The minister's wife was expected, if need be, to sit up with the sick, and I well remember one very charming family, in which there was a chronic invalid, whose attendant had one night off each week, and for the space of an entire winter Mother filled her place. It was not a matter of lack of means, for the people were wealthy, but Miss Emeline loved Mother and disliked strange faces about her, so it all happened as a matter of course, in part friendship, in part duty as it was construed.

Of weddings there were many, both inside the parish and out, though comparatively few took place in the old Broadway Church, a home ceremony in the evening seeming to be in favor. The wedding fee was held to be the perquisite of the minister's wife and great was the variation in the amount. There were also very many weddings in our own house, little groups of half a dozen who having no church connections strayed along, usually in the evening, Mother often being one of the witnesses.

Father had a sort of improvised altar in the end of his study, which gave dignity to these ceremonials. A copy of the Sistine Madonna, exquisitely done on porcelain and framed in carved dark oak with closing doors, in itself a chapelette, had been sent him from abroad by Madam Penniman, together with a combination chair and kneeling bench. The framework of rosewood had a baptismal shell carved at the top, the covering being of convent-made tapestry into which passion flowers, a cross, and a chalice in gold relief were worked. Christian symbolism seems to have been little understood among Protestants of the Puritan strain and considered somewhat akin to idolatry, but Father wrought it into everyday life, as far as might be.

The weddings themselves would furnish material for an entire volume. Some were almost sad—the widowers who, helpless to care for a young family, were marrying without impulse even, simply to partly shift responsibility. Other widowers had the impulse but no backbone, and in addition to performing the ceremony wished the minister to break the news next day to a grown daughter or a previous mother-in-law, who had remained as housekeeper. There was more than one occasion when pity for some youth, evidently in the dangerous hypnotic claws of a much older woman, led Mother to question him and advise him to wait a few days, with such good effect that the wedding was finally abandoned.

One bridal, that of a colored couple, the man having been employed about Jefferson Market and well known to us, I was specially invited to attend. It was an evening wedding. When the procession came in, even calm Father was rather taken aback. We had heard a carriage drive up, in fact I saw it, for, being greatly excited, in company with Mary Daly I was peeping out of the sidelight of the basement door.

From this single coach emerged eight people and a large covered basket; the ninth, a man, let himself carefully down from the driver's box, as if afraid of trusting his weight too suddenly on very tender feet, newly and tightly shod. By the time they had formed in line and reached the front door I had spread the news. The covered basket, carried by the groom's mother, who simply oozed flesh and smiles, came in first. Then two by two followed four gentlemen dressed even more beautifully than the minstrels I had been recently taken by Aunt Kinnie to see. Once inside the door the group of four girls that followed separated, and after much pulling and pushing, one took the lead. The bride was dressed in pink velvet and wore a pink tulle veil, which her companions pulled together over her face after the manner of a sleeping car curtain, completely concealing it.

"Now you gets along in, while I 'ranges dis yer cake. Can I trespes on your hospitableness for de loan of a knife—silver preferenced?" the head of the procession inquired of Mother. "I disfavored fetching a knife and resking to cross de bride's luck with a calamity."

Mother led the way to the small room at the hall end, which was then used for informal betweentime meals and was therefore equipped for the purpose. She had hoped the cake would be left there, but no, when its gorgeousness was revealed the bearer returned, holding it as high as possible, motioning to the party, which, in spite of Father's urging, still huddled in the hall, said, "Now we proceeds!" And the Fifteenth Amendment, redolent of musk, patchouli and attar of roses, marched in. After the ceremony the veil was thrown back, revealing a very pretty mulatto girl, who stood with downcast eyes waiting to be kissed. This the groom did promptly and then waved to his three companions that they might have the same privilege. A general kissing bee followed, the bridegroom remarking, "Ah reckons you'll get more business from outen this nuptials, Doctor."

An awkward silence, then in walked the mistress of ceremonies, who, unobserved, had gone into the side room with the cake. She carried a plate whereon was a large slice of plum cake, decorated by five much soiled one dollar bills, spread out, and pinned down by quill toothpicks that did not look entirely new. Planting herself before Mother, with a gesture of mingled respect, pride and reckless munificence she said, "Lady Minister, here am de climax, dis am yore perquisition, to be eat to de health an' happiness of all!"

Mother never flinched. Saying, "You have given too generous a slice for one meal, we must keep some to dream on," she removed the least soiled dollar, broke off a visibly large bit of the cake, ate it slowly as if relishing each bite and placed the remainder, decorations and all, in a conspicuous place on the study table. The situation was saved then and there by the gentleman in the new tight boots remarking that "an adjournment am now customary." The picture of this wedding would have remained distinct even if it had not become more than a twice-told family tale.

Christenings also sometimes happened at the house, though only for a very special reason, but the only part of death that entered the home was the funeral linen. I wonder how many people now remember this? It was the custom for the clergy of denominations not using vestments, when reading the burial service either at house or grave, to wear a long scarf of pure white linen over one shoulder and crossed beneath the opposite arm, the ends falling below a rosette of black ribbon that united them, an adjustment not unlike the regalia worn by the Ancient Order of Hibernians on St. Patrick's Day. This scarf was made of a strip of yard-wide linen, three yards in length and pleated lengthwise in large flat folds. A pair of black gloves came with the scarf, both furnished by the undertaker and being afterward the wearer's property. At one time the family physician always attended funerals of importance and was garbed in the same manner. But I have heard Mother say that in New York, at least, this ceased before or during the Civil War, as it seriously added to the expense of funerals, and gradually the rather grim humor and dubious taste of physicians being so conspicuous at this time, evidently dawned, and they themselves brought it to an end.

How do I know the measurements and construction of this scarf? Because it was one of my amusements, under Mother's directions, to unfasten the rosettes, smooth the ribbon and roll it over a piece of cardboard for future use. Next the linen was unpleated, put to soak in a small wooden tub, when, after several changes of water, the dressing was quite removed, it was pulled smooth, sun-dried and put away in the linen chest. When next seen it would be fashioned by Mother's tireless fingers into pillow slips, or one of the then indispensable articles of woman's gear, a chemise, with hand-embroidered bands for neck and the sleeve caps.

There were various happenings of which the dominie, though not a first cause, had to bear the burden—family disputes, young people who willed to marry against parental desire, and the elopements of those who actually did so. In such emergencies they often seemed to have sent for Father as today they would call in a nerve specialist. The upsets that people had were not called by the softened term of nervous breakdowns, they were out and out tantrums, which is perhaps the same thing under another name. They fought things out and the poor dominie was called to be umpire, or if arbitration was impossible to exorcise the evil in cases before which the judgment of Solomon was a simple matter.

Small wonder that poor Father fell in with the prevailing phrenological fad fostered by Fowler and Wells and had a cast of his head made with all the characteristic bumps showing in high relief and plainly labeled, though it did not seem to help him much, for my sisters soon used the thing as a dummy for hat trimming.

In the matter of marriages considered unsuitable, chiefly by the bride's family, and elopements, the last half of the nineteenth century would hold its own very well with today, except in one respect—the calling in of the clergyman as a counsellor instead of the family lawyer.

Two of these affairs would have remained clearly in my memory aside from the comments in Father's journal.

Brignoli was the favorite tenor of opera and concert in the sixties, when it was also becoming a vogue to have professional singers at private houses in the dual rôle of musician and guest. Brignoli also gave singing lessons to a favored few, the fact that his personality was considered irresistible adding to his popularity. Ye gods! how standards shift. I chiefly remember him by his hair. It was rather long, parted on the side and so well oiled that it hung in little clumps, not exactly curly, but rather like the strands of a cedar-oil floor mop. It is well to remind the moderns that this was the period when oil, Macassar oil, was used freely for hairdressing by both sexes, thereby making it necessary to cover the backs of chairs and sofas with articles in some quarters called tidies, but in New York elegantly termed antimacassars. At the same time women's headgear was protected by a sheer but oil-proof interlining called Argentine.

Brignoli had dark, full, rather baggy eyes, the conventional dark, small upturned mustache—and a voice! As I picture him he partly blends in memory with an entrancingly romantic popular actor—Lester Wallack, except that Wallack was at once more forcible, gave more of the sense of having muscle under his makeup, while his hair, being naturally wavy, did not go in clumps but broke into a few love locks, as the metaphysical poets called them, held in place only by the emotional damp of his forehead. Also Wallack's mustache had a sweep at the ends. Does any one remember him in the hunting suit he wore when he played up to Effie Germon as Naomi Tigh in the simple-minded drama called *School?*

To the pith of this: Brignoli gave singing lessons to Almira S., the daughter of one of Father's most intimate parishioners. She was temperamental, and, well—a number of the correct beaux of the time, judging by daguerreotypes, must have been very like overstuffed furniture, antimacassars and all. Brignoli was too shrewd and frugal to risk an elopement, he demanded her hand. Father being consulted took in the situation at a glance—something was bound to happen, and he advised surrender on the part of the parents. The next step was that Brignoli, being a Roman Catholic, desired that his betrothed should change her religious form. Again Father counselled against family opposition, as he had seen the unhappy outcome of many mixed marriages in the second generation if not in the first. Six months passed and the wedding was imminent, when investigation at least partly unearthed an humble and forgotten wife of the tenor living in Italy.

A few years later the lady, forgetting romance, married Frank Otis, of one of the altogether correct families, many years younger than herself, he in turn becoming a Romanist to mate evenly with her. Then was Father altogether left on the shelf! Gatha took me to see the spectacular wedding in old St. Ann's Church, but all that I remember about it was that the service was very long and that the bridegroom looked rather like Brignoli in the mustache.

The other affair was a real elopement and much more serious in every way, but very thrilling to me to whom the details sifted.

The Lampson sisters were noted for their beauty and aristocratic bearing, and of these Fidelia the eldest was of a classic but icily cold patrician type. No one of many admirers could seem to reach her, when one day a message came calling Father suddenly to the house, as Mrs. Lampson was in a state of complete collapse, for the unapproachable Fidelia had stepped out and married her music master, Richard Hoffman, the popular composer and pianist, who was many years her senior.

This was not a case for arbitration or exorcism, but for common sense, a little time, family coöperation and reconciliation. "I told the heartbroken mother," Father wrote in his journal, "that many unwelcomed events moved toward broader living and that perhaps the graft of this new, artistic strain of blood might leaven the colder New England flow to some new form of creative life."

Always looking for the best, Father then was prophetic, for of that union was born one of the great women sculptors of today, Malvina Hoffman, whose work will outlive all the petty social castes of yore.

The inauguration of the use of flowers in the church at Eastertide, and the publication of a New Service Book for which Bryant wrote his Mother's Hymn, had been two of Father's labors of love, before the old church was sold and the move made to the new building at Thirty-Fourth Street and Park Avenue. In its original form the Hymn lies between the pages of Father's journal, together with the letter that came with it written upon the paper of the *Evening Post*, of which Bryant was then editor.

Office of The Evening Post, 41 Nassau Street, Cor. Liberty.

New York: January 16 1862
— Thursday morning. —

Dear Mr Osgood —

Here is the hymn. Do what you list with it and I shall not be displeased. As it is the first thing in its way it may be a failure.

I had some trouble with the two last stanzas, and I could not di-late them. This morning, after a night's sleep on them, and before breakfast I overcame the difficulty.

Yours truly
W. C. Bryant.

Dr. Osgood.

Lord, who ordainest, for mankind,
Benignant toils and tender cares,
We thank thee for the ties that bind
The mother to the child she bears.
We thank thee for the hopes that rise
Within her heart, as, day by day,
The dawning soul, from those young eyes,
Looks forth, with clearer, steadier ray.

And, grateful for the blessing given
With that dear infant on her knee,
She turns her willing thoughts to heaven,
And teaches it a prayer to thee.

Such thanks the blessed Mary gave
When, from her lap, the Holy Child,
Sent from above to seek and save
The lost of earth, looked up and smiled.

All-gracious! grant, to those who bear
A mother's charge, the strength and light
To guide the feet that own their care
Along the way of Love and Right.

In addition to the floral decorations of the church itself, at the Easter festival of the Sunday school baskets composed of many small bouquets were placed upon the chancel steps from which a posy, together with an Easter card, was given to each scholar as the classes marched up in turn. To those adults who were in trouble or had known trouble during the year, flowers were sent, or some memorial picture or illuminated card of value. Much of this work was hand-done illumination, Beatrice having no little skill in designs such as bordered the old missals. In turn memorial gifts were made for church ornament, some one offering to decorate the pulpit or furnish the panniers of small bouquets.

One of the problems was somewhat akin to that of choosing teachers for the Sunday school—how to encourage coöperation and yet avoid unsuitable combinations and collisions. Finally at the new church it was found necessary to have a well-devised plan to be carried out under the direction of a professional florist. This plan might be examined several weeks before Easter by those interested so that each could select the portion which they desired to give.

Then something happened which put a stop to both amateur conceptions of design and their fulfillment. A very charming woman who had lost an only child offered to decorate the font—an emblem of purity—as a memorial, to which Father gladly assented, asking no questions. Mother and the ladies' committee, going to the church early on Easter morning to see that everything was according to plan, and if necessary to adjust loose ends, discovered that the emblem of purity consisted of one calla lily with a single leaf, floating in the font brimful of water. The flower itself, having become water-soaked, was head down, entirely submerged. Mrs. Post, who always called a spade a spade, said it certainly was an emblem of suicide and nothing else. The font therefore was necessarily empty and the poor mother broken-hearted at the lack of appreciation of a tender thought.

Were the old church days so very good, after all? For the people, yes, for the minister was theirs, heart, body and soul. For the dominie, no, for though he is no longer on a pedestal composed of mystic respect, superior education and right-of-pay criticism, the present parish organization and its efficiency, has made a shield to protect him and his household, so far as possible, from the rough edges of many by-products of the ministry.

XI

HOOPSKIRTS, JOY BELLS, AND THE NEW PARLOR CARPET

PRICES of the must-be's of living that flew skyward during the Civil War remained aloft, as habit is. Mother and Aunt Cinder in moments of intimate relaxation would grow reminiscent and prate about paying Mr. Nott in Boston $1.87 for a pair of street boots made to measure, while the Coits, father and son, in their little shop on Sixth Avenue, just above Eleventh Street, now asked seven dollars a pair for the same articles. As a matter of fact cheaper footwear was to be had ready-made but the selection was very limited. An abomination, called a Congress gaiter, was very popular in some quarters, in fact the Aunties had been known to wear them, though Uncle Isaac, always masculine in every detail of attire, a very protective measure for the bachelor brother of a sisterful house, wore trig, high pull-on boots that went under his trousers in dry weather and over them in wet.

The build of the Congress gaiter was quite suitable for the ready-made class of buyers. Given the correct width and length of sole the rest did not matter much, as the top, which ended at the ankle or a bit above, had elastic gores in the sides instead of either buttons or laces, and had a couple of strap loops for the pulling of them on. The material might be leather, but was usually a peculiarly hideous fabric called "prunella," a tough cloth, horsehair in finish if not in texture.

These gaiters were *oban* in our house. In the first

place Mother could not endure sloppy ankles, and after a few wearings, or as soon as they could be pulled on without a struggle, the elastic lost its tenacity. Then the exertion of working the foot through the small top invariably pulled back the sock or stocking in such a way that a hole was forced by the big toe, hence more mending to be done.

Besides the cost of material for feminine garments, it took yards and yards of goods to make a gown, the skirt being sometimes six yards full, it required at least three underskirts or else the hoopskirt to hold it out. Handling a hoopskirt, both before and after it was put on, was an art in itself, quite as much as to arrange the "waterfall" of hair that finished the toilette on top, so that it would hang properly and not, by its weight, pull the front frizzy locks out of place. These oblong arrangements of hair, that looked like nothing so much as an eggplant, rested on the shoulders well below the neck line, and were kept in shape by nets either plain or of some elaborate pattern, often made of colored chenille.

As for the hoopskirt, dainty people who considered safety slipped the two lower hoops into a double facing with an embroidered or corded edge. This facing not only kept the wearer from stepping through the hoops but kept the hoops from the street mud, for street cleaning in New York was negligible in the sixties. Thus people had at least two hoopskirts and many facings, one to wear and another waiting. With four hoop-wearers in our house, the square closet in the third story resembled a small hangar of dirigibles. Mother was the first to halt at this thraldom, and being quick at inventions contrived a single skirt of moreen that without calling attention to a revolt against custom, was both *bouffant* and convenient.

It was one of my greatest amusements when riding

in stage or street car to watch women sit down. A little hitch with the hand at the top hoop and all was well, without it a flare-up of petticoats was almost certain. Like many other fashions of later days, this should have only been attempted for street wear by what Mary Daly called "carriage folks."

Gatha, who played and sang very neatly, had a ballad of the period called "Croquet," the cover being decorated by a very elaborate lithograph of two players, girl and man, resting on a garden bench; a picture that I colored with as great zest as I had applied to the doing of the Hatter and the March Hare. The first verse of the song I think ran thus:

Out on the lawn in evening gray
Went Willie and Kate; I said, "Which way?"
And they both replied—"Croquet! Croquet!"

As for past manners and customs, in spite of the square-cut yet flowing decorum of Willie's side whiskers or the six-yard fullness of skirt that society demanded of Kate, Willie had his arm snugly about her waist, while, owing to the tilting of the hoop petticoat, her legs showed freely, being set off far below the knee by bifurcated lingerie—not of the decorous bloomer model!

In spite of the fact that Mother had long since withdrawn from evening receptions, and that I was still in the period of cut down and home-sewn dresses, the gowning of my sisters was always a problem. At weddings the bride usually gave the material for the dress to her attendants, tulle or tarlatan for a long period being the favored material. The white was relieved by colored sashes and shoulder decorations, the bridesmaids pairing each with a groomsman, might wear different colors. But even if the yards and yards of what was called "pinking" of the fluffy flounces was done at home, by means of a "pinking-iron," a hammer, a boxwood block, and much arm-tiring labor, there were still slippers, gloves, and trimmings to be counted up. Bea and Gatha had pretty, smooth necks and arms, but as minister's daughters they must not wear the prevailing bodice cut straight across the bust line and arm tops well below the shoulder. Tuckers and guimpes were therefore necessary, made of narrow lace insertion with either puffed or plain bands of Swiss muslin between, so that between protecting both neck and ankles, the sewing required was but little less than that recorded in Hood's pathetic yet popular Song of the Shirt.

Suddenly, after a period of silence, joy bells began to ring in our household and kept ringing for several months. The chimes began the week before Christmas. Mother was an exquisite housekeeper without making a fuss about it or having the machinery visible, but for once she was caught in the act.

The front door was "grained" to represent black walnut. This process, the manipulation of layers of wet paint by combs of different widths, was once almost an art, but owing to the time and skill required deteriorated and passed out with the shortening of the time of apprenticeship and the increased pay for labor. In cleaning door handles and scutcheons, the second girl was very apt to smear the varnished paint with whiting, so Mother kept bits of cardboard to fit about the various plated trimmings to save the paint. One morning, as she chanced to be in the vestibule watching the process of polishing to make sure that due care was being taken, a shadow fell across the open doorway. There stood Mr. Rhinelander in his usual immaculate attire, his polished high hat not only raised but held in his hand, in spite of the sharp weather, with an unmistakable air of deference, as he said, "Madam, I see the proof that thrift and good housekeeping are not incompatible with intellect and charm!

I thank you for your thought of my property." Naturally Mother was pleased, for the compliment was not mere flattery, but the tribute of an old-fashioned gentleman of the "Signer" type, such as we met at the sessions of the Historical Society.

Came Christmas morning and Father received a note that read:

"To Samuel Osgood, D.D.,

"My dear Sir: Accept this remembrance in token of our pleasant relations as landlord and tenant. With respect and appreciative regards to your wife, Respectfully, Wm. C. Rhinelander." The "remembrance" was a check for $200!

The next bells rang by mail during the first week of the New Year, a chime of four, and were concealed in a lawyer's bulky letter. This said that John Pickens of Boston, a friend of Mother's father, and a once-disappointed-in-love bachelor, had died, and his will distributed his property to the many thoughtful women who had shown him kindness in his loneliness, with a lesser sum to their daughters. Mother used to sing old ballads to him, Aunt Cinder made him arrow-root custard and knit him mufflers, Bea and Gatha were merely daughters and shared alike, but alas for me, I was not born when the will was made! Money has always been a Pharisee and passed me by upon the other side. The legacy for Mother and Aunt Cinder was enough to make the future interest money of some account; that for my sisters a tidy sum each for plenishing a linen chest and buying wedding gear when the time came, which for Bea was sure not to be very far off.

Scarcely had we settled down from this excitement when the last bells rang, though the final peal was a trifle out of tune. The parish was to give the pastor new parlor carpets!—a gift of some magnitude when the length and breadth of the two rooms thrown together by sliding doors were considered. The back room had been long in use as Father's formal study, and here it was that he paced round and round the central desk, broad topped like a table, when he grew cramped from sitting, hence there was a track, as decidedly marked as in an athletic field, that it was impossible to cover by readjusting the furniture. The front room was more amenable, but the sofas and chairs had been recently shifted to cover threadbare spots, so that one old friend, coming in at twilight and expecting to find a couch in an accustomed place, had sat unexpectedly on the floor.

The best of it was that Mother was to make her own selection at Arnold & Constable's—and thus she would have a chance to pull together the somewhat haphazard furnishing of the rooms. We had a few good bits of bronze, a clock, the figure of Minerva with shield and spear, balanced by side ornaments of classic urns. The mantelshelf topped an open hearth with polished grate, and four paintings held the eye from the defects of walnut chairs stiff of frame and leg, a "what-not" filled with gift-horse trumpery, and a centre table with a marble top of dismal hue and a Rogers' group.

Over the mantel hung Little Mother's portrait, always with us and as ever smiling a whimsical greeting. At the right was a sombre but impressive painting by Wüst of the old church at Drontheim, Norway, with the peasants kneeling in the graveyard. On the left, two paintings by Samuel Coleman, bought by Father when the artist was little known; one "The Foothills of the Catskills," all soft mellow light, the other "Gray's Elegy," the little church where hung the curfew bell that "tolled the knell of parting day" in silhouette against a moonlit sky. The old carpet had outraged these pictures, but now soft combinations in Oriental tones in durable Brussels weave were obtainable for almost the first time. Hasten the day for the choosing, but it was finally set, postponed and then reset for the morrow.

At six the night before, as Father went to the door to take in the paper, there was a bumping on the stoop and two men rolled some large and very heavy bundles into the front hall. They were followed by Father, who wore a rather dubious expression.

"Carpet and lining from Arnold & Constable—will be laid tomorrow—this note goes with it," said one of the men, taking the missive from his hat.

The note, from Aunt Kinnie Haven, was to the effect that, having learned from one of the church committee of their intentions concerning a new carpet, as well as the dimensions of the rooms, she, having seen a very desirable offering of extra width goods of English make, had bought it as a personal gift and ordered it sewn; the men to come the next day to move the furniture, take up the old floor covering, etc., so that Mother might have no trouble, but simply go for an outing during the transfer! Bea was already opening the end of one of the flat bundles, for the colors of the deeply woven fabric gave more than a hint from the under side. Mother actually groaned and even Father had not a word of consolation, for the pattern was of interlocked squares, two feet across, once a common design for floor oilcloth, while the colors of the alternating blocks were white, ginger-brown and a dull red, a coral pattern in dingy black striving to unite them.

"And it will last forever!" truthfully ejaculated Gatha. The Oriental proverb, "Do not worry about two things, those that may be helped and those that may not be," was put into practice and this jangling joy bell was in the latter class.

A week later, being housed by a snuffle cold, and feeling very dreary, as every one was either busy or out, Bobbie Spence came over to play with me. I showed him the new carpet, whereupon an idea seized us—it was surely created for indoor hopscotch. We pinned paper numbers on a sequence of squares and with large copper pennies furnished by Bobbie instead of stones to kick, we spent a happy and quite conscienceless afternoon until the sound of Father's latch key in the front door made us pause suddenly and wonder. Mother and Father had been paying calls together and naturally they would come where we were as the direct way to the study. Bobbie was rigid with alarm, but I kept on hopping as a courage breeder.

"Are you having a good play?" inquired Mother casually, as she took off her kid gloves and carefully pulled the fingers straight before folding them.

"I am glad that we have a young optimist in the family," Father said, turning to her. Then he went to his study table where stood an ornamental basket of fruit that Mr. Richard kept replenished at intervals, and gave Bobbie and me each a luscious, ripe winter-Nellis pear—in those days a treat for any one in January, let alone piratical children!

XII

WHEN THE BLACK CROOK BROKE INTO THE FAMILY

CAME a year that began and ended quite differently from all those that had gone before. My sisters were young ladies grown and a bit over, and Mary Daly said that the time would soon come when I must stop standing on my head and pegging tops with boys. Why, oh why, must this time ever be? Of course if it was a matter of wearing long skirts, then I would never wear them. Yet as I look back, how very comfortably the change took place, even though I perfectly remember the desperate feeling that Mary's words once gave me, like a tightening of the throat. As to boys, how could any one ever get on without them, for was not Father a boy as well as all the people who did the worth-while things, like shovelling snow and tending the furnace like O'Connell, up to the smart young man who walked home from church with Bea more often than any one else?

Considering that ours was held to be a quiet household my sisters had a very good time, at least for minister's daughters with never more than two festive gowns apiece. It was not expected that we should give parties, but they were invited to one or more every week. The Boyntons and Wallers specialized on tableaux, charades and musicals, Laura Havemeyer and Adèle Wolf gave informal dances and sometimes a real cotillion with lovely favors, while the George Havens had opera evenings followed by a buffet supper at home.

Then there was always a chance that a pair of tickets, plus safe escorts, would be forthcoming for the annual Charity Ball at the Academy. There were several young men that Mother regarded as S. E.'s (safe escorts), as Bea dubbed them, who took the place of the required chaperone, the reason why still being a mystery to me, nor could Mother herself ever say exactly why she chose them, except that they had good mothers who were her friends. At least two of them turned into reckless detrimentals at thirty, yet it may well have been because they were suppressed mothers' darlings at twenty!

One of the correct amusements that might be enjoyed without supervision was to walk home from church with people, male people. Bea had many such escorts, while Gatha would never let anybody walk with her, saying that an escort was absolutely unnecessary in broad daylight.

Very soon, as far as Bea was concerned, "people" were condensed into one "person," who not only walked home from morning service, stayed to dinner when asked, returned in time for vespers, but brought wonderful boxes of sweets from Maillard's in the middle of the week. Not small boxes but large round ones, divided into quarters and holding four pounds, one section being nougat, one French chocolates, one marrons and one bonbons. Surely in my eyes as well as Bea's, though for different reasons, this boy was a pearl of great price, for he allowed *me* to untie the box and choose two bits from each section, provided *I went upstairs to eat them.* Mother and Father liked him because he had studied both here and in Germany and knew a great deal. Then he had been in the Civil War on General Meagher's staff, a captain in the Irish Brigade, a dashing and brave officer, for his pet riding horse, Ginger, had been shot beneath him while he was delivering a dispatch under fire. Consequently he had a great deal to talk about, though he never bragged and was wholly different from some of the others whom Bea called "tame cats, that just sat and gazed, while they smoothed their whiskers as if they had been lapping milk."

Oh! Another attribute had he that counted parish-wise; his parents were supporters of the church and all its charities, and they lived in the wonderful house in Fourteenth Street, a house as big as the Barlows', with a ballroom and wide stairs, upon which his younger brothers had taught me to come down on my hands and knees, head first without turning a somersault.

Before I realized it Bea was engaged, had a diamond ring, and crowds of people came to call and made a great fuss over her, even giving dances in her honor. Bea somehow did not care for parties after this, and if she had to go to one she never danced with any one but George, Brother George, he said I must learn to call him. He was very good to me from the very first and gave me a large box of candy for myself—an engagement present, he called it; and he let me try what I had been wishing to try for a long time—if a dried pea would fit into the deeply cleft dimple in his chin. It would not. He had a very nice mouth and a crisp well-behaved little mustache, and never used a mustache cup at table. This pleased Mother for she hated the things, although she had to keep a few for visiting clergymen who came to exchange with Father. In the sixties and seventies the lack of at least the ability to grow hair on the face was considered effeminate, so it was often overdone and resulted in walrus-like mustaches that must either slop into the tea or coffee or be pushed away by a brace on the inside edge of the cup, which cup was overdecorated as if to call attention to its function. Father had smoothly shaven lips, only wearing a beard in later life because of his throat, while many trig professional men, especially physicians, were cleanly shaven except for small close side whiskers, Doctors Parker and Draper being of this clear cut type. It is said that the mouth is largely a self made character feature, but of course there is the Disraeli type of mouth with the protruding under lip, which no mental qualitites could change, and for this a drooping mustache is probably a necessary veil.

One of Brother George's great hits, as far as little sister was concerned, was when one day he heard me say that I wished to earn some money and offered me a dollar apiece for either a pair of chicken's ears or eel's feet. As all recent gifts from the Aunties had been of the to-be-put-in-the-bank kind, I was pocket-money poor. I did not know exactly how to begin the search for either article in New York, the country would have given me a better chance, but Father suggested Jefferson Market as a likely hunting ground. So the next time I went there I deserted "Cup o' Tea's" hut for the fishmonger's and poultry stalls.

Mr. Davis kindly skinned an eel for me and proved that it had not even a suggestion of feet. Mr. Tyson, however, helped me to earn one of the dollars, by plucking the head of a sturdy old fowl so that not only its ear openings but a small outside ear was visible, and let me take the head home as proof. Brother George paid the dollar very promptly, which gave me a lifelong confidence in his square dealing; Gatha had said in the beginning that he was only making fun of me. I often wonder why she was financially suspicious of every one.

Presently something quite unusual happened in New York, about which there was much talk both inside the family and with Aunt Kinnie Haven and Miss Elizabeth (Cis) Gray—who, by the way, was just engaged to Mr. James Morris. He chewed tobacco and was sometimes called "dismal Jim" behind his back. He belonged to an old New York family and I liked him very much, for once in summer when we drove out into the country he had taught me how to play "Travelling Whist" by counting the number of cattle on my side of the road while he took the opposite side, and I won.

The fuss was all about a new play that had been put on at Niblo's Garden that autumn, also as to whether Bea and Gatha might go to see it, or if Father and Mother were reasonable to forbid them unless they first saw and judged the play for themselves and not by hearsay. The matter seemed very strange to me because our family always went to see plays when they had a chance, Father often going to the Bowery Theatre with Mr. Bancroft. Mother had been with the John Paines to see Mme. Celeste dance, while even I had been taken to Christy's Minstrels over in Irving Hall.

This play, however, was entirely different. It seemed to have something specially to do with the devil—it was called *The Black Crook!* Moreover it was not merely the play itself that caused the trouble, but a Thing that was upsetting society and had broken into our family so that we had to take sides about it, for the manager, Mr. William Wheatley, was Brother George's uncle and of course we must be very polite and careful for Bea's sake.

Ah! how words sizzled around *The Black Crook's* cauldron which was evolved thus. Jarrett & Palmer had imported scenery and dances for an opera that could not be produced owing to the burning of the Academy of Music. Then their material was worked about a play, knocked together by an actor, Charles Barras, as a spectacle; William Wheatley, of the Arch Street Theatre, Philadelphia, was the manager. He was himself a debonair actor of the romantic school, akin to Lester Wallack, very courtly and charming. Well do I remember him, a typical Claude Melnotte.

Wheatley came of a dramatic family, his father an actor and his mother, before marriage a Miss Sarah Ross, after her widowhood took old-lady parts, somewhat along the lines of our Mrs. Gilbert. Wheatley's two sisters, Julia and Emma, also were on the stage in minor parts and dancing a *pas à deux* for a brief period before marriage. Julia married Edmund Miller, a well-known broker, a man of affairs, later a director of the opera, while Emma married William Mason, one of the exclusive "We-are-and-that-is-sufficient" clan—builders of social stone walls that are not worth the mounting.

Hence the production of the daring *Black Crook* had more social ramifications than met the casual eye. Wives and mothers of sons frowned upon it, preachers railed against it. Conservative public opinion ran so high that for a time even Father was a bit shaken.

A lull followed the first discussion of our family's attendance, then came the crisis—a box at Niblo's Garden was sent Mother with Mr. Wheatley's compliments, at the same time that I, aged seven, was asked to go to a children's matinée party with Ross and Lawrence Miller. The box was declined for reasons of prudence, yet my sisters went with Brother George. It must have been a fairy spectacle and would have been taken only as such by a beauty-loving child, but as a line had to be drawn somewhere, it was drawn at me. However, I played *Black Crook* with Ross and Larrie Miller, for Mr. Wheatley sent them a miniature theatre with scenic backgrounds and all the characters of the play made of cardboard with colored costumes. As these figures were mounted on firm supports that did not wobble, we could make our own combinations and the amusement was endless. That is, endless unless we made too much noise and then Grandma Wheatley would come across the great hall to the play room and call us to order. For this prim little Mrs.-Gilbert-like lady, once of the stage, was a martinet in matters of domestic conduct. Children might sometimes be seen, but *never* heard, and not one of her three nieces or their friends would dare cross their legs (excuse me—limbs) or even their feet in her presence unreproved, while her son-in-law, to whom she owed all, was only allowed to lie on the lounge, before her ever burning grate fire, if he was really ill!

. . . .

With the carefully preserved program of this play now before me, plus the mature vision that can look in many directions,—the social revolution that *The Black Crook* caused in New York is clearly cut, though scarcely to be understood by those of a later generation. Yet even today this spectacular bill of the play will rival the announcements of a Hollywood thriller.

The names of the actors of the Parisian opera mean nothing to me now, save that of one dancer, Betty Rigl, whom I saw years later when, as a young matron, I enjoyed to the full New York's dramatic life. She then appeared with her younger sister Emily, and together they expressed the highest development of their art that was known before the coming of the school of the present Russian ballet.

. . . .

New York in the sixties, strong for "the legitimate drama," was very young, as was all America, along lines of artistic staging. It was but a little over a century before that there had been a law against all acting in New England, which was not set aside until the seventeen-nineties, when an English com-

NIBLO'S GARDEN

LESSEE AND MANAGER . . . . . . WM. WHEATLEY.
STAGE MANAGER . . . . L. J. VINCENT.

Doors open at Seven. Curtain rises quarter before Eight.

September 12 1866 - First Night -

EVERY EVENING

AND

SATURDAY AFTERNOON

AT TWO,

Will be presented, after a preparation of several months, and

AN ACTUAL OUTLAY OF OVER

FIFTY THOUSAND DOLLARS

The Original, Grand, Romantic, Magical and Spectacular Drama in Four Acts, by CHAS. M. BARRAS, Esq., entitled The

BLACK CROOK

The SOLE RIGHT of which production in New York and its vicinity has been purchased by MR. WHEATLEY; who has also entered into an agreement with

MESSRS. JARRETT & PALMER

For the introduction of their Great

PARISIENNE BALLET TROUPE,

Under the direction of the renowned Maître de Ballet

SIGNOR DAVID COSTA,

(Of the Grand Opera, Paris,) who will appear in the

MOST COSTLY AND MAGNIFICENT DRAMATIC SPECTACLE

EVER PRESENTED IN AMERICA.

PREMIER DANSEURS ASSOLUTE,

Mlle. Marie Bonfanti,	**Mlle. Rita Sangalli,**
From the Grand Opera, Paris, and Covent Garden, London.	From the Grand Opera, Berlin, and Her Majesty's, London.

FIRST PREMIER AND SOLOIST,
MLLE. BETTY RIGL
From the Grand Opera, Paris.
NINE PREMIERS AND SOLOISTS,
From Berlin, Milan, and London.
TWENTY CORYPHEES,
From London, Paris, and Berlin.
FIFTY AUXILIARY LADIES,
From the principal Theatres of America and London.
A POWERFUL DRAMATIC COMPANY,
Embracing the names of New York and London Favorites.
GORGEOUS NEW SCENERY.
By those Masters of Scenical Art,
RICHARD MARSTON,
(from Covent Garden, London)
J. E. HAYES, R. SMITH, D. A. STRONG, F. W. SEAVER, W. WALLACK, and Assistants
THE WONDERFUL TRANSFORMATION SCENE,
ENTITLED
"THE PALACE OF DEW DROPS,"
Painted by the BROTHERS BREW, of London,
For E. T. SMITH, of Theatre Royal, Astleys, London, and purchased expressly by Messrs. JARRETT & PALMER, at a cost of
FIFTEEN THOUSAND DOLLARS.
AN ENTIRELY NEW STAGE AND MACHINERY,
With all the American and European improvements, making it equal, if not superior, to any in the world, have been constructed, at a cost of over ten thousand dollars, by those skilful Machinists,
JOHN FROUDE, of Her Majesty's Theatre, London, and BENSEN SHERWOOD, Of this Establishment.
ESPECIAL NEW MUSIC,
Composed expressly for the piece by THOMAS BAKER, by the courtesy of Leonard Grover, Esq., and produced under the baton of HARVEY B. DODWORTH.
GORGEOUS NEW COSTUMES.
By M. PHILLIPE AND MADAME COSTA.
THE DAZZLING NEW ARMORS AND BALLET PARAPHERNALIA
Prepared expressly in Paris by GRANGER.
ENTIRELY NEW PROPERTIES AND APPOINTMENTS,
By S. WALLIS.
THE COMPLICATED GAS CONTRIVANCES, ALL NEW,
By CHARLES MURRAY and Assistants.
Calcium Lights, &c., for the Transformation,
By CHARLES SEWARD, of Astley's, London, (engaged expressly for the occasion).

The Drama produced under the immediate direction of *W. WHEATLEY.*

THE CAST.

Count Wolfenstein, ... J. W. Blaisdell.
Rodolphe, (a Poor Artist), ... {First appearance at this Theatre in several years.} .... Geo. C. Boniface.
Von Puffengrautz, (the Count's Steward,) .... J. G. Burnett.
Hertzog, Surnamed the Black Crook, (an Alchymist and Sorcerer,) his first [appearance,) C. H. Morton.
Greppo, with Duett & Dance, (His Drudge,) | From Sadler's Wells Theatre, London. His first appearance in America. | Geo. Atkins.
Dragonfin, ... | His first appearance at this Theatre. | .... Hernandez Foster.
Zamiel, (The Arch Fiend) .... E. B. Holmes.
Wulfgar, (A Gipsey Ruffian,) .... E. Barry.
Casper, (A Peasant,) .... H. Weaver.
Red Glare, (The Recording Demon,) .... Mr. F. Clark.
Skuldwelp, Familiar to Hertzog .... Mr. Rendle.

Villagers, Peasants, Guards, Attendants, Demons, Monsters, Apparitions, Skeletons, Gnomes, &c., &c.

Stalacta, with Songs, (Queen of the Golden Realm,) Prima Donna Contralta,
| From Covent Garden Theatre, London, her first appearance in America in six years. | .... Annie Kemp.
Amina, (Betrothed to Rodolphe,) .... | From Theatre Royal, Lyceum her first appearance in America. | .... Rose Morton.
Dame Barbara, (Her Foster Mother,) .... Mary Wells.
Carline, (with Songs and Dance,) .... | From Theatre Royal, Drury Lane, her first appearance in America. | .... Milly Cavendish.
Rosetta, (A Peasant,) .... C. Whitlock.

Fairies, Naiads, &c., &c.

The Scene is laid in and around the Hartz Mountains.

A lapse of six months between 2d and 3d, and 3d and 4th Acts.

ACT 1st, Scene 1st,—A Valley at the foot of the Hartz Mountain, ... J. E. Hayes.

GRAND BALLET,

PAS DE SABOT,

Mlles. Rose Delval, Paulina, Elise, Helene, Marie, Rose, Cheri, Helene, Duclos.

PAS DE FLEURS,

MARIE BONFANTI, MLLE. SANGALLI,

MLLE. BETTY RIGL,

Mlle. LOUISA MAZZERI,	Mlles. GUISEPPE,
" GIOVANA MAZZERI,	" LUISIDI,
" AMELE ZUCCOLI,	" MARIE DUCLOS,
" EUGENIA ZUCCOLI,	" PAULINA,

And Full Corps.

Scene 2d,—A Woody Pass, ... Seaver.
Scene 3d,—Laboratory of the Black Crook, ... R. Smith.
Scene 4th,—An apartment in the Castle of Wolfenstein, SONG—"Naughty, Naughty Man," } .... Carline.
Scene 5th,—A Wild Glen in the heart of the Brocken, ... R. Smith.

GRAND INCANTATION !!

Introducing many Weird and Startling Effects

CATARACT OF REAL WATER AND RIVER OF BLOOD, ... R. MARSTON.

ACT II, Scene 1st.—Subterranean Vault in the Castle of Wolfenstein, ... R. Smith.
Scene 2d.—Lobby in the Castle of Wolfenstein, ... R. Smith.
Scene 3d.—A Wild Pass in the Hartz Mountains, ... D. A. Strong.

SCENE 4TH,—THE GROTTO OF STALACTA,
(THE QUEEN OF THE GOLDEN REALM.) R. MARSTON.

Splendid Pas de Naide,

Mlle. RITA SANGALLI,

AND FULL BALLET.

Song Stalacta,............ Flow on Silver Stream.
Do. .... Power of Love.
Do. .... March of Fishes and Dance of Mermaids.
BY THE CORPS DE BALLET.

PAS DE DEMONS,

Mlle. MARIE BONFANTI,

Mlles. BETTY RIGL, ZUCCOLI, ZUARDI, MAZZERI,
—AND—
Signor DAVID COSTA.

ACT III. Scene 1st,—Illuminated Garden of Wolfenstein by Moonlight. R. SMITH.

THE BAL MASQUE,

PAS ESPANOIL,

Mlle. SANGALLI.

PAS DE HONGROISE,

Mlles. L. MAZZERI. G. MAZZERI, ZUCCOLI, ZUARDI.

AN ORIGINAL AND GRAND

DANCE DE AMAZONS,

Arranged by Signor DAVID COSTA,

Danced by Mlle. MARIE BONFANTI, and Full Corps.

ACT IV. Scene 1st.—An Apartment in the Castle of Wolfenstein,
Scene 2d.—The Retreat of Rodolphe in the Forest,............ Wallack.

GRAND TRIPLE SWORD COMBAT.

Scene 3d.—A Forest,............
Scene 4th.—A Burning Forest,............ R. Marston.
Scene 5th.—Another part of the Forest,............
Scene 6th.—Pandemonium,............ Seaver.
Scene 7th and Last,—THE PALACE OF DEW DROPS, Painted and Designed by the............ Brothers Brew, of London.

A DAZZLING TRANSFORMATION SCENE,

REVEALING THE

NYMPHS OF THE GOLDEN REALM,

Terminating with Stalacta's Triumph

HAPPINESS AND JOY.

Treasurer,............ J. A. ZIMMERMAN.

Ladies' Dressing Room, with female attendant in waiting in the Dress Circle.

Seats Secured Six Days in Advance.

PRICES.

Admission............75 cents.
Secured Seats in Dress Circle,............$1.00
Reserved Seats in Parquette & Parquette Circle,......$1.50
Family Circle, (Entrance on Crosby St.)............50 cents.
Private Boxes,............$8.00 and $10.00

SANFORD, HARROUN & CO., PRINTERS, 644 BROADWAY N Y

pany dared to appear in Boston, to be followed the next year by the opening of the Federal Street Theatre.

There was dramatic blood in my mother's line, for English-born Aunt Susanna Rowson, sister of Great-grandfather Haswell, not only acted in the Chestnut Street Theatre, Philadelphia, and the Federal Street Theatre, but wrote a play that was put on there called *Americans in England.*

Minstrelsy long had held its place and many of our best "legitimates" started life as "nigger minstrels," even Booth and Jefferson having had their turn at it, Jefferson making the Jim Crow song famous. But *The Black Crook* was New York's first absolute "Leg Show";—beautiful, novel and very well presented. But the crux of the whole matter was, judged from afar, that a barrier was broken down, never to be replaced, for it was then discovered that some of the dancers as well as actresses could personally be really fine women, whom several of the "sparks" (ancient for "Johnnies") took honorably to wife. Thus a precedent was set for all time.

It was found that nimble feet and shapely bodies may be topped by intelligence, keen wit and real morality. This had been fully realized in England when the daughter of a Presbyterian minister, Ada Isaacs Menken, the Mazeppa against whom sermons were preached and virtuous eyes veiled, was capable of holding the loyal and aboveboard friendship of men of the intelligence of Dickens, Swinburne and the elder Dumas.

A little space ago I heard two veteran playgoers speaking of *The Black Crook.* In discussing this spectacle in comparison with the dancing of later days, it was only a certain crudeness of setting, that obtained everywhere in the theatre, which came under their criticism, not in any way the moral side. But New

York Society then felt that such things belonged only to debased oversea countries, and not to its severe Republican purist New World. It was mistaken. Americans paid out one hundred thousand dollars of their good money in a little less than a year and a half to see the play it had tried to frown down, at the rate of one dollar and a half for the best single seat and ten dollars for a stage box. Yet the coming of these dancers and the following development and change of public opinion in New York was a species of moral and social revolution; for *The Black Crook* and its train broke into many families beside ours, with a crack akin to the storming of the front windows by a mob.

XIII

PARTIES—TWO IN PARTICULAR THAT NEARLY MADE ME A SOCIALIST

AMONG many children's parties, that only differed in the color of the ice cream, or as to whether we had mottoes in fringed papers, or candied white grapes and oranges as a finale, two stood out in high and somewhat cruel relief.

The usual home entertainments of youth, before the dancing age, consisted of games that could only be played well indoors. Hunt-the-slipper, Going-to-Jerusalem, Post-office, Clap-in-and-clap-out, Hide-the-handkerchief, and most desperately romantic of all, Pillows-and-keys.

The forfeits that fell to the loser in many games seemed to take a kissing form; also the little printed mottoes that were wrapped up with the bonbons in the colored tissue paper petticoats all bore in sickly verse upon love, sweethearts and marriage. I cannot remember that the words made the slightest impression upon the children, it was for me merely a matter of rivalry as to how many mottoes I could collect to take home in the little bag made by tying together the four corners of my best initialed handkerchief.

Pillows-and-keys was a game in which kissing was

the only motive, also it was the reverse of all other games in that to be the odd number, the one left out, was an honor, not a discard. Armed with a sofa pillow and a large door key that usually had a very brassy odor, the little boy, if shy, wandered up and down the row of expectant girls, preening birdlike in their white party frocks and gay sashes. If he was resolute he made short shift and choice, going straight to his three goals as directed—"Kneel to the wittiest, dance with the prettiest, and kiss the one you love best."

This triple performance was somewhat complicated and required quite a bit of steering with some one at the piano to supply music, either for a few dance steps or a ring-around-a-rosy whirlabout if the children could not dance. Usually it resulted merely in kneeling once and kissing the best beloved; so on and round and round until much duplication ended the zest of the game. The keys being thick and sizable the kiss itself through the loop of the handle was a rather remote affair, not as unsanitary as it would seem, and one was lucky not to receive, instead of a caress, a hard bat on the nose from bad aim. Still, rivalry was the spice of this game as in many other indoor sports, for the real fun of Fox-and-geese, London-Bridge-has-fallen-down, and of all the others that require muscle or speed, were not thought good for the parlor furniture.

So long as basement dining rooms obtained there was a thrill and excitement about choosing partners for the grand march downstairs, always with the hopeful chance that the odd girl, there seemed always to be one, who was led by the lady of the house, would be some one you did not like. Thus early do social amenities enter the female heart!

Gradually the party atmosphere cleared and evoluted to better things; a juggler, a story-teller, or a Punch and Judy show drove out the overworked sofa pillow. Mottoes grew long, were wrapped in colored isinglass, paper caps replaced the pallid, rose-flavored candies, and the snappers were sufficiently powerful to justify a shriek, if pulled off near one's ear. Also little frosted cakes and macaroons were mingled liberally with the customary lady fingers. These parties cost more, but what would you have? Even in the sixties and seventies youth, if not vocally asking for more, craved it, and the parents were thus bidding, half unconsciously, for prestige through their children.

Presently there came to me an invitation to a birthday lunch party from Aunt Kinnie Haven at Washington Square for one of her grandchildren. Long before the day arrived various details had leaked out sufficient to whet anybody's appetite. A sit-down luncheon at one; afterward jugglers and, oh bliss indeed, performing dogs! Gatha, who took a great interest in my clothes, made me a new dress, a light blue silk poplin, with a full skirt and bretelles, trimmed with rows of narrow velvet ribbon that formed a waist, low front and back, worn over a muslin tucker, and Bea, too busy with her own bridal linen to do any other sewing, but having her "Pickens money," bought me a pair of smart ankle-tie slippers with heels. Very flat heels they were, to be sure, but heels all the same, quite an upward grade from the slippers that I had previously worn. That "Pickens money!" I hope the dear old man has caught up with his lost love, somewhere, somehow, and knows how happy he made a little bit of the world when he left those women the very own pocket penny that let them, in turn, buy something for some one else "unbeknownst like," as Mary Daly would express it.

When the great day came I was dressed and waiting before noon and by the time I arrived at the house I was almost dizzy with excitement. I only hoped that my new dress would not attract *too* much attention. It did not. In fact, as fat Ann, Aunt Kinnie's much enduring maid, took off my coat, the glances that fell upon the blue poplin, and then travelled the length of my spine with a shiver, were not of admiration. I was the only girl there who was not dressed either in elaborately embroidered muslin or light-colored silk, with silken socks or hose to match.

It proved to be exclusively a girls' party, so there was no scrambling for partners as we filed into the dining room and took our places. I found myself seated by a very pretty girl named Minnie Griswold, who, after looking me over critically, said, "I live in Fifth Avenue, where do you live?"

"In Eleventh Street," I replied.

"Don't know where that is. Is yours a big house?"

"Oh, yes—very, and it has a yard in front and another at the back; we have lots of fun playing in the front yard."

"I'm not allowed to play in the street. How many servants do you keep? We have five and a butler."

"No servants. We have help, two of them. Is your mother sick? Can't she do anything?" I asked. Then she gave a little laugh and a shrug of the shoulders at the same time, and the soup, a delicious broth with noodles, being served, conversation stopped, much to my relief. That course was successfully accomplished, only I observed that a very richly dressed girl, with a much capped nurse behind her chair, put the whole spoon in her mouth, unreproved, something that I had known was a must-not-be ever since I could feed myself.

Next came plates upon which a beautifully roasted squab was surrounded by a nest of water cress. How my mouth watered! I waited and watched. Everyone had an attendant back of the chair, busy with the anxious business of dismantling the bird, save me alone.

The two waiters, who had at least twenty children to serve, did not notice my plight. I waited I suppose five minutes, it seemed an hour. Grief overcame me and tears began to ooze more quickly than I could lick them up unnoticed. Then anger followed and braced my spirit with iron. I stuck my fork into the bird with all my strength, raised it from the plate and began to gnaw the breast.

"Don't do that, my pretty, that is not the way little ladies eat. Let Ann help you," said a buttery voice close to my ear, while strong hands quickly disjointed the squab. "Now you can pick it fine. You're the minister's little girl, yes? Well, Ann will stay by you and help you out, as your nurse didn't come."

"I haven't any nurse, I never had one! I don't want one! I like my mother and Bea." And the unusual snarling sound of my voice has remained in my ears as clear as a sound of yesterday.

Ann did as she promised, and moreover when the dessert came, wonderful ice cream in the form of a hen sitting in a nest of straw-colored spun sugar, surrounded by eggs of many hues and little chickens, she spoke to one of the waiters and my portion was the hen's head, that had a fine red comb of raspberry ice also a chocolate egg and an extra helping of sugar. By the time the trained dogs came on I felt better, but a germ had entered my soul, to be developed as the years went by into a positive hatred of social ceremony and form. Even that night as I told them at home about the wonderful party, I knew in my heart that I had really had better sport at the simpler neighborhood birthdays, with the games, one kind of ice cream and lady fingers.

Again a birthday party. The sixties had slipped away and a couple of years beside. The same people but a different house, Thirty-fourth Street and Fifth Avenue; a smaller group of young girls able to dissect a squab politely; perfect table service and harmony, some bits of gossip, rather below or above my understanding, but packed away for digestion and reference.

After the luncheon a May party in carriages went to Central Park, the entertainment being rides in the merry-go-round, on the Shetland ponies, and in the pony carriages. One of the birthday gifts had been a sleek pug dog, small of size and perfectly equipped with a harness studded with shining nail heads, and a leading leash with a padded loop that would not cut the hands.

One can almost fix a date by the breed of the pet dogs then in fashion. Black-and-tans, the one pound weight kind, were passing. Enter the screw-tailed pugs. They grew stout too early and wheezed painfully. Then succeeded the French and Boston Bulls. (Weak-eyed white poodles always have been the favorite of elderly widows, through several periods.) Next the yapping, snapping Pomeranians, carried in the muff along with the handkerchief. Enter the Pekinese, intelligent and able to stand on their own feet. Exit the muff! Now Police dogs!

The birthday girl wished to take her pug to the Park; there was some objection on the part of the governess who was to be in charge, but the young lady prevailed and off we started. A leisurely drive up Fifth Avenue was always worth while to me. I loved horses and nowhere in America were so many fine horses to be seen. Men and women on horseback coming from the side streets on their way to the bridle path, open landaus with beautifully gowned women, more formal coaches with high springs and double folding steps to bridge the greater distance, gave a truly Victorian touch. Elderly people usually rode in these, and the smart young men and women who were not on horseback were frequently seen driving the two-wheeled dogcarts, sometimes with single horses, sometimes tandem. Indeed Fifth Avenue was akin to a horse show, a very gay place of a May afternoon, and even of a morning, and as far down as Eleventh Street might be seen the beautiful if somewhat mysterious Mrs. Hicks-Lord going up the Avenue, her groom riding exactly so many paces behind, a distance that was never allowed to vary. Perfect in figure, hat and habit, a faultless mount. As an equestrian picture the entire combination was notable.

There was some hitch about the ponies, for though they had been engaged ahead the supply was insufficient. Finally it was decided by the rather distracted governess that we should take turns, part using the merry-go-round while the others rode, and *vice versa.*

I patiently waited my turn for the pony ride, seated on a bench and being well amused by all that was passing. Then as my time came at last the young hostess rushed up and, putting the pug dog in my arms, threw her coat on the seat beside me and said, "Here, you hold him and wait, I want to ride again before you do"—and dashed off, leaving me entirely alone. Then I realized that all the other girls had taken two rides! For a few moments I sat perfectly still; my only desire was to get away, to get home, but how? I had never yet been allowed to walk in the streets alone, also I had no money for car or stage fare. Never mind, I had legs, though at the time I was so lanky of limb as to be dubbed Spider, by Nabob the Magnificent of Washington Square.

I folded the coat carefully and set the dog upon it, fastening the leash to a bar of the settee so that he should not stray away and be lost. The happenings were not his fault. For the first few minutes I trembled all over, but when I got safely out of the Park and past the many empty lots and open places, I knew that I only had to keep straight ahead to reach the home goal. Three miles or so was not a long walk for me in the country, I had gone much further, but alone in New York streets for the first time, and choking with the sense of injustice because I was considered the most humble of the group, made each breath I drew painful. I was almost spent when I reached the gate of our yard and I had to steady myself by it before I could go in.

Only when I found Mother did tears and relief come, but they were merely a vent, not sad tears now, for even to look at the expression of her face gave me backbone. Oh why did not I too have a Roman nose instead of a no-account pug? Very gently she questioned and soothed me, suggested that I should go to bed at once as I was growing feverish. Then as soon as I was tucked in she dispatched Father to tell of my return. As he reached our gate the family carriage and Aunt Kinnie drew up, having come down in such haste that the sleek horses were all afoam. I never knew what passed between them, but when Father returned there was a flash in his eyes that I had never seen there before; they quite played up to Mother's nose.

Next day Mother took me to see Dr. Draper over in Twelfth Street. She told him how fussed up I had been by the party and how I had not gone to sleep, also that I did not like the food that was good for me but craved strong tea, sips of claret and liked cold-slaw with vinegar on it. Of these crimes I knew I was guilty and I hung my head, until, looking sidewise, I caught a glimpse of the doctor's face. It wore a lovely smile such as he alone could give forth, half amused, half sad, and wholly comprehending. His finely shaped hands busied themselves with balancing his eyeglasses between thumb and finger, a habit that he always had when deep in thought, though he sometimes varied it by snipping the binding of his vest with his pocket scissors.

"It is not freakishness but nature guiding her," he said in a low tone to Mother. "She needs a tonic, fruit acids and green salads."

"Come here, Ma*belle;*" he always emphasized the last syllable of my name thus. "Look at me." I raised my eyes to his.

"What do you like to do best? What do you love best? I mean aside from your people."

I thought a moment before I answered, "I think flowers, and dogs, to live in the country, where you don't have to wear best clothes, and—some kinds of music, and—I love you!" I added, "because you always know the reasons why of me without being told!"

Then he really laughed aloud, and putting his arm about me he said, "My child, hold fast to all those things—for they will never turn a cold shoulder." Wheeling about he seated himself at the open cabinet piano that was in the room and began to play and then sing in his sympathetic, tenor voice, song after song from a newly published English book of rhymes for youth:—

I had a little doggie that used to sit and beg—
But doggie tumbled down that stair and broke his little leg:

The North wind doth blow,
And we shall have snow,
And what will poor robin do then?

The King of France—Lullaby—Mistress Mary—and ended with the eery tune of—

My Lady Wind, my Lady Wind
Went about the house to find
A crack to get her foot in!

Singing it to the end. "My Lady Wind and her doings are what you disliked about the parties, Ma*belle*," and he got up, closing the piano.

I understood him partly even then, and, since, completely. Moreover I have kept all the loves, and this "beloved physician" was the first among those of the most comprehending of all professions in which I have always found true and loyal friends. I had been understood; this in itself is the anti-toxin of socialism and all discontent.

XIV

AUNT CINDER MAKES A LANDING:—ENTER UNCLE CHARLES

THE family had not really become accustomed to the fact that Bea was engaged to be married, when, all of a sudden, Aunt Cinder came down in a place from which she had flown up many years before, and, finding the same man had also returned to the trysting, was not only engaged but married before she had time to again change her mind. The circumstances were a little different, however, in that when she had flown up she was twenty, and when she made her final landing she was forty and more beside. At that age, at least for a woman, I do not think that it can possibly be the altogether, moonlight-moss-rosebud-bouquets-stolen-kisses-in-the-dark affair that it is at twenty. Especially when the man has married in the interval and has several well-grown, motherless children. A woman must necessarily resent these children of an old lover whom she once sent away, because they must remind her of the lost years during which they might have been born to her.

Aunt Cinder cried when she left us, in spite of the fact that she was going to a house of her own and that the Prince had at last come for her. She gave me a pair of roller skates and a puppy—with a family tree, not a street purchase—for a "wedding present." Yet even though she was happy, no doubt, in her heart, she was always restless in her body and took it out in moving from house to house instead of flying up into the air.

Be this as it may, Uncle Charles was a very welcome addition to our scanty stock of relations. He was our only uncle now, for Uncle Isaac, the quaint family bachelor, whose purchases at auction sales were always exciting gifts, whether of books, crockery, or old prints that the Aunties sometimes considered unfit to hang upon their walls, had slipped away exactly as he would have wished. He broke the ice in the River Charles for his before-breakfast swim once too often. Returning home to dress for the day, and perhaps sitting down to rest from an unusual sense of weariness, he had made a final entry in his mysterious diary—strangely enough the only one in English:

"I have rather overdone my cold-weather plunge. I begin to feel my y-e-a-r-s"—here his pen failed; as with so many of our family tribe the heartbeats not backing up the will to do.

Dear Uncle Charles Emery Soule (the son of Gideon, of Exeter Academy fame), what a joy his coming was to me. He too went on before age marred him, holding my hand in the going. From first to last he was the most loving and thoughtful of kin. In spite of a keen legal mind he was transparent by nature and really wore his heart on his sleeve, so reachable it was and easily tuned to childhood's needs. He was in truth a "first aid to all injured" feelings—a bouquet for a birthday, an absorbing story book for one housed with a snuffle cold. How mercifully he came of an evening to read aloud to me when I was blinded by the measles and must lie with bandaged eyes, leading me into the light along a gold trail by way of Hiawatha, until the poem was a reality in which I lived and had a part, the rhythm following his deep, rich voice with all the unction of intoned Latin. If there was no special reason, he would drop in merely for a cheery greeting to the house and a "What can I do for you?" in spite of the fact that from first to last, through no fault of his own, his life road was hard marching, something akin to the old cobblestone pavement when one had to tread it in thin shoes.

With the coming of Uncle Charles my New York expanded both in territory and through new experiences, for though short and stout he was a great walker and rather prided himself on trying never to go twice to a place by the same way if it could be avoided. To him I owe my first experience in riding on the elevated railroad, a contraption looked at askance by conservative folk in the late sixties and well into the seventies, very much as the present generation looked upon dirigibles and aeroplanes.

This single track structure, with turnouts at intervals, ran only on Ninth Avenue and for a short distance (it having been first called the West Side and Yonkers Elevated R. R.), I do not remember how much, above Fourteenth Street where we took it, but it ended abruptly at about Chambers Street. Aunt Cinder and Uncle Charles were then living in Brooklyn and he proposed that we should walk from the terminal over to Fulton Ferry. I was fascinated with the idea of such an adventure, yet afraid, for neither Mother nor my sisters had trusted themselves to the elevated. I was a good climber of trees, haystacks and the sloping roofs of barns. When I looked up at the tracks they did not seem very high, but yet—?

When the fussy little engine started with a jerk and we began to speed past buildings on a line with the second-story windows, and swaying considerably, something loosened in my chest, very much as it did a short time since when I unthinkingly stepped into an express elevator in a tall office building, meaning to go down only two floors and suddenly found myself at the street twelve stories below. If I looked as pale as I felt, it was no wonder that Uncle Charles asked me, when we stopped a moment in our walk across City Hall Park to the East River, if I was hungry? I was by no means sure what ailed me, but this was at least a tangible idea, so I said yes, looking expectantly at some ripe pears that a woman of the standard "Apple Mary" type was peddling.

"Then we will stop at Dorlon's at Fulton Market and have some oysters. Being September there is an R in the month, so it is quite safe. Do you like oysters?"

"Not cold ones," I quavered chokingly, remembering the fat, cold, slippery things that O'Connell had fed me from the shell, the memorable day of the lumber-yard fire.

"No, piping hot ones, a Saddle Rock pan roast, or a broil, right off the fire," he proclaimed reassuringly.

At that moment a diversion happened that now helps me to locate the date 1872 as the time of my first ride on the elevated railway. A man hawking toy balloons, pinwheels and fans, pushed one of the latter square into Uncle Charles' face. He halted abruptly and began to laugh, for the fan was a life-sized mask of Horace Greeley, then running for President. It was well colored, spectacled, sparse hair and throat-latch beard being closely imitated by white yak fringe, then fashionable as a trimming, which blew to and fro in the wind with lifelike effect. A short, stout wooden handle coming from under the turned-over collar finished what was a perfect portrait, yet at the same time a caricature by suggestion. With childlike enthusiasm that was so typical of him, Uncle Charles dropped the overcoat that he always carried but never wore, upon the grass, together with his satchel of law papers, and after looking at the fans for a minute bought the man's entire stock, six in number, which, when they were secured by a string, he gave to me, saying, "Youngster, we will have some fun with these."

So it proved, for they were not merely a fleeting fancy but outlived poor Greeley himself; their last appearance being several years later when they furnished heads for an old man's chorus in a play that was staged by budding dramatists under the back porch of the West Eleventh Street house.

When we reached Fulton Market the salt air began to put my insides back into place, its tonic and pungent odor of fresh seaweed in the oyster baskets discounting the fishy smell. Though this market was then a famous retail place for general food merchandise, I always remember it as a fish market pure and simple, which it became later on strictly wholesale lines.

Picking his way carefully, Uncle Charles led me into a rather large, low-ceiled room, filled with plain wooden tables and the sort of chairs that we used in the country kitchen. The floor was strewn thick with sawdust, and I noticed that there was a brown, glazed earthenware spittoon by each table, an article that Mother loathed and which was *oban* in our house, even though many conservative families had very handsomely painted ones in their libraries and even sometimes in the dining rooms. This custom will indicate that men other than Dismal Jim chewed tobacco, also expectorated freely when they smoked, and yet were rated as gentlemen.

Hanging up my coat and hat as well as his own, and pushing in my chair, Uncle Charles looked at the small bill of fare quickly and gave the order, "One pan roast and one broil," saying to me jokingly, "I suppose you do *not* want a glass of milk?" While we waited for the pan roast, the waiter brought two plates of cold-slaw, some round crackers, larger and thicker than those now served with oysters, also a brown mug, shaped like the top of a man with a three-cornered hat, only there was foam oozing where the brains should have been. This he placed by Uncle Charles. To me he gave a glass of water, a thick glass, and the water was not very clear. Now Mother was always particular about the drinking water, "fussy" the careless called it, and long before filters were in common use she had a series of narrow cotton flannel bags, that were tied to the drinking-water faucet and often changed. Being myself very thirsty, and the water repulsive, I was much interested in the foaming little brown jug and asked what it was.

"A Toby of Bass ale, I always take it here with oysters. Yes, you may taste it, but it is bitter and I doubt if you will care to swallow it—" this said, the Toby was put within my reach.

I tasted, swallowed hastily, then began to drink! As soon as the ale reached my stomach the two became chums. I was saved! I touched ground, I was no longer swimming through the air behind a spitfire of an engine. I now thought of the coming oysters with joy, I saw that before me, in a rickety merry-go-round castor, were the makings of French dressing for the cold-slaw. I bit into a cracker and quickly put it down, lest Uncle Charles should look over the paper he was reading and take back the dear, cheerful brown Toby. This happened a moment later—"Here! what are you doing? Put that down, child. I never heard of such a thing! They will never trust you with me again. You will be ill, and there'll be the devil to pay!" Then he grasped the Toby, upon the edge of which I had set my teeth very firmly. When he retrieved it his was but a half portion. When my broiled oysters came at last, closely crumbed, brown, and showing the marks of the grill, my appetite was keenly edged. We ate in comfortable leisure while I asked questions about the many pictures that hung upon the walls. Crude they were, no doubt, those colored prints of crafts of all sorts, from fishing-smacks to merchantmen, but now methinks I have seen collectors squabble over far less worthy specimens for den or dining-room decoration, during the present fad for all things maritime.

When we had finished the meal and were preparing to go I thought that Uncle Charles was looking at me a bit anxiously. Was it because he had said "there would be the devil to pay," and he expected him to be standing close by, as the waiter had stood for his tip? Now really the myth called the devil had long befriended me by nonappearance, at times when others had seemed to expect him, this occasion being no exception to the rule. Even in Norah Goodnuff's grim reign her version of him, called diversely Baal and Beelzebub but never recognized by Mother or Father, had seemed far less real or possible than Alice's Cheshire Cat. At the door I turned back regretfully to look at the sturdy little mug that had ended my first land attack of seasickness. "Could you buy me one?" I unblushingly begged of Uncle Charles. "I think I should—like to drink from it better than from my silver mug, and it would not need polishing," I added, by way of an excuse. So when Aunt Cinder greeted us at the door she found a brown spider of a girl of thirteen on the step, one arm grasping a six-headed Horace Greeley complex and the thumb of the other not over clean hand firmly hooked through the handle of the precious Toby!

Lobster palaces, oyster houses or oyster saloons, as they were variously called, have come and disappeared, in sequence, but to me none at any time during the long years between then and now could excel, either in quality of the sea food or the atmosphere of the salt waterways, the old-time Dorlon's of Fulton Market. Gone alack! like the Brown Toby of wholesome Bass "on draught"—together a lasting flavor and a memory.

Uncle Charles knew of a great many places where

rather unusual food could be had, other than the real hotels that had restaurants. As Aunt Cinder had a great deal of trouble in keeping cooks, while mother's always stayed forever, Aunt Cinder dined about constantly, while for us it was a party that only happened when Boston people came. Then we sometimes went up to the St. Denis Hotel at the end of Eleventh Street and Broadway, where we usually had *meringue glacée* for dessert, while the bread or rolls and butter were free and so good and they gave so much, that one had to be careful to leave room for the real dinner. There was one little shop on University Place, kept by a real French woman, I think her name was Mme. La Rue. Almost all the people who came there were French, and the special dish that they went for was either of boiled snails or creamed mussels. The snails, Uncle Charles said, were grown in France and brought over in a basket of grapevine leaves by one of the petty officers of the French liners. When they arrived word was sent around to the patrons of the place and they gathered for the feast. I did not know what they were until after I had eaten a portion and found it very good. Then Uncle Charles told me, and all I could think of was of the slimy things that stick under stones in the garden and at once I began to feel crawly inside. The mussels, however, were not unlike creamed oysters, the sauce *à la marinière*, in which Mme. La Rue smothered them, bringing fame to a notable restaurant in Paris even today.

Another excursion that we took the week after we went to Dorlon's, Aunt Cinder, Uncle Charles and I, must be recorded here. It was out of rather than in my New York, though now well within the city lines of the third borough, that I had my first taste of a new food that belonged partly to the water and yet was neither fish, flesh, nor fowl.

Aunt Cinder had a desire, the second since her marriage, to move into the near-by country, from which Uncle Charles might reach town easily by rail. Armed with a list of possible houses to be had, we took the Harlem Railroad, getting off at Morrisania, one of a chain of half-country towns, including Melrose, Tremont and Fordham, that reached from Mott Haven to Williams Bridge on the Bronx, now the lower boundary of Woodlawn Cemetery. Engaging a driver who knew the neighborhood and had a sturdy team, we started across a dreary stretch of country where there were no consecutive streets broken through or graded until we reached the Boston Road, which I remember was our aim, the drive being very like playing a game of hopscotch on wheels. Squatter shanties, swamps, here and there a shabby bit of woods, or an old dwelling once of dignity and now falling to decay or threatened by the cutting through of unsewered streets, is my memory of the tract that we skirted with difficulty that day. After the house hunting was ended we were driven to the station at Williams Bridge, the only place on the Harlem road where the New Haven trains stopped, as I was to be taken home to Fairfield that night.

It was yet early afternoon and Uncle Charles found that we had more than a hour to wait. Our lunch of sandwiches was a thing of the past, I was very hungry and did not hesitate to let Aunt Cinder know it. It is something that grownups should never forget, that hunger—natural hunger and childhood travel hand in hand, especially upon all-day excursions where the active brain absorbs vitality rapidly via observation. Never say "Wait until you get home"—do it now! Aunt Cinder understood this and after some conversation Uncle Charles set the doing in motion. A little river, the Bronx, picked its way along with many curves, not far from the station. I had often watched this stream from the trains, coveting the many wildflowers that followed it, seeing the ducks and little boys with no bathing suits swimming with equal freedom, and envied both, but it never occurred to me that some day I might go a boating on it, or even that it was deep enough for boats. But the early fall rains had swelled it, and presently Uncle Charles was pushing us down stream with a stout pole in a boat that wobbled and swung about, this way and that, while Aunt Cinder gathered her petticoats about her, cautioning me to keep still and sit in the middle of the narrow board that made the end seat of the homemade leaky craft. We had not far to go when we brought up at the sloping bank near a small building about which were several rustic arbors covered with grapevines under which there were tables. A name—The Hermitage—was formed of letters in rustic work. Soon a short thick-set man with snappy dark eyes and a pointed mustache came out, pulling on a short jacket as he ran, and fastened the boat as if he had expected us, and led us toward the house. "Would we be served within, or would Madame and the *jeune fille* prefer to partake outside with the landscape?" To my regret Aunt Cinder chose indoors, for almost at once some ducks and chickens began to gather around as if expecting scraps. However, as four tiny white poodle puppies and their very stout mother appeared in the doorway, I was resigned.

While Uncle Charles talked in French to the proprietor, or rather the man in charge, for a stout woman soon appeared and gave directions, we looked about. It was unlike any place I had ever seen, and from memory I can only describe it as impressing me as an artist's studio where people lived, or else a scene in a play; bits of color here and there, blue smoke clouds veiling and lifting. Some artists' gear was lying on the floor, while the men who owned it were sipping red wine and rolling cigarettes idly as they talked—cigarettes,which I thought,until it was explained to me, were lamplighters. When they presently began to smoke, the odor was quite different from Brother George's cigars or Uncle Charles' pipe: softer, a bit sweetish, more clinging and persistent. Then and there my hunting-dog nose first began to sense the difference in tobaccos, so that in time I have come to be able almost to identify well-known friends by the odor of their tobacco smoke.

The meal arrived. First an omelet, with sliced tomatoes surprisingly cuddled into it, yes, and just a mere breath of onion. "No garlic," Uncle Charles had said. Crisp French rolls and sweet butter. Delicious! A wine card was handed to Aunt Cinder, which she waved away, but presently I saw that both she and Uncle Charles had flavored their glasses of water with claret, the tart red claret that I had been reproved for craving when my Dr. Draper had said "The child needs fruit acids." Ah, yes—Aunt Cinder had remembered this and presently there came a tall glass of lemonade, in which a blend of both orange juice and pineapple syrup was evident.

Next a deep platter was brought, and as the cover was lifted Aunt Cinder, after looking at the contents, put on her glasses—and looked again. What were the two-legged things? They were not put together like either pigeons or chickens and they stopped at the waist. Uncle Charles laughed, while the woman proprietor, who seemed to take a great interest in us, now stood behind my chair wearing a smile of expectancy.

"I cannot guess what they are," said Aunt Cinder, who had looked both with and without her glasses.

"Your turn, three guesses, youngster," said Uncle Charles, moving the dish nearer. All at once it flashed upon me—partly the effect of the action that the frying had given the legs, partly, probably, the association with my usual view of the river outside. "They are like boys' legs when they are in swimming and drawn them up to push back, just as frogs do. They *are* frogs!" I almost shouted.

The proprietor clapped her hands in Gallic glee. "Ze *jeune fille*, she is observant, *anatomiste*, she sees all through ze cover of batter!"

"Where do you get so many of them?" inquired Uncle Charles when, the dish being empty, he ordered another round.

"Everywhere, ze *garçons* bring them in to sell each night in season. Ze country, he jumps wiz ze *grenouilles*, Johnny Frog you call him, yes?"

As a matter of course, I could not have the strong black coffee in the tiny cups that followed the dessert of pancakes rolled with jelly. This also was my first introduction to the demi-tasse, for at home we had coffee only at breakfast. In fact I now realize that the New Yorkers of New England blood clung quite loyally to tea even at breakfast, long after the Holland and Huguenot strain used coffee freely. And what horrible mixtures were compounded under the name! Even then I realized that the fragrance of this coffee in the little cups was quite different from that at home—almost like a perfume. While I meditated upon it and as to whether a sip would be possible, the proprietor, who had taken me under her wing, placed beside me a large cup, of a tall and unusual shape, and a plate upon which was a long, stick-shaped roll of French bread.

"You eat him so"—she explained, dipping the end of the roll into the cup of rich, sweet chocolate, and indicating that I should eat the moistened bread. This I did with great pleasure, but never again did I meet the exact combination, until, in Paris on my honeymoon, it was served to me for the *petit déjeuner* at the old Hotel de L'Empire, in the kitchen of which I also learned the making of the "dripped" coffee that flavored the breakfasts of all our following happy years.

Thus came my introduction to frogs' legs as food. Frogs' legs eaten at the vanished Hermitage, seen from a young materialist's viewpoint, no doubt, yet in many ways the surroundings have lingered with me more poignantly than the food, and been revived each time I read Hopkinson Smith's idyl of a day spent in a like riverside shelter. The Hermitage that was, on the banks of the untrained and vagrant Bronx, is gone. The river is now put through many paces, groomed and garnished with "just-so" shrubs, curbed and harnessed to a Parkway system. Beautiful—in keeping with the expansive grandeur of the Greater New York. Yes, but nevermore to be the wilful, sometimes dancing, sometimes sluggish sleepy stream, sowing along its banks the seeds of wildflowers from afar, marsh marigold and sweet-gum burrs, according to season, and cooling the naked stomachs of little swimming boys, who, however, still manage, in spite of police mounted and afoot, to shed their clothes and play at being frogs. Improved? This depends upon one's temperament, age, and memories. The answer lies in the viewpoint. Zoo and Botanic Gardens cover the land of the Jumping Frogs. The river that has named its borough is itself now a city dweller. What is your answer, River Bronx? Have you, too, memories of Youth?

XV

AND SO THEY WERE MARRIED

For a family not to fossilize, its soil must be stirred, and plantings and transplantings be made in it. All these three things happened to us within a single year.

Sister Bea was married in the autumn and went to live that winter in the big house in West Fourteenth Street, the ladies thereof having been among the pioneers of that now hackneyed American cruise—touring Europe with grown daughters, and, incidentally, accumulating more or less dubious husbands, and world weariness en route.

It has been very interesting, this having of an engaged couple in and out of the house, and there was a certain etiquette about things which an engaged girl did and did not do that set her quite apart from her heart-free companions, even before marriage. Bea never after danced with any one but her betrothed, and he was bored with dancing, as he had been through quite a course of wild German "spieling" in his Heidelberg days. Also he was a bit tired at the end of day, after the camp fever that was a result of the war, so they often sat the evenings out in the front parlor with no one to watch them but the portrait of Little Ellen, much to my elder sister's disapproval.

The ruling of the day required that a bride should walk with her husband either to or from his office or place of business, sometimes both, if the distance was short as it usually was in the sixties. Engaged couples did likewise if the houses of the two were in the same neighborhood. Very soon after breakfast Brother

George, who was then a teacher of chemistry at Columbia College at Forty-ninth Street and Madison Avenue, one of a group that under Charles Frederick Chandler founded the School of Mines, would appear at the door, and after a discussion as to whether it was likely to rain, etc., and a little fussing and preening, perhaps to loop up the uncomfortably long walking skirt over the shorter and gaily striped Balmoral underpetticoat, they would start off arm and arm. Walking thus in the street was quite as much a habit by day as by night, while at neither time would any one who even pretended to be a gentleman smoke when in the company of a lady.

Brother George, wishing to be married, presently gave up the struggle with chemistry, the job that he loved so that it was a part of him, and yielded to his father's wish that he should become his partner and a stockbroker—practical but deadly for one who had no jump, but instead the temperamental patience to weigh and measure and watch distillations for hours—days. I know this patience well, for he was the only human being who could help me to even an uncertain footing in the morass of algebra. I also know one other thing, that it is as bad for a man's morale, and also ultimately for his family, to adopt a profession or job he does not love, simply because it may pay, as to marry a girl that does not in any way thrill him, simply because it seems a prudent and common-sense proceeding.

The wedding was like many others, except that it was ours, but as I look across the years I realize one serious difference in the social technique of the church procession. The bridesmaids, three of them, were dressed in long trailing tarlatan skirts, six yards wide (that is, if anything could be said to trail that stood out as stiffly and undrapably as a wire cover to keep flies from food on a lunch counter). The bodices were cut low on the straight-across-below-the-shoulder-top model and the sleeves were mere frills. The men wore full evening dress, though it was a midday ceremony. Each bridesmaid paired with a groomsman, chosen from the near friends of the groom, corresponding to the present-day ushers. The bride and groom followed at this wedding, although I have seen them precede the others, the bride with father and mother bearing the groom company, the makeup of either form of procession being, to my mind, a much more intimate family affair, and less trying to the man, than the present custom of waiting at the altar.

Yet this ruling must have been quite out of date, even then, as in a letter to Mother dated October, 1861, Father, who had been dining at the Bridges' and learning the details of Pauline's forthcoming wedding, wrote, "There are to be four bridesmaids at the wedding to-morrow and no groomsmen. The newest mode!"

Bea did not part with me easily and I went to her for my lessons all that winter, which put off the dreaded confinement of school for yet another season.

Presently a plowing up of the home garden came suddenly, an upheaval, as it were, both a planting and transplanting, followed by new growth. Father's health drooped, the results upon his sensitive nature of the tragedies of the war, parish differences concerning his liking of a certain formality of service and reverence for Christian symbolism in the church edifice, and the heavy weight of debt caused by the building of the new church, in Thirty-fourth Street. Dr. Willard Parker ordered: "A long trip abroad, new places, faces and ways. The time is ripe, go! You have made friends everywhere, some by pen whom you have never met. Also you must resign from your parish; it has reached the point where your spiritual development and liberty is being checked. I know you and these conditions through and through, though you have never voiced them. Go!"

There was a great to-do, but Dr. Parker prevailed; and it seemed to me like world's end when the next May we went to the dock, and a tubby-looking boat, called the *Scotia,* having side wheels like a Brooklyn ferry-boat, carried Father out into the unknown. Did Mother go with him? You would say "certainly," how could she let the ocean part them? This, their first separation, though it was in silver-wedding days, really came through love and self-sacrifice on Mother's part. Yet so carefully disguised was it that Father did not realize at once what it was costing her. Going alone he would meet many men, theologians and other scholars, and do many things where a wife would be a hindrance. This Mother saw from the letters of introduction given him and the invitations to visit received as soon as his plans were known. Also double expense, double everything, was undeniable. At first it marred his pleasure, but her reason could not be offset. "Bea is not strong, and she will need me long before your return."

To Mother this parting gave a double responsibility—she had always been the domestic head of the house, but now she must be the financial manager as well, something entirely new. She must have a check book and draw the money from the bank instead of having it placed in a certain corner in her desk for her to help herself. It was a little sentiment of Father's, this method; it kept away even the shadow of anything like pay or material considerations from between them. Mother hated money business, checks and bills; "pay as you go and if you can't pay, stay at home and don't look into shop windows"—might have been her motto, or at least the pith of it. This novitiate condition of her mind concerning checks evidently inspired the ending of the steamer letter that came the day after Father sailed, which, being on ship paper, so interested the postman, one of Father's "home wedding" bridegrooms, that he not only rang the bell instead of slipping it in the box, that he might put the precious envelope into Mother's hand, but waited a moment for "news of the dear Doctor." How vital handwriting is and how characteristic the hasty note—years do not rob it of its magnetism.

Dearest Ellen:

At dinner, between Mr. Blight and Mr. Roosevelt, charming company, his wife and four children on board. Trunk and bags all safe and the promise good. All my arrangements speak of your care. You are my good Providence. The peace of God be with you. Sunday is Whitsunday, the day of the Comforting Spirit. Send to our communion table from Wilson's a basket of red and white flowers from their late pastor. . . .

Remember this, in making out checks, do not leave any blank space after the figures—thus $100.----, to avoid fraud!

All love, faith, hope,
Your husband ever,
SAMUEL OSGOOD.

. . . .

It took Mother some time to use her check book freely; the Roman nose did not give her courage in this respect. It is said to have taken all Uncle Charles' logic to keep her from drawing all the money at once and keeping it in the usual drawer.

We hurried to the country that year before the violets bloomed in the back yard, strawberries were cried in the street, the chain of purple wistaria festooned the three-story balconies, or the horse-chestnut tree across the way began to swarm with the alley boys. Bea went with us to Mosswood, and this summer everything was done for her pleasure—no one else was of any account, not even Brother George. It was so strange to be without Father, but then there were his letters, and the going to the post office for them was an event, that is until the *great* family event happened. Of a Sunday morning, the September day before we were returning to the Rhinelander block, a son Edmund was born to sister Bea.

No cablegrams then, only the slow-crawling, cold-hearted mail bore the great news to Father, then in Italy, and this was the reply that reached Bea when she went back with us to West Eleventh Street to be brooded over by Mother and adjusted to new conditions before she went to her own home in Fifty-fifth Street, then almost the country, where Brother George could take her out driving in a low buggy with Belle the mare, thus being able to keep away from city hustle.

Florence, Oct. 14, 1869.

My dear Daughter:

Great was my joy last evening on reaching here to find the letters announcing the birth of your son and my grandson. I am so happy that I do not know what to say or do and I was awake half of the night thinking the gift over. You may not deem it strange in me, after I have finished this letter, to go to Dante's famous Church of Santa Croce to give thanks for the bounty of God and to ask his blessing upon you, the boy, your husband, and all of our house.

I know nothing so magnificent as this capacity of maternity. What is like it—the power of bringing a human creature, a living, loving, rational soul, into the world? A book is nothing in comparison with such authorship, and I rejoice that my dear girl has gone so well through this grand publication." . . .

At Christmas we were back in New York and Father had returned. I was the first to spring into his arms, almost before the gangway of *La Pereire*, a quite forgotten boat, touched the pier. Father was bronzed, bearded, mustached and almost stout, who had always been spare and rather ascetic in mien; mentally and spiritually well, filled with new incentive and eager for work. But in spite of appearances he was ever after to feel the ill effects of some Alpine climbing done with Sir John and Lady Bowering, stout-limbed Britishers who did not realize what the strain would be to one who had led a student's life much indoors.

. . . .

It naturally came to be that Father's first home service in New York on his return was a christening, his grandson's. There were several first babies that year among Bea's friends. On the social side these christenings for a brief time were called caudle parties. I wonder how many of the grandmothers now living remember the function or the beverage? It was too thin to eat, too thick to sup, so it was served like porridge or gruel. Its composition was smoothly thickened milk spiced and flavored with sherry or Madeira and filled with raisins. Thin sweet wafers were served with it, the combination taking the place of the customary glass of wine or the modern cup of tea. The use of "caudle" doubtless came from the idea that it was a suitable food for the nursing mothers, who might be expected to gather at the early times when baptism took place within a few days after the child's birth, and those who came to congratulate the mother would find her in bed. Be this as it may, "caudle" soon evoluted into a sort of hot spiced milk punch, served from a conventional punch bowl, much to the relief of the guests in general.

Then came the third event, the upturning of the soil in our home garden, the transplanting of Father from the Congregational Channing-Unitarian form of worship to that of the so-called Church of England. Not that I can discover did he change his belief, his faith—merely the outward expression of it. The fellowship of men whom he had visited in England, like Stanley, Dean of Westminster, and the glorious liturgy of that Cathedral, with its background of the prayers of the ages, gave his spirit rest and peace. Long had his soul had its love of the beauty of religious symbolism misunderstood from within his fold, and he had suffered the mental and spiritual agony of forced extemporaneous prayer constructed to please a many-minded congregation. He had found individualism too lonely when contrasted with enfolding brotherhood. Having taken the step, he paused a while for meditation rather than speech, turning to his pen for occupation. Meantime the words that bind many as a fettering chain he interpreted in the spirit of luminous vision.

A modernist? When has any thinking being truly accepted the man-limited interpretation of another concerning things of the human soul? Many lifelong friends walked beside him in the new way. Some praised at first, then doubted and even jeered, as has been the world's way ever since the Sunday of the Palms and its sequel.

Not living in a parsonage, thanks to Father, we did not have to leave the house with its garden, but ah, for me liberty and learning were no longer to travel together! I was to be sent to school, to sit on a seat and not curl up where I chose, the Green School, at Number One Fifth Avenue, which had kneaded, moulded and finished Bea and Gatha and many more beside. Not all children went to school; there were many among our friends who were educated entirely at home by a governess and various masters who came in for languages, music or dancing. In fact, the English governess system was preferred for years by the most conservative people. Of course we could not afford this, and if we could I should have missed the most joyful periods of youth—two seasons at Dodworth's Dancing School, Allen Dodworth's, the courteous, gracious gentleman. There were several years between these periods, for dancing was a luxury for which savings must be built up, but this only served to make the days more precious and the memory pictures of them more distinct.

XVI

DANCING SCHOOL—IN TWO PANELS.
1,—JOY; 2,—SELF-CONSCIOUSNESS

NO.1 JOY

BROAD steps with a deeply porticoed main entrance over which the letter **D** was carved led to a substantial building on the southwest corner of Twenty-sixth Street and Fifth Avenue. A ballroom, which seemed immense in the late sixties and one that would hold its own even in this day of superlatives; long square-topped windows lighted it on the street and Avenue side. A parquet floor smooth as ice. A man of medium height and slender, lithely muscular build, hair a bit gray, as also his mustache; wearing faultless evening clothes, walks to and fro, now glancing at a moon-faced wall clock and then at the wide doors thrown open toward the corridor. When the hands point to three, he together with his gracious wife, shorter by more than a head, dark-haired, dressed in black velvet with a stately sweep of skirt, will take their places to receive a group of young people, boys and girls from six to fourteen. For the **D** over the door stands for Dodworth and the graceful man is Allen Dodworth himself, the founder of the dancing academy, a man who in the last half of the nineteenth century created the type of dancing that was both a joy and an art, and a part of the social-life training of Better New York. To see Allen Dodworth walk was in itself an education in motion and spoke of something more than mere technical training.

The time being ripe, at a signal the musicians begin, perhaps a march, perhaps a galop, a more rapid version of the present shuffling pushing-a-carpet-sweeper two-step. The pupils enter singly or in pairs, curtsying or bowing to the Dodworths, according to sex, then walk to their places at the seats on the floor level, in front of those elevated and directly against the wall, reserved for parents and friends. I said *walked* to their places; walking was the inflexible rule, and it was no small part of the drill, but always it seemed that the temptation of the polished floor would prompt some lad or lassie to take a run and a slide. Together came the slender nervous hands of the master in a sharp clap! The music stopped and with all eyes fixed on the culprit, the order was given to walk back to the door and make a fresh entrance. The slide was delightful and thrilling, when, as very rarely, it was accomplished unseen. But chilling was the return walk when detected. Having experienced both sensations many times, I know.

The dancers were divided in four classes, number one being for beginners. There was an evening class also when the numbers justified it. This was more of the nature of an assembly. In it young women of the last school year were perfected in all the graces and intricacies of the German, later called the cotillion, and the young men put through the necessary paces for leading the same, but to us youngsters this was only hearsay.

The before-ten-years-old period of dancing school might be called Joy—pure and simple. The girls were dressed pretty much alike in washable white, with ribbon sashes and shoulder knots, long white stockings and heelless black kid ankle ties, kin of the present strap pumps, except that the strap held the shoes firmly about the ankle itself, preventing a wild kick from sending them flying. Some of us had small silk bags that hung from the wrist for holding gloves or a handkerchief, for though gloves must be worn on entering it was permitted to remove them later. Lulu Gregg had a chain that hung from her belt with a wrought silver shell on the end that clasped the handkerchief, and she was the object of concealed envy. To carry any form of candy in these bags was a grave crime, and a repetition of the offense meant confiscation, bag and all. As there was a candy shop either under or next to the hall, memory fails its exact location, where Ridley's famous hard candies, permitted to children, were sold, the temptation to tuck in a few with one's handkerchief was great, as was also the risk of their appearing with the handkerchief at unsuitable moments. I have known a gumdrop discovered by Mr. Dodworth's foot when illustrating a sliding step to cause the entire class from which the spiller came to be kept seated during a dance period, and at the day's end to be made to march out one by one in silence after the music had stopped.

The dressing room was a place where sweets were covertly exchanged, or given outright by the very small boys who were admitted to the girls' section, to their favorites. There were several only sons who were always well supplied. There are two whom I remember by contrast—"Teddy Spectacles," as we called him, and another, a really beautiful lad of the richly colored, Oriental, dark-eyed, long-lashed type, Boisé Hendriquez, who was generous to everyone, boy and girl alike, including my lean, brown self. We had missed him for a whole month and when he returned he wore new gloves which he did not make the usual haste to remove. On being pressed for the reason by our little group, while we ate the long missed candy, he said that he had been ill with scarlet fever, and his hands had not yet "peeled," so his mother said that he must keep on his gloves. After examining the hands we eagerly offered to hasten the peeling process and I was allowed the first attempt. It was an entrancing job, which I did so thoroughly that, among others, I developed the fever in due course. It is now held that the breath and not the skin transmits this disease. Well! There was a fair combination of both in this intimate operation, so an argument as to which did it is not necessary.

As for the social relations between girls and boys, we girls were very independent and hopped along quite as gaily without boy partners. In fact we rather snubbed boys when it came to dancing, however much we liked to play marbles, peg tops, or fly kites with them. They were so often clumsy with their feet and got out of step. To equalize this indifference, Mr. Dodworth when teaching position and steps caused the first class (all of youngsters) to stand in two lines, boys and girls opposite each other, heels together, toes as nearly at right angles as possible without toppling over. This "first position in dancing" being exactly contrary to the toeing-in, pigeon-toed step of the Indian and other fleet-footed races required by the present-day orthopedists to prevent falling arches. Another custom of the time, this strange mincing gait based upon tradition instead of knowledge.

When a sharp hand clap ended the drill, each boy was required to take the girl directly opposite him as a partner for the following dance, either polka or galop, for one must be in the second or third class before attempting the waltz. If there was an odd child Mr. Dodworth became its partner, much to the elation of a girl and the deep distress of a boy. Usually I was quite fortunate in drawing opposites, but there was one boy of great assurance, an only son, who did not like me. This was "Teddy Spectacles" and "I'll get my own way anyhow" determination. If I fell to his lot he would go half around the hall and, as soon as we had passed inspection, give me a quick but decisive kick under the ankle bone, that sent shivers up my spine and made me glad to sit down. That I was not alone in this elimination made it at least less marked!

I never knew precisely what became of Boisé of the soft eyes and courteous manners. He was too beautiful for a male, his type seldom survives long, at least in New York. Rumor said that he never amounted to more than a well-dressed *flâneur*. But "Teddy Spectacles" achieved and resolutely put away everything that he considered undesirable from his path. In a reply from the White House to a note of mine written in 1903 T. R. wrote: "I am much amused to think that I should have met you at Dodworth's in the old days. Even now I remember how dreadfully I danced!"

Panel 2—Self-consciousness

The same master but a new location—this was the third change of habitat of the dancing academy since Allen, one of the Dodworth trio of brothers, founded the school down in Broome Streete before the middle century, later moving up to Broadway a door above Grace Church, then to Fifth Avenue and Twenty-Sixth Street, and finally in the late seventies to 681 Fifth Avenue near Fifty-fourth Street. This location was on the upper edge of the ultra-fashionable district, allowing, of course, that Washington Square and lower Fifth Avenue still held their own, even though new families were jostling the old and trade was waiting its chance to elbow in.

Of the three Dodworth brothers—Thomas the band master, Harvey the musical leader, Allen the dancing master—the latter is the best remembered of the family.

He was now white-haired and rather frail. His son Frank, who usually taught in Brooklyn and outlying places, sometimes came to aid him, but he was not fancied by the older girls. He lacked his father's personality. He was short and the tails of his dress coat were too long and flopped as he danced, a grievous fault to critics of seventeen, who though painfully self-conscious and sensitive when under criticism themselves take great thought of the details of raiment and stature in others, especially males.

There was the same general arrangement of the hall here as of yore, except that there was a gallery for the musicians over the entrance door, near which was a desk at which Mrs. Dodworth sat with her record books, when not occupied in flitting about the hall making little calls upon mothers and guardians. Here paying a compliment upon good deportment or dancing; there explaining to a grasping parent that it was impossible to make a money allowance for irregular attendance or long absence when the required notice had not been given; using the same courtesy and moderation in both cases, thus often forcing the impolite and unreasonable into ladylike behavior through the force of her own courtesy. I think that it was at this time, through watching and listening to the semi-social and financial tactics of many women of really good ancestry, that I began to realize how impossible it was for me to understand women as a sex, or at all, except in rare and individual cases. I wonder, and the wonderment increases daily, if, following the allegory of Eve's creation, it was not a very curved, floating rib of Adam that underlay her and made us, temperamentally at least, take the form of a question mark to keep the world a-guessing?

The joyous, happy children of the three lower grades were now grouped on Monday and Thursday afternoons. Ours was the Tuesday and Friday set, devoted to the fourth and fifth class pupils from sixteen to eighteen, girls of what might be called the conscious age; conscious of their clothes, conscious of the desirability of male dancing partners, and conscious that the schoolboys of a like age are in reality very much younger than themselves, and for some subtle reason totally inadequate. "Willie boys" was a term applied by our group, who had all passed seventeen, to males until they had entered either college or business.

Mr. Dodworth now introduced much variety into this class. The cotillion, danced to both waltz and galop steps, held its vogue, the figures constantly growing more varied and elaborate. There was the polka-redowa and the five-step waltz, a hybrid of the schottish, invented by Dodworth himself who also composed the music for it. Lancers of course remained, and the plain quadrille, while the climax of the season's work was in perfecting oneself in the *Minuet de la Cour*, beginning with its many graceful poses of leg and arm, and stately sweeping curtsy, and leading up to the swift whirl of the lithe gavotte finale. From a hall full of pupils there were never more than a dozen couples who could be trusted to do credit to this dance at exhibition time, and, strangely enough, it was usually the "Willie boys" who failed, unless they had taken lessons in fencing, for this court minuet demands a like flexibility of wrist and ankle.

The waltz had many phases—glide, dip, Viennese, the Boston, etc. The final test after the minuet, which constituted the "finishing" of a pupil, giving entrance to the evening class of social amusement plus ice cream, was the waltzing of a single couple at a time, in a figure eight about two chairs in the middle of the hall, reversing frequently without change of direction. "Oh! for a well-balanced partner," when this day came, was the thought of every girl. He must be a bit taller yet not too tall. He must be able to hold you lightly but firmly, without pressure, for not only was this a forbidden thing in the school, but being hugged made graceful reversing impossible.

Silence and anticipation! The strains of Waldteufel's "Manola," "Mon Rêve" or Strauss's "Blue Danube" floated through the hall as the first couple was selected, never for the perfection expected but rather as a lesson. If the intricate reversing went amiss Mr. Dodworth would drill the dancers separately until his rhythm became contagious. The Christmas and Easter vacations seemed especially chosen for these tests because there were sure to be some extra fellows at home who were welcomed as dancing guests.

Ah! The door opens and a young man enters the hall, without either noise or fussy caution. He is of medium height and spare, muscular build. Brown hair with golden glints, a genial face, a smiling mouth roofed by a crisp mustache. He wears a well-cut tweed suit and thick-soled tan shoes. Quiet as is his entrance all eyes are instantly turned on him, mothers and girls alike, for it is Evart J. Wendell, a student at Harvard, home for the holidays, who has run in to visit his old haunts and perhaps—(yes, the Dodworths are inviting him)—have a dance or two for old time's sake and because he loves both dancing and making himself agreeable.

Whom will he choose to waltz around the chairs? Arriving at this particular moment he comes as a gift of magic. Consciously or otherwise every girl begins to prink mentally, sits a bit more carefully, or points her slippered feet more acutely—sprawling legs not then being a recognized method of attraction—and glances nonchalantly in an opposite direction. It was a heartbreak if one had not chanced to wear one's nicest gown. Why, oh why had the Aunties sent me a violent magenta plaid silk instead of the pale blue that I had so craved?

On went the strains of "Manola" as each couple either passed muster or failed. Around the hall moved Evert Wendell, merely shaking hands with some of those on the raised seats, pausing for a seemingly intimate chat with others; always debonair, always welcome. The first dancing partner chosen was characteristic of him. She was the very bulky, clumsy, unsought daughter of a prominent judge, but through his skill she navigated the shoals and beaming and perspiring was returned to her seat, having received the silent nod from Allen Dodworth that meant promotion. Next! The music changed, the "Vienna Woods," less languorous but more stirring, replaced "Manola." Margaret H. and I, who were sitting together, became conscious without looking up that someone had woven his way around the room toward us. To have crossed directly would have been too abrupt and conspicuous to suit his methods. Pausing in front and exactly between us, he bowed and holding out a hand to each, asked, "Which comes first?" A moment later stately Margaret H. was drifting easily about and between the chairs, I being well content to feast my eyes in looking until my turn should come, for these two were the poetry of well-bred dancing, Margaret flexible without abandon, he leading her confidently but without force, and dancing as lightly in double-soled street boots as in evening shoes. As a matter of record, be it said here, the wearing of tan footgear in winter was then in itself an entire novelty.

Known socially by every mother who gave dances, many girls fancied themselves in love with Evert Wendell, for he had charm at the same time that he was the most impersonally and universally attentive cavalier of his day, yet it was his dancing, perfect even in thick-soled boots, that they were chiefly in love with, his dancing—plus! What they suffered in consequence was from the naturally inexperienced discrimination of youth. It was always so—flowers—bonbons—the play plus an agreeable escort—all these cross-current young emotions. So many voices call to us in youth. Which one shall we follow? How answer when we do not fully understand the language that they speak? For surely at seventeen of all the lures that of the dance is the most direct.

Thus through a dancing school of yore, a third type, that of the faultless gentleman, was painted in memory: one who never intruded yet never forgot; who, no matter what lapse of time between the meeting, remembered all, so that years later when, verging on old age, he crossed the ocean never to return, remembering my love of dogs he sent me a quaint copy of *Rab and His Friends* to add to my dog library. Now when I take this book from its shelf and open the cover, I again hear the strains of "Manola" and glide blissfully around the chairs at Dodworth's Dancing School. Ah, how the memory of a gentleman outlasts all else!

XVII

NUMBER ONE FIFTH AVENUE, A SCHOOL THAT WAS

"Live, old life! Play the part that looks back on the actor or actors!" WHITMAN.

ONE must have led a meagre life to say in the evening of it that "schooldays were the happiest"! Not that in this crowded period of the world I owe any particular grudge to that necessary institution called school. I am quite sure that it made my spirit more flexible by the constant bending process, even though it failed in any way to break or even angle it. To see, to hear, to ask questions, to be nourished and led forth by the answers, whether spoken or absorbed from the silent printed page—that is education. The personality of the teacher was everything. A human being lacking it, or a badly printed or soiled book were equally valueless to me, as well as the rigidly standardized thing of the seventies called school—save as the means of finding personality in the teachers as individuals. Else it was nothing more than a shackle, a chain of many stout links to be broken one by one, a path so narrow and cramped and stuck with thorns for thorns' sake that walking it grazed the elbows when it did not bruise the heels.

Doubtless I am putting the cart before the horse or framing a picture before it has been painted, but as I think of my schooldays—all of which were enclosed in the substantial and orthodox brown-stone house known far and wide as Number One Fifth Avenue—the constant though then unconscious struggle against moral and spiritual narrowness pushes to the fore, and for the moment casts a veil over the earnest and sometimes really inspiring and splendid group of men and women whose teachings made the struggle worth while and finally led back into the sunlit open of real living where I was born.

Until the winter after Edmund's arrival sister Bea had continued to give me regular lessons, which as ever were supplemented by Father's eternal patience in answering questions and practically illustrating the answers as far as possible. But at this time there was very little material in New York available for demonstration of either natural science, or art, aside from a few private collections, while at best the art idea in America was bound fast in the tightest of bellybands, and Father was considered by some to be in a precarious state of laxity and almost an unfit guardian for youth because he took me when I was somewhere near ten years old to a rather private exhibition of Powers' Greek Slave! The outstanding memory of this day, that grew with my years until it became intelligible, was a discussion between the sculptors, Launt Thompson and William Story as to the treatment of the human figure via the Venus di Medici, Venus di Milo and the Greek Slave, and how in the latter mere sleek prettiness had taken the place of the underlying vigor of the classic sculptors. Never a thought or a word of nakedness was there, until I heard the statue condemned in whispers by some women who seemed quite frightened to be there and who stood in a corner by themselves.

As for natural science, the germ of the American Museum of Natural History was lying dormant in a few rooms of a building, the old State Arsenal, toward the east side of Central Park near the only zoo that New York possessed, while all that existed of the Metropolitan Museum of Art was housed in the high-stooped brown stone Cruger house in West Fourteenth Street, later a part of the Salvation Army Headquarters.

The time had come at last! To school I must go, for regular discipline and the companionship of youth, and Number One Fifth Avenue was the place selected. Not but what there were several other schools equally good, but sets of people foregathered closely, travelled clannishly in community groups then, theological, medical and social, and the girls, not only of the family and its associates, but all my friends along Banks, Perry and Eleventh streets were headed toward Number One. Considering the breadth of Father's viewpoint I now wonder at his choice, but it was doubtless his keen yet always kindly sense of humor that made him overlook a narrowness that to him could only seem superficial and of small account compared with the good to be gained from the really brilliant instructors that at this time gravitated about Number One. This institution, founded in the early eighteen-twenties, was more recently kept by the Misses Green—Lucy and Mary, sisters of Andrew H., who was something of a figure in local civics and politics. Miss Mary finally withdrew by means of marrying the drawing teacher, Mr. Knudsen, and when I began my schooling Miss Lucy was also preparing to retire in favor of the Misses Frances and Margaret Graham, but for some years she remained a power behind the scenes, much to my distress, for she never seemed to travel about in the broad light of day, but appeared from shadowy corners and doorways at inopportune times. Not that the appearing would have been amiss if her point of view had ever been free from suspicion, but her principle was, in a matter of evidence, to consider a girl always in the wrong until she was proved to be right, while in my upbringing the very reverse process had been my portion. Praise and blame had both been open and aboveboard, hence pussy-footing for evidence was something quite new to me. I bitterly resented it as I always have any form of injustice, hence school black ball number one was cast while I was still a "primary," cast but temporarily forgotten under the charming influence of Miss Frances Graham.

For two or three years the same joy that surrounded the first dancing-school period possessed me. I found girls in plenty for the companionship that a solitary youngster passing over the bridge from childhood to the teens craves. Lessons not too important or too difficult; healthy competition for the head of the class, neatly written essays upon rather abstract subjects easily transcribed from Appleton's *American Encyclopedia;* texts from the Bible recited one or two a day and grouped at the month's end, made up the slight mental strain. Deportmental requirements were satisfied with curling up the fingers and grinning to show clean nails and teeth before Bible class in the morning, refraining from whispering as far as in us lay, and week by week each in turn carefully sweeping up the crumbs after lunch time. During this period we sat in a hollow square of benches and munched away until our baskets were empty and then, at the call from Miss Isabelle Priest, head of the primary department—"Now go and play, little girls, go and play. Be quiet, little girls, in going through the hall. Be quiet, little girls!"—we marched to this hypnotic formula down to the playroom where stood the great piano used at exhibition time, leaving behind the crumb sweeper of the day to finish her job as quickly as possible and follow in company with Miss Priest.

For this crumb sweeping by a pupil I have never yet been able to discover a plausible motive. A lesson in housekeeping, humility, economy in school service—what? From the dustpan the crumbs were deposited in the great scuttle that stood monumentally beside the enormous hard-coal stove which was expected to heat the room with some slight assistance from a hot-air furnace in the cellar. When the afternoon supply of coal went into the stove the lunch remnants either smoked, sizzled or were sautéd according to their kind, permeating the air with a crude kind of incense that caused a window or two to be dropped, thus driving the odor into one's petticoats and whirling an icy draft about our dangling legs. As there was no place for hand-washing, the fingers of the sweeper remained soiled for the rest of the session. In fact I never remember to have washed my hands in school hours during the seven years of my stay! It simply could not be done. Yet the crumb-sweeping requirements continued all the way from the white-aproned and ribbon-tied, pigtailed girls of the primary to the graduating seniors, to whom it was no easy task, considering the wasp-waist aspirations of those who were developing "figures," to stoop and scoop up crumbs from a bare floor with a brief switch broom and dustpan. All this may seem unimportant, but it is an unforgettable detail, and a side light upon the forms of discipline of the day in a New York school for girls.

One other strictly physical impression made upon me during these first years of school was the extreme discomfort of the chairs upon which we had to sit. Nature has provided the sitting hinge of even a child with a comfortable curve, but Number One Fifth Avenue ruled otherwise, and the stiff, narrow-seated, high-backed chairs were so constructed that to more than perch on the edge, one must be hinged at an acute angle like a sharply folded paper doll. To seek spinal support would be to fall to the floor on one's face. It really did not matter in the end, I suppose—yet unanswered queries are always annoying and I still wonder why, oh why, to the chair as well as the crumb question. Was it because a certain type of Puritanism held that physical discomfort should form a part of the mental discipline yclept education? In my whole school life I never knew what it was to be relaxingly warm at any time during winter. We all either wore sleeveless knitted jackets, the tight uncomfortable garment from which in due course the sweater evoluted, or we kept small plaid shawls squeezed in among the books in our desks and it was no unusual thing to pad one's chest with an extra supply of handkerchiefs to supplement those the pockets might hold. A snuffle cold in schooldays seemed a must-be of winter. Now who has them? No one that I know. Herein is today greatly better than the-years-before-yesterday—no heavy woolen or cotton flannel underthings, air-tight coal stoves or snuffle colds!

At fourteen I arrived at the senior department, which was fortunately provided with fairly comfortable seats, and the portals of responsibility closed behind me. Each morning at quarter of nine I was left at the door of Number One, either by Father or some other member of the family, for it was not until a year or so later that I was allowed to walk alone from West Eleventh Street or even form one of the group who were gathered from houses along the way.

This morning walk itself was more varied than would seem possible from the short distance, and often for three months each winter there were days when the snow-blocked streets made going at all a problem. We had deep and lasting snows these days and no attempt at public snow removal. Householders made paths along their frontage in a haphazard sort of way and were supposed to keep their street gutters open. But if snow fell in the night the early morning pedestrians had to tread their own paths in the cross streets, while on Fifth Avenue the snow was banked like a fort in the middle of the way, each storm adding to its height, so that at times only the ears of the horses that drew the sleighs and omnibuses on runners were visible. While there was an attempt to cut a roadway through this barrier at the cross streets, in times of stress and lack of workmen it was only completed at every two or three blocks, forcing one to calculate before starting how to reach the destination without too much retracing, thus giving a foretaste of the one-way traffic regulations of today. The lucky children who had butlers or coachmen were often drawn to school on sleds or else emerged from the buffalo robes of the deep, high-backed sleighs which would take the father of the family down to his office.

The senior department was graded in five courses of a year each, the various studies being grouped about the history selected, beginning logically with Greece, Rome, England, America; a universal summary following. Botany, geology, astronomy, physics, the standard mathematics, rhetoric and composition, literature, Latin and French, all followed in turn. German under Helene Hesse was an extra, also drawing and music, the last two accomplishments pertaining chiefly to "the young ladies of the family," the term by which the boarding pupils were always called.

French now became the required spoken language of the school and we were supposed to converse in it even during the hour for luncheon. When the roll was called each morning, prior to Bible class, we must answer either *français* or *anglais* according as we had spoken the previous day. This forced many of us either to lie, to keep an impossible silence, to answer *anglais*, or speak a jargon to which the confusion of Babel was nothing. We had excellent teachers of French, but the periods for conversation were all too brief and the subjects chosen too technical to give social fluency of speech, so we verbally hopped, skipped and jumped along, that is with the exception of a few who had either lived abroad or had French maids or governesses, and acted as anchors to keep the rest of us from hopelessly drifting out to sea.

One serious decision had to be made on entering the senior room, and this followed almost immediately after the newcomer had committed the Golden Text of the school to memory—1 Thessalonians, 4–9, 11 and 12. This concerned the type of handwriting to which one was to be moulded, angular or the round hand, trimmed, if one so wished, with many pigeon wings and flourishes. The upright block formation had not yet made its entry. The angular hand taught by Miss McLauran was esteemed the most feminine, but the round hand taught by Mr. Dolmage had many followers and in fact was preferred by West Eleventh Street, Clinton Place and a section of lower Fifth Avenue, and varied traces of its influence may be seen today in the third generation, so does handwriting cling to families. Mr. Dolmage had personality and discrimination in the copies that he wrote for us, stooping his great height as he did so. He was very tall, with a large head of heavy hair, but his shoulders stooped and he dropped away suddenly, his black swallow-tailed coat and trousers increasing the effect until he reminded me of nothing so much as the shadow of a jack-in-the-pulpit. Once when I asked him for a special copy giving the different forms of capital S, as it was Father's first initial, he wrote "Slander leaves a Slur behind it—Something Surely to be Shunned." Both the letters and the words hold fast, and I can see his long fingers forming the capitals with his round-tipped gold pen as plainly as when he wrote them. Ending with a much shaded flourish like a bird's tail, he wiped the pen on the tail of his coat and passed to the next desk.

The third curious and reasonless custom of the school was the daily morning ceremonial of Bringing in the Ink. The house was of the type known as English basement, the entrance door being only one or two steps above the street level. This floor, being used for the various offices, reception and living rooms, left the rest of the building free for school use, and the senior department occupied the main part of the second floor. Of the four large windows fronting on the Avenue, two belonged to the "Young Ladies' Parlor," which boasted of a carpet, and the other two were at the end of the long assembly room, which had many others on the side that overlooked the "Stable Alley" now known as Washington Mews—then a very interesting place but not strictly on educational lines. The desks faced Fifth Avenue, an aisle dividing them and stopping at the principal's throne, a desk between the windows, raised a step or two and commanding the length of the room.

At this time Miss Graham was in full command and precisely at nine she rang a small bell after which anyone entering the room was marked tardy. When all were seated a girl was detailed to bring in the ink, before roll call. For some occult reason this was considered an honor. One went to a store closet just off the Young Ladies' Parlor, where upon a shelf were ranged a series of long black wooden blocks each containing two small wells, one for black and the other for red ink. A groove in front of the wells held two pens in plain wooden handles. This crude stand must be carried very carefully in both hands and placed in the middle of the flat space atop the desk; as the bottles never fitted very well there was always the exciting, sporting chance that they might spill over. It would have been much simpler to have had the floor maid supply the desks with ink each morning when she opened the shutters and dusted out, but—?

At the beginning of my second week as a senior my turn came. I stood up rather of a tremble, for the eyes of all five assembled classes, for lack of other occupation, followed the ink carrier. The return trip was safely made, the stand carefully raised above the desk edge and I was still standing but about to take my place again when in clear, penetrating tones that seemed to cut through my head from ear to ear came the words:

"Miss O*r*sgood, what have you done?"

I looked quickly at my fingers and at the floor and then faltered, "Has the ink tipped over?"

"Miss O*r*sgood, you have set the ink stand upon the Word of God!"

I was struck dumb for a moment, not grasping the meaning, or I might have asked why the Bible was where the ink belonged. I was conscious of the shocked silence that surrounded me; I closed my eyes for a second to see, it seemed, the figure of an irate deity with horns of light-rays such as those that Moses on the Mount is depicted as shooting from his head, while into a giant struggling mouth I was cramming the inkwell! I opened my eyes, the scene and silence were the same—then Love o' Laughter, the most useful of all my fairy godmothers, put an arm about me and suddenly I laughed so heartily that I hid my face in my handkerchief and slipped out of the room as quickly as I could, but not too soon to hear Miss Graham say, "Miss Raymond, will you follow Miss O*r*sgood to the dressing room? This painful happening, I fear, has brought on hysterics." When Aimée Raymond, one of the loveliest souls I ever met—eighteen and a privileged "parlor boarder"—joined me (also she had actually written a story that had been published in *Harper's Weekly*, of which Mr. Conant was the editor, for which she was paid twenty-five dollars! What more could one ask of an idol?) I had laughed until I really cried, and presently, usually self-controlled as she was, she had laughed herself into the same condition, having only voice enough left to suggest that I would better go home for the rest of the day and she would go with me. Right glad I was to have Aimée corroborate my story, Father seemed to find it so nearly unbelievable. Mid-Victorian era do you say? Don't blame the beloved old Queen for it. This was superstitious, free America, New York in the middle eighteen-seventies, and even then the Puritan ice was melting in its New England fastness and retreating before the warm sweeping transcendental wave.

From that day on Aimée was my dear friend and ally, a great honor for a first-year girl and of no little importance as an educational factor. Straightway I began to "love my book" and fall in step with the many lecturers and teachers.

Lyman Abbott opened the door to history. Literature both English and American became a reality through the sturdy personality and beautiful enunciation of Clarence Cook, the littérateur and art critic, who once ably backed Feuardent in his renowned contention with Di Cesnola about the Cipriote antiquities. Dr. St. John opened the self-printed story of the earth in his courses of geology and natural philosophy, and flower meanings were interpreted by gentle Harriet Marshall and Hannah Smith, who sometimes in summer came to Mosswood and went afield with me. We forget a great deal of schooling and are obliged to unlearn much more as years go by, but the personal sources of inspiration and first knowledge remain as clear well springs, and lovely Aimée Raymond was the mediator.

For all this, two Puritan ghosts that I called the Regicides still intermittently snooped about the halls at Number One and kept one on the watch. (I was a staunch Royalist and preferred the Stuarts, in spite of all the Nell Gwyn ladies, to the Cromwellians, and the Regicide Cave in Connecticut, yet supposed to be haunted by their ghosts who walk at uncanny hours, bred this conceit, which if you had known the shadowy doorways that opened on a certain hallway you would have understood.)

Schoolgirls in order to be healthy minded must have a certain amount of romance rationed in their daily lives, just as they must have the other bodily foods that growing youth requires, and blessed are the parents and teachers who recognize this fact. The girls at Number One were very clean minded—I realize that I never heard a smutty word from any one of them. We spun several stories from our imagination about the various spinster teachers, where their personality made it at all possible. This one had lost her love in the Civil War, that one had heroically renounced matrimony to care for an old mother, while another who was pretty but like a faded rose, and always wore a look of expectancy, we decided was waiting for a long delayed letter the writer of which had been shipwrecked on a desert island. Once even we imagined romance between the middle-aged secretary of the school and a young physician who taught universal history, the only basis being that she often asked him to hand her books and other supplies from the shelves in the store-room adjoining the "Young Ladies" Parlor in which latter room his classes were held. I was deputed to enshrine this very brief affair in verse, thus:

Dr. Dillow stood on a stool,
Miss Dean gazed at him hard.
Alack, that's all there is to say,
For I'm but a budding bard!

It was by way of the theatre, or the drama, as Father preferred to call it, that my longing for color, romance, and the beautiful things in life was first satisfied and unconsciously trained. Both Mother and Father had the keen insight that told them of the proper use and value of this form of education. To see some type of pantomime or occasionally a good play had been one of my favorite "Rewards and Fairies" onward from my tenth year, when Edwin Booth owned his theatre at Sixth Avenue and Twenty-third Street and lived in a suite of rooms in the same building, where the family were always welcome. From then on we had sittings wherever and whenever he played. Thus during my years of school I saw him many times as Hamlet, as Richard the Third in the romantic and unusual double bill of *Richard II*, a personation little known, but he claimed it as his favorite rôle; as Ruy Blas, as Julius Cæsar, with Lawrence Barrett as Antony; as Cardinal Richelieu with Barrett as De Maupas, and as Shylock. Blending with them came Jefferson as Rip van Winkle and Bob Acres; Lotta Crabtree as Little Nell and the Marchioness, a double rôle; *The School for Scandal*, with Charles Fisher as Sir Peter and Fanny Davenport as Lady Teazle; *Oliver Twist* with Miss Davenport as Nancy, her brother as Bill Sykes, and Bijou Heron as Oliver. *The Lady of Lyons* at the Fifth Avenue Theatre with Mary Anderson in the title rôle and Plympton as Melnotte, filled out my schooldays, together with a goodly share of opera, both serious and *bouffe*. But strange to say, submerged as my parents were in the Civil War and unquestioned workers by word and deed for the abolition of slavery, I was never taken to see *Uncle Tom's Cabin*. Nor by some strange chance have I ever seen it played. In speaking of this book and play in later years, I remember to have heard my Father say, "The stressful needs of war justify the use of much propaganda which to continue makes for bitterness and hatred."

It was midway in the senior course that the theatre accidentally raised a curtain in full view of my Regicide-in-chief at Number One Fifth Avenue, and the happening came in this way. Two plays had long held the attention of Better New York—*The Shaughrau*, at Wallack's, in which Dion Boucicault took the part of Con, and Harry Montague as Captain Molyneux, the fascinating, played up to Ada Dyas. The other was a splendid production of *Henry V* with George Rignold as the King. Female interest ran high, for both these English actors seemed created for their parts and which was the most attractive type was a matter of opinion. At school we were divided into two bands, a sort of tug-of-war of admiration, carried on verbally at recess in our hybrid French. Slowly we began to accumulate Sarony photographs—the Montague clique, having more pocket money, had a better collection until one day most unexpectedly the Aunties, who, being quite old, had come from Boston to live with us, gave me enough shining half dollars to buy three new Rignold photographs, which threw the balance to our side, for mine were large cabinet pictures. These were the Prayer before the Battle of Agincourt—Henry returning to London through Temple Bar, and the Courting Scene of Henry and Catherine of France. At recess I was triumphantly showing my prize and had set the photographs side by side on the ledge of a window in the long hall outside the dressing room. I made no attempt to conceal them, for I knew no reason for so doing, and when a draft of air came down the hall and ceased quite beside me, and looking up I saw that it was my Regicide-in-chief, I was in no wise embarrassed, though I noticed that one of the Montague girls had slipped her pictures into the book she was holding.

"What pictures have we here?" asked the low, cool, smooth voice.

"Photographs of King Henry V and the Battle of Agincourt," I replied, being quite glad that they were historical and not of Humpty Dumpty Fox, or a Christmas pantomime.

"But, my child, Agincourt was in 1415, quite before the invention of photography or even printing; they are copies of paintings, I presume, and as such most interesting."

"Oh, no, Miss Green," I hastened to assure her, "they are from the Shakespeare drama at Booth's Theatre. George Rignold plays King Henry and he is wonderful. It is such a good likeness, too."

"You have been to a playhouse? You have seen this actor? Who took you to such a place, may I enquire?"

"Oh! Yes, and I have been twice, though we had to buy the tickets. Father took me, and he loves the Battle Prayer picture, he picked it out for me himself." With pursed-up lips the Regicide-in-chief moved swiftly away, evidently to spread the baleful news.

Next day I was beckoned very mysteriously into a corner by two model girls of the graduating class, Isabella Banks and Lily Paxton, whose father was then pastor of what in my youth I had called the "Wicked Church." Solemnly they asked me if, for their sakes and the good of my own future, I would read a little story and think it over when I went home, at the same time handing me a tract called, as I remember it, *The Evil of the Theatre*. I said that

I would not! They shook their heads and seemed truly grieved. I'm wondering what they think of their attitude today? Or if it has vanished from much broadened minds as the School That Was has passed from Number One Fifth Avenue, now the street of the Washington Arch.

The inconsistent and socially impolite part of this whole matter was that Mary and Gertrude Barrett, daughters of Lawrence, the most scholarly of the many players I have known, were at this time pupils at Number One, Mary being one of the most brilliant girls there. When I told them very frankly about the rebuke that I had received, Mary only laughed and said, "Poor woman, she has sat on a narrow shelf of prejudice, and never lived, so she doesn't really know, how could she?" Then came the grand finale, which might not have happened but for school—I was invited to luncheon by the Barretts the next Saturday, at the New York Hotel where they lived and where also Henry V was stopping. What if I should meet him? *Would* Mother and Father let me go? They did!

In going in the elevator from the Barretts' rooms down to the dining hall, a stop was made to admit a tallish broad-shouldered man with auburn hair and a rather rough skin, I think slightly pock-marked. Mary nudged me at the same time that Mr. Barrett, shaking hands with him, said, "Ah, Rignold! just in time, we have an ardent admirer of Henry V here who would like to meet him." Turning toward me with a pleasant smile he said, "I'm sorry to disappoint you, young lady, but King Henry never leaves the theatre. I am only his understudy, who is sure to disappoint you!"

The disillusion was complete, and yet with it came the understanding of the entire separation of the player from the man, that has stabilized and made life safer for one much stirred by dramatic art as well as beauty in every form.

Next week when Miss Graham asked me some questions about the episode of the photographs, I told her the story in every detail. For she was human and warm-hearted in spite of the iron framework underlying much that she must do and we well knew, by the rosebud flush that would come to her cheek and a sympathetic twinkle in the eye, when some harmless escapade called for reproof, that away from school ethics she would have laughed with us instead of chiding. In fact in spinning our romances we had given her the very noblest of our dream lovers. Hers was a captain of cavalry with a sweeping mustache, curly hair and wonderful blue eyes. His horse was coal-black and named Thor, and when he rode up to her father's door to say goodbye on going to the war she threw her arms about his neck, kissed him and clung to him—but he never returned! So we thought of this and excused her in our hearts when she was severe. Even now I like to make believe that in the beyond where there is no war the dream captain came back and that he again kissed her, as a reward for being crucified by having to teach school on the ancient one-pattern plan demanded in the middle century. After she had heard me out this day she sat quite still, the rose tint coming to her cheeks. Then drawing me to her she gave me an almost unheard-of kiss, saying simply, "Mere books cannot teach us life. My child, your father is a very good, wise man."

XVIII

MUSIC AND THE FAIRY PRINCE

MUSIC lessons were a part of the must-be education of every young girl once upon a time, irrespective of any talent she might possess, or inclination to be so trained. Also there was no distinction made between the instruction that gives the ability to appreciate music and the merely forced technical training that produced such an appalling regiment of piano pounders and thin-voiced, bleating singers nominally intended to produce "music in the home" and therefore add to its attraction. (Distraction would often have been the fitter word, and those who have had to bear with this should thank God for the victrola.)

In Grandmother's Murdock's day—the eighteen-twenties and thirties—her harpsichord and guitar, or lute, as I find it should be called, for I have it still and it is esteemed a "collector's piece," sufficed for the really good, straightforward arrangements from Handel, Mozart, and the rest, and as an unpretentious accompaniment to her singing. A childish amusement, allowed me when kept indoors by some little ailment, was to look over Grandmother's music books and make-believe play the airs on the guitar. The first printing of "The Star Spangled Banner" was in one of these much worn books, the coarse paper, brown and crumbling, and the text much blurred by the offset caused by time and dampness. But like all of America's patriotic songs the words alone belong to us, for on the title page was "Set to the music of the Ode to Anacreon in Heaven," an English glee.

Mother and Aunt Cinder revelled in ballads, both British and our very own, for these books of bound sheet music, many with ornamental lithographed covers, were sprinkled with the songs of Stephen Foster and Dempster, and no one ever sang "The Old Folks at Home," "Old Black Joe" and "My Old Kentucky Home" more truly than Mother, when Father was resting and the room was dark except for the firelight, and the closed shutters quite kept out the noise of the jingling bells of the Sixth Avenue street cars. This was the real home music, effortless and sincere. "We Are Coming, Sister Mary," was another favorite. The old books of bound music refresh my memory, telling that the darky melodies written by Stephen Foster were collected in a series called "Christy Melodies as used in his American Opera House, New York, 1853," and many years later they were still in everyday use. Among them are "Massa's in the Cold, Cold Ground," "Jim Crack Corn," "Virginia Rosebud," "Way Down South," "Uncle Ned," "Oh, Susanah!", "Carry Me Back to Old Virginnie," "Rosa Lee," and "Darkey's History." These darky melodies were a great relief from the serious and conventionally pathetic songs that made the backbone of the polite parlor repertoire in Mother's early days in Providence where for a time she taught music and singing, going up to Boston for lessons from Dempster at the same time. He taught her the music that he had written to Burns' "Mary in Heaven," Mary Howitt's "The Dying Child," Tennyson's "May Queen," "I Canna Lo'e Him Less," "The Ocean Burial," etc. How refreshing the swing of even the saddest of the darky melodies must have been. One duet Mother and Aunt Cinder sang together that was halfway between classic melancholy and melancholy romance—"What Are the Wild Waves Saying," by Stephen Glover, a duet supposedly sung by Paul and Florence Dombey. "Old Dog Tray" always caught me in the throat, while "The Knight Looked Down From the Paynim's Tower" moved me to raise a regiment and go to his rescue. A rather dilute sort of sentimental ditty presently worked its way in—"Willie, We Have Missed You," being typical of this period vocally followed by "Poor Carlotta," Maximilian of Mexico's unfortunate wife, and led the way in the sixties for "The Maiden's Prayer" and "Monastery Bells" for the piano and an elaborate variation from *Martha*, featuring prominently "The Last Rose of Summer," these being among Gatha's show pieces. Amateur music in general had not then become the serious brain-racking classitude that the Wagnerian epoch of the last twenty years of the century required of it; it was a recourse, an amusement, not a career. Then (I am guided by memory aided by Gatha's music books) there must have been a sort of musical explosion following soon after the coming of *The Black Crook* and Lydia Thompson's Blondes, for into Music in the Home bounded "Champagne Charlie" in a red and gold mantle, "Shoo Fly," "Paddle Your Own Canoe," "Paddy Duffy's Cart," the "Mabel Waltz," "Jolly Brothers Galop," "Croquet," "Five O'Clock in the Morning," the latter introduced by Parepa Rosa at Steinway Hall. Songs from the Grand Opera House over at Twenty-third Street and Eighth Avenue, where the George Havens often took Gatha but from which I seemed to be excluded, introduced La Belle Hélène, the Grand Duchess of Gerolstein, La Perichole, Madam Favart, etc.

J. R. Thomas, who was the basso at Father's church at the time of Bea's marriage and before, had composed the music of two ballads that were heard everywhere—"Rocked in the Cradle of the Deep," and

"Happy be thy Dreams." Even today they have not been suppressed, by Time, the Wagnerites or by jazz. I was not yet ten when, crouched in the organ loft, where, if I was very good, I was allowed to sit during service on a small bench, I heard Thomas sing the first of these songs as an ending to the vesper service, the *vox humana*, then a rather new stop in the great organ, carrying on the air after he had ended. I can see the whole scene as plainly as if it were yesterday. Edward Howe, the organist; soft blond beard and hair touching his shoulders, neither combed back nor yet untidy, with the type of face that is so often given by the painters to Christ; a loose collar, his tie undone and his long thin fingers clinging to the keys as if he could not bear to be parted from them. On and on he played until the church was quite empty and the lights were lowered one by one, the volume of sound growing less and less until only the *vox humana* was left. That too faded away when suddenly great chords swept like a final roar of the ocean—then silence. Father had come up the stairs to the organ loft in search of me. Not seeing me at once in my corner, he laid his hand gently upon the shoulder of the organist, who was sitting quite still, his head bowed upon his hands. "Over-fatigued, Howe?" he asked.

"No, praying!" was the reply. "The organ speaks the words for me, and God hears!"

When I crept out of my corner I was crying happily—one can, you know, without knowing the reason. Always have I thanked Edward Howe for the birth of the sustaining love of organ music, for sitting in that choir loft and in others later, it grew until it enveloped me and protected my emotions. I never hear "The Lost Chord" of Sullivan's inspiration sung with organ accompaniment but what its setting seems that scene of childhood in the Church of the Messiah.

Ah me! The sequel was not so pleasant—music lessons with Mr. Howe for the master. It was sad that he should have to teach stupid children, but there were several little Howes to be fed. It was, I think, the only mistake in judgment that Mother and Father ever made concerning me, this enforced learning of the piano. I wanted to write, to draw, to paint with a very wet brush and plenty of color so that it would splash! To try to catch, prison and express some of the feeling and beauty of the out-of-doors that I loved so that it was a pain to be parted from it. I did so long to create beauty of form or word, yet I could not voice it then. To begin with, the practice time required was too long: two hours each day with only scales and five-finger exercises. Bea having gone, Gatha was the practice mistress; she had a dreadful metronome that tick-tocked to whatever speed you were expected to keep and paced you heartlessly as a machine must. Oh the agony of the lessons that first spring, when April left soft May green in the front yards! I did my first hour in the morning; the second had to come after school.

Twelve years had struck on my time clock. I did not care so much for marbles and tops, but some girls from school walked up and down for exercise, opposite our house, that first hour after school and talked and talked—when I must count one—two—three—four! I could see them and the front garden sidewise from the piano stool, and the dandelions were beginning to close as the house shadow fell on the grass plot. A belated woman still cried "Strawberries!" and the plant wagons were coming up from the supply market on the river front loaded with the morrow's wares, and for almost the first time pans of Dutch bulbs and forced Madonna lilies were displayed with a lure not to be denied. I opened the long French window a crack to get the scent of them; I lingered a bit, but tick-tock went the metronome which had no nose, no eyes! How *could* Gatha stand over me so that I couldn't even let the scale of C go softly and drag in places and make believe that it was a tune? How could she? How could she? But she could and did! Oh, why didn't a Fairy Prince come and rescue me? In those days all the rescuers of misunderstood youth were of a fairy origin, I had not as yet even sensed real male humanity in relation to a future.

Yet at this very time love, life, liberty, color and music were on their way to me, sailing overseas from England in the *City of Montreal* in the shape of a very homesick, seasick, misunderstood lad of eighteen, with a Glengarry bonnet set crosswise on his head, a soft bit of a mustache across his lip and changeable sea-gray blue eyes. He dreamed as little about me as I did of him, or, had he seen me, would have quickly passed a lean, brown girl not yet in her teens. At this time his was the advantage, he could get away from what he did not wish to do; I could not. But my fairy godmothers were watching us and weaving the thread. For unless one has these fairies for godparents one cannot see a Fairy Prince through a rough tweed suit, walking about the street like other men with no golden luck penny in his pocket, doing everyday things. But with them on your side to guide your sight you may see him through overalls or khaki.

Mr. Howe left New York presently and a new teacher tried me out, who hailed from Maine; with him I struggled along for a few winters. I never have cared for the piano as an instrument at any time—under his touch it became an agony. He smelt of mice in an attic. He was very fidgety and held a pencil in his left hand which he constantly rubbed up and down with his thumbnail making a disagreeable squeaking noise, as an accompaniment to a nervous sniff. "Repetition,

repetition," was his constant cry. He would say that I had done my lesson very well and in a few moments when Mother came in tell her that what I needed was "interest and repetition," that my fingers worked but not my mind; in fact he quite doubted that I had any music in my makeup.

Presently, there came a dispensation that proved to them that I truly loved music, in part as I loved dancing —as a rhythmic emotion but not as a vocation. The Edmund Millers being much abroad, the opera box at the Academy of Music that belonged to Brother George's father was exchanged for orchestra seats, two of which fell to our part of the family. Straightway heaven opened, for in those days if a young girl folded her legs under her carefully the ushers pretended not to see her and she was allowed to sit in the aisle close beside the orchestra chair of a parent if there was not a chair for her. Thus the dominie's daughter came to be a participant in one of the great opera eras of New York, that of the eighteen-seventies, and though I have followed both Opera House moves and singers ever since, I think the combination that passed across the stage during those years has never been excelled—Christine Nilsson, Ilma di Murska, Lucca, Cary, Italo Campanini, Del Puente, Gallassi, Nanneti, Victor Capoul et al. *Faust* was the first presentation that I heard, the Faust legend having been read to me by Father via Charles Brooks' translation. Each time I heard the opera through the years that led to womanhood it had a new meaning—for in childhood, through Father's interpretation, it was a sort of fairy legend, all unpleasant complications passing unnoticed. Thus should all classic literature be treated rather than made a mystery and shut away from youth, the meaning deepening with the years.

Nilsson has always remained the typical Marguerite

to me as Del Puente has the Mephisto. Campanini had the unromantic figure of Caruso, but he took his breath better, never bawled his high notes, and seemed less conscious. Jean De Reszke as Faust had the ideal personality. The most consistently romantic of all the operas was *Mignon*—for as the student Wilhelm Meister, Capoul was beyond compare, and Nilsson, as ever, born for the simple peasant characters, with fire in reserve but never forced.

Then in the middle seventies in the spring I saw my first Wagner opera—*Lohengrin*, with Nilsson as Elsa, and Campanini as the Knight of the Grail; Ortrud I cannot recall, for I gave our stock of librettos and play-bills to Evert Wendell, who craved them, when we left the Rhinelander Gardens. But through those blissful years came Patti, Minnie Hauck, an early Carmen but one who never equalled Calvé. By way of all this I learned what music meant and stirred in me. The organ or a rich bass voice ever made the highest appeal. Violin, according to the theme and tempo, touched either my heart or my toes, as gypsy music must.

Then too Steinway Hall lured with concerts. Ole Bull, Wieniawski of the violin, and Theodore Thomas, who led the Philharmonic there before Damrosch was a name, and who also had a wonderful summer garden near Central Park with a cascade falling over rock work—a novelty in the seventies, where smoking was allowed and tall glasses of lemonade might be bought that had floating strawberries or cherries atop and straws to drink through to prevent the ice from tickling one's nose.

Gatha took singing lessons of Paolo Georza, a one-time organist of the Jesuit Church of St. Francis Xavier in West Sixteenth Street, and, as he utilized his class to swell the church chorus at festivals, by tagging on I heard much of my beloved organ music. Then there was always Trinity with the best choir master that could be coaxed from England. At this time Gatha's music took an operatic turn and her serious songs were in Italian, some of which were written by Georza, as "Mia Stella," "Repeat That You Love Me," and one, "Were I an Angel" that Brignoli the fascinating dedicated to Minnie Parker, whom Faganni painted as one of the Nine Muses that, as art improved and outdistanced social favoritism, became an embarrassment to the Metropolitan Museum to which they were given.

There is usually something truly funny about amateur efforts at either opera or theatricals when the performers take them too seriously. As I write there comes before me the performance of a cut-down version of the opera of *Romeo and Juliet* given under Georza by his pupils at the Union League Club Theatre in their building that was once at Madison Avenue and Twenty-sixth Street. Then it seemed a wonderful event, and Gatha stood several inches taller in my sight because she was to be a lady of the chorus, kin of either or both the Capulets or Montagues. Imagine it, wearing a much frilled party gown at least six yards wide and hair in a waterfall! Fannie Powell, who was Juliet, also wore evening dress, and Antonia Henne, a contralto and therefore cast for Romeo, wore high riding boots with spurs, the rest of the costume, wig and all, belonging decidedly to the time of Charles II; while the tomb shook ominously and was a very tight fit. Yet how the whole family thrilled!

Yes, for ten years until the eighties, when part of our world ended, we revelled in music, largely through the kindness of friends but sometimes paid for by the result of much economy and scrimping. One optimistic prediction of Father's was that the next generation would be able to hear nationalized opera or the drama plus an orchestra seat for one dollar, the only price possible per capita for a middle-pursed family's pleasures. It has not yet happened and we can, in this instance, truly say, "Those were the good old days," when two dollars bought a fair opera seat and five dollars was thought sheer robbery for an orchestra chair for one of Patti's numerous "Farewell" performances.

With this foundation to work upon, in the late seventies came my third teacher, George William Warren, the organist and choir master of St. Thomas's Church, who by understanding rescued me emotionally in things musical. For though his manner was that of a gay gypsy violin, the spirit beneath had unexpected organ depths and harmonies, known alike to his pupils and the choristers, gathered near and far, whom his slender purse supplied with luncheon each day of double service, that they might not go hungry and thus have the double strain of body and mind so hard to bear by the temperamental.

Organ music and wallflowers! When did I first learn of the combination? I think of them and Old Trinity as one, why? I did not know then, but my birth fairies, Love o' Music, Love o' Nature, and Love o' Home knew. They saw the once homesick, seasick lad, now in full manhood, clad in formal Sunday gear, a wallflower at his coat lapel, his top hat on his knees, sitting behind a pillar of the church; his heart swelling as the organ music surged, and his eyes, that devoured the young choristers as they came out two by two, blinking lest they overflow—shaken by the memory of that last day when he, as a chorister in a great shadowy English cathedral, was singing the soprano solo, "Oh, for the Wings, the Wings of a Dove," with his voice soaring high, thrilling with fervid emotion, when upon his throat had come the sudden grasp of impatient adolescence that had broken voice and spirit together. Ah! but the wallflowers at least were true, unchangeable, and their fragrance unforgettable to the English born, be they where they may. Then the three Fairies, beckoning to the fourth, Love o' Laughter, who had stood aside but was now needed in the fabric's perfect planning, began to snip loose ends and work in earnest on the fateful life garment, adding color and perfume as they wrought.

XIX

THE OWL AND THE EAGLE
CHARLOTTE TEMPLE AND OLD TRINITY

ANCESTORS and old furniture had been a spasmodic topic of discussion ever since the days of the Cookie Jar Sewing Society, the greatest rivalry being between families of English and Dutch descent. Really you could hardly expect the latter to be pleased that New Amsterdam should be so completely submerged in New York, especially from the literary viewpoint. On both sides those families who had an ample store of furniture, plate and good family portraits never put them aside, but those who had but little treasure, younger sons and the newly married side branches of these families, also women who sought smartness in the new, from the eighteen-forties well up into the eighties, when setting up housekeeping, discarded or packed away in the great attics the dignified old maple and mahogany of so-called Colonial design, together with pewter plates, flagons, and much solid brass in the form of candlesticks, andirons, etc. To replace all this the furniture of The Age of Horror was evolved. Oh, yes! I know, for at least fifteen of my discriminating years were spent in this atmosphere, to which I contributed my share of painted plaques, vases of appliquéd design and "crazy" patchwork table covers. There were mantel and pier mirrors heavily framed in black walnut and gilt, presiding over emerald-green curtains looped up with gold cord over dizzily figured Nottingham petticoats. The same brightly polished black walnut everywhere, centre tables for the parlor with white or gray marble tops and acutely bowed legs. Haircloth sofas with walnut frames, awful bureaus with funny little drawers atop their marble slabs. Beds with high backs like double tombstones, étagères with curlicue-supported shelves placed at random to hold dust and inane ornaments, while as for color combinations!—sister Bea's parlor suit, given by her mother-in-law when she went to housekeeping in 1870 and quite expensive (the draperies by Marcotte), had a black walnut framework with gold lines and was upholstered in bright scarlet silk reps banded with black and gold; the red damask curtains striped with black were lined with yellow.

Logically, after the Centennial celebration in Philadelphia in 1876, when all sections of the country had their first real chance to go a-visiting, to see, be seen, and know both the work of their hands and the fruit of their lands, the first general groping about for origins began, both in life and in furnishings. Roots, feelers, anchorage in the new soil became desirable—the deeper the better—as well as a knowledge of the trees from which the thrifty cuttings and grafts came. Of course there were and always will be some undeveloped minds that will continue to take pleasure in trying to twist the Lion's tail rather than in educating themselves in a way that shall veil to alien minds some of the unpleasant (even though ornithologically correct) attributes of the national emblem, the American Eagle, in obtaining its food, etc.! Stimulated by the new interest, collectors began to go about the country rummaging attics, and by the time the eighties were on their feet, the Age of Horror was beginning to pack up its wall plaques, plush albums, etc., and start its Westward Ho!

It was not that New York was ignorant of either history or art, people had long since made the grand tour and brought back decently executed copies of old masters though usually of impossible size, but it took a long while to apply the knowledge to general home products. What was called the Hudson River School of pretty landscapes had broadened and deepened, and the time was ripe for Winslow Homer, Kensett, Smillie, and Whittredge.

The New York Historical Society over at Eleventh Street and Second Avenue was one of the few places where history and art both received impetus, and it held an important niche in the bygone days when a good lecture was classed as an amusement. The first Tuesday in the month was always the public meeting and lecture night, and I can remember first begging to go with Father when I was hardly in my teens, not so much for the knowledge to be obtained as the chance to go somewhere and sit up until ten o'clock. Also after the meeting there was the "social hour" of primitive days, when we all went up to the picture floor, or downstairs where there was usually a small loan exhibition of either portraits or historical paintings in addition to those belonging to the Society, and a few curiosities, which numbered several Egyptian mummies visible and encased. Cups of good chocolate and sandwiches were then passed about, and people separated into little groups to chat while they stirred the chocolate until it cooled a bit. It sounds now very like a small-town affair, but among the people who foregathered there were always men of note. It was here that I met Edwin Arnold, at the time his *Light of Asia* was framing a new cult; General Custer, the Indian fighter, who was on his last furlough before his own rashness and Sitting Bull wiped him out; Bryant, Parke Godwin, William W. Story the sculptor and the Shillabers, whose guest he then was, also John Hay. There were the many Fields, Cyrus of Atlantic cable fame, Henry M., and Judge David Dudley, with Frederick Talmadge, his brother-in-law; also the dry, witty and unexpected Mr. John Hamersley, who wore a long cape of wide sweep and a small round cap for street gear and was both brilliant and eccentric. These, with Father, made one group, on the outskirts of which I would linger, making my chocolate and sandwiches last as long as possible. These "historical sandwiches" as we called them were crustless, very thin, well spread with butter, tongue and a dash of mustard, and of half-loaf size, whereas the sandwich one associates with the middle and later seventies was a heavy split roll, a jab of butter, a slice of ham or corned beef, hurry, a railway station and indigestion! Those "good old times" sandwiches and the little red schoolhouse have happily faded away together.

It was at one of these meetings that Mr. Hamersley invited Father to a "man's character party" which he was to give the following week. "Come as you are, Doctor," he said "your costume will be waiting and I assure you that the performance will be quite clever, in fact Olympian!" Father went and when he returned he brought with him a gilt lyre, a laurel wreath and a Roman toga of white linen bordered with purple. I never learned the details of what happened on Mount Olympus, but it must have been a very original affair judging by the way in which Mother and Father laughed together about it.

The formal business meetings that preceded the lectures were quite solemn and yet they had a funny side. The makeup of the hall was very like a church, with a row of chairs for the executive committee in front of the regular seats. A high-backed throne-like chair for the president was in the middle of the platform at the back, while the desks of recording and corresponding secretaries were toward the front on either side. One president alone fills my memory, Frederick De Peyster. Upon the theory that every man resembles some bird, I called him The Owl and never had the Great Horned Owl a better understudy in man, for he was well feathered by whiskers, two horns of hair were brought from the sides to conceal baldness, and his full eyelids drooped and blinked, closing his eyes in sections in a perfectly owlish manner. Andrew Warner, the recording secretary, was of the fine aquiline type of "the Signers," clean-shaven face save for a trace of side whiskers, and the merest tinge of rosy color in his cheeks. Keen-eyed though rather harsh of voice, he figured as the Eagle, and, save on rare occasions when the corresponding secretary (George H. Moore, I think) had some letters to read, the Owl and the Eagle had the preliminaries of the meeting out together.

Meanwhile the executive committee would squirm and wriggle down in their chairs, until the two excitements of the moment would be watching to see who would slide completely to the floor, and waiting the joyous possibility of someone's saying No, when a motion was put in a mumbling tone by the Owl, after an unusually long and unintelligible bit of reading by the Eagle. The *Ayes* always had it, though I lived in hopes until I was twenty odd, and the only real casualty from the front row was a few explosive snores quickly covered by ostentatious coughing by a neighbor.

These may seem trivial details but they were all a part of the panorama of New York life. Slow-moving? Yes, but for that very reason the more clearly to be remembered. Dull, those evenings? It never seemed so to me. Men who are interested in anything are always so worth listening to, especially the middle-aged and onward who have the balance of experience. A word here, another there, and fabric for the city's history, political, social and intellectual, was gathered for the weaving, as time required.

One of these clearly pictured evenings was in the spring of 1875, when Thomas Crawford's heroic statue, The Indian, the gift to the Society from Frederick De Peyster, was unveiled. The hall was packed by an unusual audience that waxed enthusiastic over this majestic marble, which even in this day of changed standards holds its own and will repay a visit to the present building of the Society on Central Park West, from any one interested in the development of American sculpture or the lost possibilities of the vanishing American race. It seemed then as if the revelation of this work by Crawford, who was called by the orator of the evening "the master sculptor of America," was the corner stone of American sculpture itself. New York was the place of Crawford's birth and in New York he learned the technicalities of his art, though his inspiration came from Thorwaldsen whom he met in Rome in his early twenties. He was but a little over forty when he died, but he had achieved the statue of America on the National Capitol, and that of Washington on the stately monument at Richmond, Virginia, beside some sixty more. He married a New York woman and was buried from old St. Johns Church that he had attended when a boy, yet I have met many staunch New Yorkers of today who knew him not, or else confused him hopelessly with his son Marion, the novelist.

Month after month I went with Father quite eagerly to these meetings. The return trip that led us past St. Mark's and its churchyard in the night's quiet—which was then, indeed, silence—was always fraught with the thrill of mystery. I would cling to Father's arm and walk a space with closed eyes, trying to picture when this was the heart of gruff old Peter Stuyvesant's pleasure farm, his "Bouerie" with fruit and flowers and grassy paths reaching up into the wild, well-nigh untrodden fastnesses of Manhattan. I sometimes wondered if Peter would not like to come out of the family tomb and kick away the enclosing barriers with his wooden leg and call the present-day New York to order with sound Dutch oaths?

Often we had company across town, Mr. Bryant, whose house was west in Fifteenth Street, or Dr. George Moore. One night they both bore us company. It was in early April, we walked quite slowly, for Bryant was growing a bit feeble and showed it in his gait in spite of his unbending austerity of will, so that Miss Julia, his daughter, often relied upon Father to see him safely home. It was in these many homeward bound walks that I came closest to this poet whom most of the world thought cold, because his personality was always wrapped in a cloak of reserve, which was not pride or self-consciousness, but like the shyness of the very young who hesitate to express themselves in words. In walking through the quiet streets at night, however, he often spoke what was in his mind without forethought, even his very wonderments being those of straightforward unsullied youth, with the added yet slight tinge of an austere melancholy belonging to one not wholly in congenial surroundings and always beyond them. "Thanatopsis," the crystalization of his young soul, serves as an expression of his mind for all time.

One night in particular do I remember; it was in the early spring, I think, of that last year of his life, 1878. There had been a meeting of the Goethe Club—a small group of the lovers not only of Goethe but the classic literature of Germany—that met chiefly in private houses. We, Father, Mr. Bryant and I, crossed Fifth

Avenue at the middle sixties, and walking down the Park façade paused near the spot where now stands Sherman's statue. Leaning on his cane, half in meditation, half to gain breath—for subtle change was coming over this rugged man now well past fourscore—he looked about, first into the Park and then at the line of Fifty-ninth Street, where the first building, on the site of the Plaza Hotel, was rising above the lower roofs behind it. Sighing, he said, "They have covered the earth and now they are reaching up to the clouds. I shall not see it, nor you, Doctor, but," turning to me, "you may, when this beautiful Park, this gift, blended of nature and art, to the people of New York, may be surrounded on all sides by buildings eight, nay possibly ten stories in height, until the spirit of the Park's loveliness will go from it." I have lived more than long enough, and I have seen the poet's prophecy come true. The spirit of the Park's loveliness has indeed passed with its once splendid trees, as if, dryadlike, it could not forsake them. This particular evening on the return from the Historical Society and suggested by St. Mark's graveyard the talk turned on monuments, hero-worship, and as to which had the greater potency in attracting, valor or romance. The final judgment is forgotten, but I remember one remark of Dr. Moore's: "They say that of those who visit Old Trinity, ten pause at the simple slab of Charlotte Temple and again return to it, for one that gives more than a passing glance at Hamilton's monument. Meanwhile the little book goes on selling by the thousands though published nearly a century ago. Though a real person lived under the fictitious name of Charlotte, Mrs. Rowson's story is the most primitive of romances, while Hamilton himself was mystery, history, and romance all in one. How can her hold, I might say her grip, be accounted for?"

I knew that Grand-aunt Susanna Rowson was Great-grandfather Haswell's sister, also that she had made history and fought with William Cobbett, and Mother had a copy of Charlotte Temple among her family treasures, but it was so badly stained and blurred that I had never had the perseverance to more than glance at it. I must ask for it and go to the stone that so rivaled Hamilton's. I too began to feel a curiosity to know which way the roots of me were grounded and in what direction the tree top might chance to grow. In the sun of course, I thought, with plenty of room and plenty of air! Then and there I prayed that I might be let grow in the open and never be like Stuyvesant's old pear tree, which, though long cherished, was enclosed by streets and finally replaced by a stone monument.

I suppose that unless one has grown up in an overpowering and almost restrictive atmosphere of heredity, the desire to investigate one's roots, and, feeling them, test them out as moorings, does not come until life becomes somewhat serious. I was seventeen when I first felt this impetus and it was born of a blending of the Historical Society, a love of all things romantic, and the sending to me as "an omen" by Great-aunt Rebecca Clark of a cornelian pin that had fastened the velvet headband that Mme. Rowson was wont to wear, and a copy of the life history of Mrs. Rowson that had been printed from private family papers; this because of some girlish verse that I had written which pleased Aunt Clark.

Next time that Father travelled far down town I went also, to wander about the churchyard of Old Trinity while he had some affairs in near-by Wall Street. From the Astor House, where the Sixth Avenue cars stopped, we sauntered pleasantly down Broadway, pausing as often as I could reasonably manage it, for after that almost fatal day of Father's Alpine climbing, a heart lesion had followed and fatigue must be avoided with as little visible curbing as might be, while thus feeling that I could help, made our precious friendship doubly close and dear.

Halting at a curb stand where, in addition to papers, dime novels new and old were sold, Father picked up a rather ragged specimen and held it toward me, saying, "Take it with you and read it while you wait, the print is vastly clearer than the one your mother has." It was indeed a copy of *Charlotte Temple!* Less than a hundred pages bound in dull lavender paper, on the front a half length woodcut of a young girl, her short curling hair topped by a hat with three Prince of Wales plumes. *Munro's Ten Cent Novels No. 7* above the picture, the title below, and George Munro & Co.'s Ten Cent Publishing House for the Millions, but no date. On the title page: *Charlotte Temple. A Tale of Truth*, By Mrs. Rowson, Author of *Victoria, the Inquisitor*, *Fille de Chambre*, etc.; below, a verse foreshadowing the moral of the story:

Her form was faultless, and her mind,
  Untainted yet by art,
Was noble, just, humane and kind,
  And virtue warmed her heart.

But, ah! the cruel spoiler came—

I own many other editions of this book, including the first English printing of 1794, bought at the sale of Augustin Daly's library, but no other has the meaning of the dime book, read for the first time in the close of Old Trinity.

The church gates were locked, but in the vestibule Father found a verger who let me in, closing the gates behind me but telling me to come to a rear door when I was ready to leave, for he would be near, as there was to be a wedding in the noon hour. There had been some recent pillaging of mementos by relic hunters, it seemed, and at the time there was no outside watchman. For a while I wandered to and fro looking at the various monuments and simple headstones grouped about the church as if seeking sanctuary from troublous times after the old-world meaning of the word. Almost every class of service in the freeing and upbuilding of New York was represented, and yet until I reached my destination I think that the simple slab of William Bradford, the first printer of a city paper, of whom I had only lately heard through George Moore, appealed to me the most directly.

There was very little street noise even from busy Broadway. A curious group was swarming about a novel vehicle for New York, a private hansom cab, the so-called "London gondola," imported probably by some wealthy man of "the Street" eager to outdistance his social rivals. Pigeons flew overhead and settled here and there to pick at the bits of food left from lunches that passers-by had thrown to them; they tiptoed about prettily, cooing, a pair or two preening as if with mind to mate. A lonely robin perched in some overhanging shrubs, no doubt a bird of passage only. Then I came to the stone I sought, flat on the ground, only the dateless name—Charlotte Temple—and spreading my coat upon the dry rough grass close by, for it was a day when April played at being May, I began to read. An hour passed and the chimes were ringing noon when I had finished the story, simple and direct in everything but the stilted wording of the time. "Are you for a walk?" said Montraville to his companion. "Are you for a walk, or shall we order the chaise and proceed to Portsmouth?"

With this the narrative begins. Two English officers, about to sail for America; a group of young ladies from a boarding school, encountered as they leave church following the school mistress. Glances exchanged. One officer impressionable and foolish, his friend calculating and heartless, both careless of consequences, as happens on the eve of war. An unprincipled governess in charge of the pupils, thirsting for adventure. An evening meeting or two arranged by her, an elopement of the governess and Lucy (the Charlotte of the book) to Portsmouth, thence to New York. Treachery of governess, treachery of friend, whom Montraville believes too easily when it suits his convenience. Montraville, about to marry Julia Franklin, while in a strange but humanly inconsistent state of mind often found in a weak but plausible character who really believes himself excusable, writes this bombast to Charlotte in a letter she never received: "Can I, dare I tell you that it was not love that prompted the horrid deed? No, thou dear fallen angel, believe your repentant Montraville, when he tells you, the man who truly loves will never betray the object of his affection!" Which must have reflected the curious attitude of the day in placing the entire responsibility for seduction, as Susanna Rowson before leaving England lived where viewpoints were a matter of observation, not hearsay. Destitution and despair of Lucy follows, now abandoned by all concerned; then the birth of a daughter, and the arrival of the distracted father from England before Lucy dies. The pitiful funeral in Trinity churchyard almost at dusk. The arrival just before the burial, of Montraville, who has meanwhile married. He has learned of the schemes of governess and his friend to defame Lucy, who was attached to him alone—of letters undelivered. A dramatic and extravagant scene at the grave between lover and father. Returning to his lodgings Montraville finds his faithless friend (Belcourt) and challenges him—again following the actual wording:

"Belcourt was intoxicated; Montraville impetuous: they fought and the sword of the latter entered the heart of his adversary. He fell and expired almost instantly! Montraville had received a slight wound, and overcome with the agitation of his mind and loss of blood was carried in a state of insensibility to his distracted wife. A dangerous illness and obstinate delirium ensued during which he raved incessantly for Charlotte; but with a strong constitution, and the tender assiduities of Julia, in time he overcame the disorder. He recovered but to the end of his life was subject to fits of extreme melancholy, and while he remained in New York, frequently retired to the churchyard, where he would weep over the grave and regret the untimely fate of the lovely Charlotte Temple."

For a little space I remained, seated on the ground, in part stiffened by crouching, in part almost rooted by thoughts, that flew to the time when the now important church and graveyard had been the centre of a straggling village, and that one of my own far-away kinsmen had been the bombastic, faithless lover, fighting a duel and then weeping at this very grave. For a "tale of truth" was Charlotte Temple, born Stanley, and Montraville, Aunt Rowson's own first cousin, John Montressor. There is some strain in the blood of each one of us either to be developed or driven out, and we alone can do it for ourselves. Herein lies freedom of will, the will to choose. Had Father put a paper-covered sermon in my hands this April morning? He sometimes preached thus silently.

After the carillon had ceased and the noon hour struck, organ music came through the now opened doors of Trinity. Choir rehearsal, I thought, then I remembered the wedding. At this, some carriages, not very many, drew up before the church and the wedding party passed quietly in. It was a cheerful family group, well-bred and free from ostentation. The bride in a travelling costume had one little attending maid, perhaps younger sister, who carried a basket of roses, and as the bride crossed the vestibule I saw that the child was clinging to her hand. It seemed but a short space before the organ pealed again and suddenly the carillon pealed joyfully, in recognition, I found, of the marriage, howsoever private, of a daughter and son of old New York!

In going to the carriage the flower basket had let fall a single pink rose. Seeing my eyes fixed on it the verger, who had now come to release me by the nearest gate, handed me the flower. "One minute, please," I said—and going back I laid it on poor Charlotte's stone in the little groove where once the metal tablet with her name had been, that it might last the longer for moisture lodged there.

Ah! the mystic magic circle of the wedding ring! No logic, law or psycho-analysts will ever break the subtle meaning of it. "With—without? Without—with?" called two bells, as the chimes dropped away. "With!" rang the single bell.

XX

THE BUYING OF BOOKS AND WHAT CAME OF IT

ONLY when schooldays are over does one really begin to live as an individual. Then the school process, a background that has shut in and limited the horizon, breaks away like sunrise clouds before clear daylight, yet leaving, if one is fortunate, impressions and motives that walk out into life, keeping pace with one as invisible kindred belonging to the clan of fairy godmothers.

The chief of these new pacemakers was Love o' Books. Not alone for the matter they contained, romance, history, pure literature, the natural sciences—all these were long-time friendships beginning in the days of *Alice's Adventures* and *Little Women* and *The Legend of Undine*. The arrival of *Our Young Folks*, that delectable yellow-covered monthly, was an event. Indeed there has never since been quite such a lovable magazine for youth. The direct boy side of me revelled and swam through the serials—*Winning His Way*, *Afloat in a Forest*, *Jack Hazard and his Fortune*, Aldrich's *Story of a Bad Boy* and the like, while *A Summer in Leslie Goldthwait's Life* and *We Girls* set my heart beating decidedly *girl!* I have some well-worn volumes of *Young Folks* now and the thrill still lies between the pages, or else, is it in me? For I feel it as I open them each time. Second childhood? May be—if so I'll answer joyfully "Yes" when the roll of second youth is called. *Round the Evening Lamp* kept one content to be there, while as for the department for

Young Contributors, did they not send me a wonderful two dollar check for a poem, which so elated me that I must have been temporarily unbearable?—*but* the magazine was discontinued before it was printed!

The new love of books, which not only for their contents, but for the shape, size, feel and type, enthralled me and still does, was born of the dainty well-bound, well-printed volumes from which Clarence Cook had read to us at his literature class at Number One Fifth Avenue. His Chaucer and Shakespeare, in English editions, by their form seemed to give more meaning and importance to the text. His Tennyson also, in tree-calf covers, printed on heavy paper in clear text, was such a contrast to the odd volumes of our own copies, "pirated" editions and printed cheaply, like so much of the work of overseas authors before the honor of publishers and the law of international copyright prevailed. Then and there I joined minds with Father in the reclaiming and reclothing of his library. From the beginning he had always bought books, and Mother gladly pinched to have them, if it came to a choice between this or that. Uncle Isaac, who haunted auction sales in Boston, sent books on sometimes in barrels, but though usable they were chiefly poorly printed and "foxed" copies, which through being in damp places showed the offset of the text that blurred each opposite page.

At this time a new peal of joy bells rang for Father personally. Mr. Rhinelander added a library across the entire end of the Eleventh Street house, and at the same time an old parishioner in Providence left him a handsome sum of money "for some personal use" which made the replenishing and furnishing possible. Then there began a joyous hunting, and, within bounds, free from qualms about the cost of ammunition!

At last Father would have an adequate place for his treasures instead of the long-time condition of books, books, everywhere but where they could be easily reached. Books to be really friendly should be as high as one's heart, when sitting or standing, but never above reach of hand. For to mount a ladder to converse with a beloved book is as awkward and chilling a formality as to compose a love letter by consulting a dictionary. Mother entered into the sport, in so far as it permitted a move up from the basement dining room, the old back-parlor study taking its place. Also she rejoiced at the freeing of nine-tenths of her closets from the overhanging menace of books, that when hastily replaced often came tumbling down on her head when she opened a door that was not well hung and bound at the top. Also she was always glad of anything that gave Father pleasure, but aside from this she could never understand quite why he preferred to collect, as the term stands, one by one, volumes that had been printed many years and have them rebound, if necessary, rather than go to a bookshop and buy something fresh from the press, in commercial garb, or a new subscription edition sold by an agent of glib speech. In this she was thoroughly feminine, for it is something, this collecting of books and almost greed of touch, that many admirable housewives not only misunderstand but quite resent in their mates. So when we went a-hunting, Father and I, we were a bit careful not to bring the game home in too large quantities. It did not look as profuse on the shelves as in a package!

Then followed halcyon days, two or three each week, between times of special Sunday preaching, lectures, or writing. The sales catalogues of libraries from the various auction marts piled upon tables and overflowed onto the floor, in company with the thin, ill-printed, paper-covered monographs in German that were being constantly sent up by Christern or Westermann, costing, it seemed by the bills, several marks a leaf. For after Father's visit to Berlin in 1869, where George Bancroft was then American Ambassador, Father's interest in German philosophy was revived, though he was far too sane and American to be upset by it. Yet he did go so far as changing the name of the country rest home from suitable Mosswood to pompous Waldstein, which word was interpreted by an Irish dog fancier who wished a local name for registering our St. Bernard and suggested Waldstein, "which I do hear be's the Dootch for sthone fence!" However, a stone-mason's chisel restored the name Mosswood at the beginning of the World War. But I believe that this one emotional exception was necessary to prove the rule of Father's straight thinking.

We would often start the week by going to see pictures, the Tenth Street Studio being the first stop. We did not go as guests to an exhibition, but passed in and out, having the advantage of watching creation, as it were. Le Clear worked there with his portraits, father being one of his sitters, Albert Bierstadt sometimes doing a wide canvas of western scenery, or sometimes an almost *genre* bit of detail such as an eight by ten inch sketch, "The Golden Gate"—the entrance to San Francisco harbor. Appreciating our admiration of his treatment of light upon the sea he sent the painting around to the house before we returned, with this message on a card: "What one truly appreciates is a part of one—so this is yours and your words are therefore mine." Hall's smooth still-life work, full of color and cheerfulness, held me, as did J. G. Brown's impossibly clean newsboys and street gamins, plus the always appealing haphazard dog. Of course time and a better sense of values have led beyond both, but how pleasant it is to have been able at some time in one's life to be frankly pleased, without the required responsibility of the criticism that study brings! Whittredge's exquisite landscapes, his New England woods and brooks, remain as true as does the sunlight that flecked the tree boles and filtered through the birch branches. I never could understand how, seeing beauty as he did, his face had such an eager sadness, for he rarely smiled—perhaps because the thought that he must earn money by his work was ever present, and it is difficult to "aim a star" with the dollar mark intercepting the vision. Beard's animal combinations were always amusing, but when Father craved something of past times we would go over to Fourth Avenue where Louis Lanthier, a dealer, who had both an intuitive sense and a picked-up knowledge of art, kept a curio shop and a small gallery of really worthy paintings, gained by importation and the flotsam and jetsam of exchange.

Schaus, now that America was ripe for pictures, showed the cream of foreign ateliers, the time being over for copies of paintings in the great European galleries, or Prang's chromos. Then Leavitt's Sales Gallery on Broadway was also a stamping ground, and I think that it was there that I first saw and craved a Winslow Homer, "Rocks and Sea," and learned the rich sunset glows of J. Francis Murphy's early period. The S. P. Avery Gallery, too, made a specialty of exhibitions, when possible, of the portraits of Copley, Rembrandt Peale, etc. A haze of picture combinations floats about this period, rather unfocussed, but it all nourished, with a craving for beauty, the roots of life that were gripping fast and finding anchorage.

For books David Francis, of course—he was now in Astor Place, having moved since I had saved enormously to buy *Plutarch's Lives*, complete in one large volume, which cost the appalling sum of six dollars. But this was during ancient history year at Number One

Fifth Avenue and the place was starved for books of reference, so that my six dollars gave me the worth-while importance only known to students of that particular age. Scribner's, on the west side of Broadway, was now beginning to cater to collectors and always had several long tables on the main floor where such books were displayed. "Second-hand" books, the unknowing persisted in calling them disparagingly, and wrongly rated them with the junk and waste paper of sidewalk stalls and rag sellers. Scribner's array was fascinating, and a quiet Englishman named Coombs was the human catalogue of it. While Father went about armed with a list, I browsed and again listened, for many other men beside Father gathered about these book tables. One whom I remember in particular (because through him, if two "ifs" had happened, we should have been cross-over kin to a President of the United States, an office then much esteemed) was Samuel J. Tilden, the astute lawyer, famous for his routing of the Tweed and Canal rings. He was very dry and immobile but well-meaning, doubtless; in fact he gave me several valuable books and a colored Audubon print. Occasionally a twinkle would flash from his heavy-lidded eyes, that at other times seemed to be closed at the outside corners, as if to prevent any one from possibly reading his thoughts or getting an opinion in advance. In appearance he looked very much like an old-time farmer come to a country fair, rather than a New Yorker and politician who had been governor; a farmer whose best clothes hung between-times on a nail in a closet but were never pressed. The two "ifs" were, *if* he had married Brother George's beautiful sister Emma, and *if*, after the close election when he ran against Rutherford B. Hayes, the Electoral Commission had not counted him out. His courting, however, came to a much more sudden end, if it could have been said to have had any responsive beginning on the lady's part.

Being a bachelor, for whom a quiet widowed sister kept house, it occurred to Mr. Tilden, that, as he was not an adept at ceremonious functions, a youngish wife who had these attributes would be a suitable addition to the campaign and after. As he was a close friend of Brother George's father, often spending whole evenings at the Fourteenth Street house in playing billiards and chess, his eyes fell upon Emma's blond curls and so falling, decided. Up to a certain point Emma was what was then known as "worldly," and possibly thought it a good thing. She had gone rather quickly through society in New York, *The Black Crook* having had a somewhat blighting effect, and had also "seen Europe." So it came to be a habit with the elderly wooer to linger in the richly upholstered library, where Boydell's Shakespeare had a place of honor on the table, and sitting comfortably before the fire, he waited, when the lady would presently join him.

One night, however, there was no preliminary game of chess. He arrived before his due time and the lady did not hasten. It was cold and the wooer wore heavy low shoes of the type we now call oxfords. Evidently hearing no sound of skirts on the stairs he pulled a deep easy chair up to the fire and slipping off his shoes rested his feet on the fender, stretched them luxuriously and leaning back dozed off, his hands resting on his chest, fingers neatly matched. Presently the lady arrived, glanced into the room and saw no one until an ear-rending snore guiding her, she saw the empty shoes—saw the shoeless feet spread out in their gray woolen socks, and turned and fled. There was no need of a Commission to pass upon this defeat! That the word "worldly" should be forever severed from her character it must be told that returning to Italy a few years later Emma met a very handsome and charming dilettante artist whom she married. He being the nephew of a cardinal, old Roman society received her, and the atmosphere not being that of politics, mere money and gray yarn socks, "they lived happy ever after."

Then came the art, print and book sales at Leavitt's in Clinton Hall. For many years it was quite the custom for women as well as men to go to the sales of rugs, bric-a-brac, Oriental wares and porcelains frequently held there. In fact it was a fashion, a novel form of sport for the women, with a relishing spice of risk in it, especially when at times they would bid against themselves in spite of restraining relatives, being overjoyed at downing a rival at a high price, which rival was none other than themselves. For in spite of good intentions, the best of auctioneers and watchouts could be confused as to the identity of the bidders, when the same woman alternately waved a catalogue in one hand and an umbrella in the other.

Though the book sales were held in the same long hall, the important libraries and collections of prints were received, catalogued, and arranged on the floor above, which contained several rooms. These upper rooms had been something of a mystery sometimes, as when, sitting through an afternoon sale with the Aunties, who, though in the seventies, were enjoying New York to the full and to whom the buying of an occasional rug or some plates at auction had all the reputed excitement of Monte Carlo, I would watch grave and scholarly-looking men climb patiently up the narrow stairs. But I never discovered them coming down; what could be the spider-and-fly attraction? The only one who came down was a slight, tallish young fellow, usually dressed in tweed with a tailless Scotch cap set on somewhat awry, clean shaven save for an unusually well-curved mustache, very heavy brows and sea-gray blue eyes that seemed to take in the whole room and its audience, in the brief time it took him to do whatever errand brought him down to the office. He returned two steps at a time without a backward look.

One day Father and I went up those stairs and discovered for ourselves the secret, which was that of a trusted few being allowed to examine at their leisure and intimately, the rareties of books and prints before the dealers and the general public had their turn. Nowhere did I see Gray Eyes, however, and wandering about I presently discovered a small room full of odds and ends that interested me but were not books.

"Just rubbish that comes mixed in with things of value; when the place gets too full we pitch them out," said a coatless attendant, pausing in his job of unpacking a case in which every book was carefully wrapped and padded at the corners.

"Could I go in there?" I asked. "Sure, if you don't mind mice; only it's mighty dusty."

I went, poked about and stayed, retrieving a small vial of almost powdered old glass that showed exquisite opalescent colors when shaken, some lumps of amethyst and rose quartz, a stuffed humming bird, one glass eye missing, and last of all a small tree branch about which a glistening-scaled black snake was coiled. Time must have passed very quickly, for after I had brought the plunder into as good a light as possible I realized that the afternoon was waning and that the gas was lighted in the long room, where Father was one of a small group to whom the gray-eyed man was showing page by page some book of great value as to contents and binding also, as there was a piece of velvet on the table where it rested, and he held a crumpled-up silk handkerchief in the hand that turned the leaves. Later I learned that it was a very perfect tall copy of the

First Folio of Shakespeare! Then I was only amazed at the youth of the man about whom graybeards were gathered, taking counsel in booklore; I had thought such people must be old like Dominie Samson, dried-up, black-beetle sort of folk.

The book being closed and put away in a safe, the session ended and Father came to look for me, my whereabouts having been told by a backward jerk of the thumb from the man unpacking the cases. Slowly Father and Gray Eyes strolled toward me, Father evidently explaining my mania for collecting anything belonging to outdoors for my treasure room up in the country. I began to feel rather foolish, as if I had been caught playing with dolls, I who had passed my nineteenth birthday. Moreover, though I had had no "coming out" like other girls, I had gone to a sleighing party at Christmas where we all went in cutters and soon lost sight of the chaperone's slow double-horsed team, the lady then having wisely returned home and had supper ready; also, in spite of Gatha's eagle eye, I had made a few friends who were not "Willie boys," and I had received a basket of Maillard's bonbons, little tongs and all, twice in one week, and some written valentines!

Father introduced me as "my out-of-door girl," adding, "Are you going to try to carry those things home? If so we will have to leave some books behind, so I can lend you my pockets. I draw a line at the snake, however, for you can prove yourself beyond a doubt a daughter of Eve without its company." As I came forward and Gray Eyes saw a fully grown person and not a little girl, as he evidently expected, he looked amazed but the only part of his face that laughed was his eyes and they fairly danced. The humming bird could not go in a pocket, so when he took it over to his desk of many drawers and cubby holes to find a box,

I ventured to ask the name of some golden brown flowers that filled a cylinder-shaped vase of blue Sèvres porcelain standing next his inkstand. They looked rather like single stocks done in velvet, but the perfume outranked the freshest violets—something quite unforgettable.

"They are wallflowers. At home in England they grow wild everywhere, in every wall chink that holds moisture, though the finer sorts belong to gardens. Here they are forced indoors like these; they tell me the winters are too sharp for them outside"—and he handed me a few sprays. "I knew that you must be English from your speech," said Father, "and for the reason that few native-born men, as young as you are, know books, old books, so well, so thoroughly. You must lack many years of thirty. Are you here to stay or as a bird of passage merely?"

With the merest shrug and a sudden sadness falling across his face he said slowly, "I do not know, time must settle that. I've been going to and fro these eight years. My mother, a widow, lives in England and she has an older son—to an American, however, that fact means but little."

"And what do you like and what dislike most among us?" asked Father, with that bid for criticism so prevalent among us even to this day.

"What do I miss would be the easier question," he answered with a ready tactful wit. "In spring cowslips and wallflowers, then deep shady streams where one can row a boat for miles, also the lack of organ music such as we may hear in every cathedral or minster the land over."

Then fell silence, for this was unanswerable, and taking the carefully done-up box from him we went down the mysterious stairs, now often to be trodden, Grey Eyes following, for it was the hour for closing, though he said that at times of important cataloguing he would return and work late into the night for the sake of quiet.

"You must dine and spend an evening with us when my bookcases are in place," were Father's words as we parted on the sidewalk. But beyond a slight bow that might be taken as assent, he said neither yea nor nay, and never looked at me at all.

XXI

TRANSITIONS

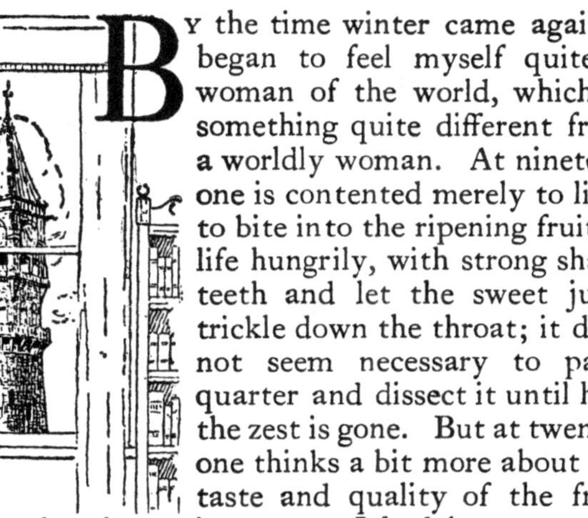

By the time winter came again I began to feel myself quite a woman of the world, which is something quite different from a worldly woman. At nineteen one is contented merely to live, to bite into the ripening fruit of life hungrily, with strong sharp teeth and let the sweet juice trickle down the throat; it does not seem necessary to pare, quarter and dissect it until half the zest is gone. But at twenty, one thinks a bit more about the taste and quality of the fruit and as to what is coming next. I had been to some good parties that first winter, besides the so-called "sociables" where the neighborhood young folks danced, ate ice cream and cake, or, if the occasion was a birthday or the like, wine jelly and charlotte russe, and reached home not later than eleven.

Eighteen seventy-eight and nine were years of turmoil in my New York, not unusual at the end of a decade. The time-honored custom of making New Year's calls in flocks was dwindling and becoming confined to the elderly, and in restricted localities, for the growing city was rapidly dividing east and west of the Park, while at the same time the younger people began to rebel at the monotonous round of either receiving or making duty calls, and the competitive excitement of having the longest list was dead. Then the entering wedge of holiday parties in the country began, which, proving so delightful, has finally disrupted New York's week-end social life.

The evening reception, attended by the family friends and visiting guests of various ages, fathers, sons, mothers and daughters, the women hatless and with elaborately dressed hair, still held sway in some sets, but afternoon teas began to appear, and spread quickly in popularity like grass fires, for at these teas bonnets and street dress might be worn and several visits accomplished in a single afternoon without dragging out the family men, though some old beaux and professional men attended the function. Yes, I said bonnets, for the head part of my modest outfit contributed by the Aunties consisted of two bonnets from the elect Misses Dorsey in Twenty-second Street, born Philadelphia gentlewomen and the last word in conservative headgear. For morning wear a gray felt trimmed with garnet satin ribbon. For dress, a black velvet poke with a fall of peacock-blue satin pleating, both being tied firmly under the chin, the first with short, the second with long, sashlike strings.

The general afternoon tea was probably the evolution of the St. Valentine "Kettledrum," a form of entertainment for the benefit of a charity, begun very simply back in the middle seventies, and ranking next to the Charity Ball as an important function, it being socially desirable to be upon the list of managers of either.

Two very distinctive evening receptions punctuated my first winter; one was given by the Cyrus Fields in November at Gramercy Park for Arthur Penrhyn Stanley, Dean of Westminster Abbey, who had received Father so kindly nearly twenty years before. The second was given by "the Owl," Frederick De Peyster, at his great bare house in University Place, for President and Mrs. Rutherford B. Hayes, Mother letting me take her place as I was very anxious to see a President of the United States, other than bluff, everyday General Grant, almost at whose feet I had chanced to sit tailor fashion, on the rough platform when he laid the corner stone of the American Museum of Natural History back in 1874 and I had as usual tagged along with Father, who was one of the speakers.

My ideal President must be a man with Washington's dignity and Lincoln's humanity; but since that night I have not cherished official ideals! The room was filled with expensively dressed women, the custom in skirts being that, much beruffled, they should flop on the floor at the front and sides, so that each step was a kick, while a train, tightly confined above the knees, so as to add intensity to the "bustle" effect, flowed out behind in loose folds like a bolt of silk that had fallen from a counter. The bodices were cut very low and every woman seemed to wear a tight band of velvet, preferably black, about the throat from which a heavy locket, either jeweled or a cameo set in pearls or precious stones, was suspended. The seventies was a locket era, a favorite daytime ornament being a monogrammed tortoise shell locket and chain. Hair dressing was elaborate and much decorated, and fans of spangled tinsel or ostrich plumes waved everywhere—why, I do not know, as the house was of the temperature known to seldom-used drawing-rooms where we sometimes called and the maid would light the fire while the hostess was making ready to come downstairs.

There had been some previous entertainment, I think at the Academy of Music, and these guests were late in gathering, so while I stood for a few minutes in a corner of the stairs I had a fine chance to see them before they merged in the crowds already in the parlors. Moving slowly through the rooms I looked anxiously for the celebrities and found myself being presented, without realizing it, to a most ordinary-looking man, bearded, of medium height, with hair neither short enough to be neat nor long enough to be picturesque. He wore an evening suit of a general looseness that suggested he expected to gain much flesh while in office. There can be quality even in the most casual grip of hand-shaking; it is better for men having moist hands of a flipper consistency either not to remove the glove or merely to bow. The formal greeting was followed by a sneeze, the pulling of a voluminous silk handkerchief from the coat-tail pocket, and foghorn blowing of the nose. Mrs. Hayes was what is termed "motherly" by the kindly critics when describing a middle-aged woman who is inadequately dressed for a particular social function. She was wrapped in a vague cream-white gown, long of sleeve and high in the neck, except a slight turning away at the throat. She smiled pleasantly, oh! such a weary smile and said, "I'm pleased to meet you, but are you not *very young* to keep such late hours, my dear?"

The changes that affected us all the most came from the greater elaboration of living that followed when the "sheep of the golden fleece" had begun to assert themselves, and the frank and cordial understanding that had existed between congenial groups of widely different financial standing was being upset. A new and quite un-American way of making money on the one hand and being received socially on the other, developed quite under Mother's Roman nose, the founder of the new order being none other than a friend of her early Boston days, a woman of fixed position and ancestry, but who lacked the money for liberal New York living. One day an invitation to a reception came from a mother and daughters, almost strangers, who had but recently moved from the Middle West; enclosed in it was the card of Mother's one-time Boston friend. People were puzzled, which of course piqued curiosity. The house of invitation was of the best, and fashionably located, so people went to see for themselves. The music and collation were well chosen, perfect and subdued, and by the time that it had leaked out that the introduction was a purely financial arrangement, an investment like the buying of stocks, many people had become involved and the deed was not only done but served as an accepted precedent.

There was much that was amusing and interesting in our own New York, however, beside the drama, opera, or parties of any kind; pleasure that could be had for merely the capacity of receiving it, little bits of the byplay of home life, among people of the old school. Up on Madison Avenue, Number Seventeen, facing the square, lived two loyal parishioners of middle age, stately gentlewomen, and the very old gentleman who wore a stock and whom in their youth their father at his death had left their guardian, the time never having seemed ripe for the arrangement to end. It was a household that would have given Thackeray finely drawn backgrounds. They lived in steam-heated rooms, had thick velvet flower-strewn carpets, and double windows between them and any possible fresh air. They dined off a rich porterhouse roast of beef every Sunday the year round, a thick soup, four heavy vegetables, three kinds of dessert, nuts, raisins and sherry wine—they disapproved of green vegetables and fresh fruit as too acid. They were immensely charitable, the household ran as if by machinery, and the lights were turned out at precisely 10:00 P.M. Notwithstanding this, twice a year revelry broke into, or rather out of, this clockwork establishment, and in strikingly opposite directions, one revel being the day of the Coaching Club parade, and the other the eve of the annual ball of the Sixty-ninth Regiment, the celebrated Irish "Fighting Sixty-ninth," as it was and is still known the country over.

As the start of the Coaching Club was between the Union League Club and the Hotel Brunswick, and the coaches had a way of wheeling around the Square in forming, Number Seventeen was a very likely place for observation. Each spring Gatha, Bea and I, when my time came, were invited to ask as many as twenty of our friends to a luncheon, banquet would be a better name, at Number Seventeen. All prejudices against food and fresh air were put aside for the time, their wide windows were thrown open, and for one day we were all young together. We came and went as we pleased, walked out and returned, vying with each other in naming the different whips and seeing who would first spy De Lancey Kane with his famous coach, the "Tally-ho," which soon came to be a name given to these coaches in general.

The ceremonial preceding the ball was more private, though Mother had seen it on several occasions. The family coachman of Number Seventeen who drove the C-springed, high-hung, blue-satin-lined carriage was no less than Major Patrick Phelan of the Sixty-ninth and a war veteran. Miss Mary and Emmie's personal maid was Bridget, his far-away cousin. Each year Bridget, though grown middle-aged in service, was given a new gown of whatever was the latest material and mode, to wear to the ball, the making being superintended by the ladies, who dearly loved fussing with the pretty finery they were loath to give up.

When the night came, Bridget's hair was arranged by a professional, and a florist's bouquet appeared at the right moment, which was handed to her by the old gentleman of the stock, when she appeared in the long parlor that she might be seen by the ladies and also see herself reflected in the wide mirror between the windows by the dazzling light of the crystal chandeliers. Presently the door bell would ring (this was a part of the "ball night" ceremony) and Major Phelan in dress uniform would enter, his wife on his arm, a second bouquet being in readiness for her. After the trio had been sufficiently admired they left for the ball in the satin-lined coach, driven by the Major's understudy. There was no breaking down of formalities the next day, and no aggression on the part of either coachman or maid, who always spent that night at her cousin's, so that the ten o'clock closing hour might not be broken, or the other younger maids be obliged to wait up. A latch key? Even Old Gardy himself was not allowed one!

Behind this kindness and recognition of family service must have lurked a desire, an instinct, for the dramatic, that has survived, for now a great-grandniece of the two dear ladies is Constance Binney, a charming woman and more than clever actress, "The Sweet Little Devil" of a year or two ago.

The Century Club also furnished entertainment to us as well as to Father. After the monthly Saturday nights we would wait up (for midnight was "waiting up" then) and gather about, Mother, Gatha and I, to hear what he called "his story." Sometimes it would be told before the fire in the precious new library. Later, however, when Father began to grow tired so easily, he would undress, put on his "double gown" of Mother's making, and we would come about his bed where, resting comfortably, with lights out and the fire for cheerful accompaniment, he would tell us of every one he had met that evening (and in those days the Century was the place where the worth while of all professions and crafts foregathered), what they had said, and what the trend of public opinion was upon any current matter of importance, ending with telling who had prepared some special novelty in the chafing dish for supper, while he had thought it wisest to keep to a few raw oysters and a single glass of sherry. Thus Father brought his friends home to us, many of whom we could not otherwise have known, sharing his man's world with his women. Ah! those happy Saturday nights! Memories? Yes, but realities as well.

The library meanwhile was nearing completion, that is as far as filling the shelves; such a thing as a general library is never really finished, it always moves on ahead, though one of specialties may be, and these too often the owners, having no more worlds to conquer, wish to sell and begin at some other angle. At least that is what Evan said. Evan? That was my name for the blue-gray eyed old-young man who lived with the books over at Clinton Hall. No, it was not his own name, but one of a flower-loving Welsh kinsman, Evan Campbell, which he used sometimes in writing odd bits of book lore for his amusement. Seeing it signed to something that he sent Father to read, I christened him privately, for it has always been my habit to have my own names for people I like. Did I like this bookman? Rather, I think, from the beginning; at least we both liked and disliked the same things, and that makes friendship. Also Mother and Father must have liked him, for they let me go to hear *Pinafore* with him, without a chaperone, the first winter that it came out. It was at the Standard Theatre at Thirty-third Street, close to the present Herald Square. If I remember, Verona Jarbeau was in the cast and Mrs. Whiffen was the jolly, plump, ogling Little Buttercup. It surely marked transition, this going alone. It was not done then in New York, though if you lived in Brooklyn, even on the Heights, you could, and nothing be said; quite the same as if you were in the country and went buggy or sleigh riding. To be sure it was only to a Saturday matinee, which is a poor substitute for coming into the brightly lighted streets when a play is over, still it was a big jump. I'd never done it before except with a very safe, much older, family friend, who, strangely enough, was also a great book collector. But as I have noticed, ever since I can remember anything, Mother was always one page at least ahead of the times—that is, with one exception—woman suffrage—which brings up an amusing happening at our house a few years back of this time when we still were degraded by using the basement dining room, and the so-called back parlor was the formal study.

The *dramatis personæ* at the start of the scene were Miss Elizabeth Peabody from Boston, George William Curtis, Father and Mother. Miss Peabody was for equal suffrage, as was also Mr. Curtis, politely but firmly, suavely and immovably. Father was neutral, or you might call it wobbly, if you did not know him. He wished woman to have every possible privilege but did not consider this to be one. Mother, notwithstanding her pluck and her nose, was against it tooth and nail. The conversation was growing heated in spots, though Mr. Curtis with charming serenity kept rancor from entering. Presently at the moment that he was leaving, as he went out the door he let in Robert Bonner of the New York *Ledger*, who, though quite an all-round sport, often dropped in to chat with Father, for they were good friends.

The smoke of battle was fast clearing, but of course Mr. Bonner could discern ruffled feathers and the expression of his face was a question mark. Miss Peabody was rather short-breathed at all times, so Father explained, saying that his wife was a privacy-loving woman who disliked publicity of any sort, and that her hands and heart were more than full as matters now stood, etc. Mother very quietly and logically gave her reasons in very few words, adding as an afterthought, "One right I do claim for all married women, the right to have and hold, or if they do not have it, to earn it, a bit of money not given them by their husbands, of their unquestioned *own*—to make surprises with"—she added, her mouth smiling at the corners as she glanced at Father's rather bewildered face, until he remembered the Pickens money and the joy bells of it and returned the smile. Mr. Bonner sprang up and said, "Mrs. Osgood, if you will put all that you have said on paper, sign it and let me print it in the *Ledger* I will give you a check for one hundred dollars before I leave."

One hundred dollars! It meant ten times the sum it would now. There was a moment's silence and I, who was seated behind the study desk, where I was copying some business letters for Father, drew in my breath; of course she *would* write those few sentences. I began taking some suitable paper from the drawer, expecting her to come to the desk immediately.

"Thank you, Mr. Bonner, but it is impossible," she said as quietly as if refusing a second helping of pudding.

"But, wife"—began Father and then stopped suddenly.

"Why not—what are your reasons?" persisted Mr. Bonner.

"The ones my husband gave you for my objection to woman suffrage—" and Mother put her finger on her lips, though in another minute the old dimples broke out, and the corners of her mouth which the Roman nose guarded loyally, and everyone began to laugh, even Miss Peabody, until the purple wistarias hanging from the back of her black lace poke bonnet waved as if in a high wind.

. . . .

There were many things that made a change in the Rhinelander Gardens that would mean little now when everyone is more or less on the move, but seemed very serious in the seventies. The city was beginning to move uptown slowly but surely, and only needed to gain impetus to make it a rush. Something as impossible to be stemmed by any group of individuals as for a person to think by sitting down on a moving stairway that it will stop. The Union League Club had gone from Madison Square to Fifth Avenue and Thirty-ninth Street. The Century was stretching itself uneasily in its Fifteenth Street quarters; house rents were rising and apartments, called at first "French flats," were becoming more and more general, and offered temptation for the easier housekeeping that in the end breaks up all real home life. Then too the little group that had gathered in our old study and once made the winter evenings so charming, was dissolving, nay, had dissolved; Bryant was dead, Bancroft lived in Washington, Curtis came up less often from Staten Island, and the younger, energetic group of which E. C. Stedman was quite typical, came now only by invitation or appointment, having no leisure for dropping in. In fact the old custom of making evening calls, husbands and wives together, had also fallen into disuse, and one might know a woman fairly well and yet have never met her husband. However, in these days the new library was a household magnet that made up for many other changes, and through one of its windows the face of the clock in the graceful tower of the new Court House at Jefferson Market kept us time true. Even Gatha, who resented innovation and change of any sort, took pleasure in arranging the books evenly, neatly, as they were wont to be shifted and pushed back at random.

When Father, his hand cramped by writing and the day's work being over, would go out for a short neighborhood stroll, Mother would come down with her sewing; not "fancy work," so called, but always some useful garment as in war days, though of daintier fashion. For now that even I, the youngest, was well out of hand needlewise—or supposed to be—though it was almost proverbial that I did not love my needle and was much more dexterous in the use of hammer, rake or spade—there were grandchildren coming on who needed stitches. Sister Bea had, beside Edmund, a second son, Father's namesake, and a little daughter. After Mother had sewed a while in contentment, I could see that her ear was tuning for the sound of Father's latch key and his step in the hall. It was in these days that I learned, as far as might be, the secret of the love that bound them without fetters, the wonder of the true married love that is really like music or art, a form of genius, inborn but to be developed by counter-personality and care. It is beyond all else to have been born of it, and so surrounded as to breathe its atmosphere. What other inheritance could be so precious to a girl groping her way to complete womanhood? I was then but half conscious of its subtlety—but now I know. Of this love, sex is but the blending ingredient, not to be suppressed, neither made the whole of life. And where are we now drifting, back to phallic worship and paganism, led by the young Bacchantes as scantily clad as of old?

Sometimes on his return Father would bring home some pears or other fruit, which even in those later days was a winter luxury to us, and, taking out his pocket fruit-knife, which most men carried then, would peel and quarter a pear or one of the rusty-skinned Florida oranges that were crowding out the woody-fibred and often juiceless Havanas, and feed Mother bit by bit, so that she need not soil her fingers, she taking more pleasure in the action than in the fruit. One of these intimate days, when Gatha had gone out "paying calls," as the round of uninteresting brief visits with card case in hand and the hope of speedy release was called, the talk turned on love and marriage, something that never flourished when Gatha was near.

"How can you tell when you are glad to see a man, to be with him and hear him talk, and love has never been spoken of, if it is love or friendship?" I asked at last.

"Your heart will tell you—that is, if you have not tossed it to and fro in idleness until it has ceased to feel."

"Then stop a bit until your head can read clearly what your heart really says," amended Father. "A man must love his work, be sure that it is his vocation, and in seeking his wife be sure that she understands his work."

"And he, hers," said Mother, stabbing her needle into her emery cushion and putting down her sewing.

"Of course an even balance is understood."

"With a decided tip toward the love side of the scale," added Mother.

"With a decided tip toward the seriousness of gaining butter for the bread," said Father, his nose twitching at the point, as it did when he was suppressing a smile; I could always tell by this, even when a small child, if he was serious or only thought he ought to be.

"You can spread butter thinner than you can love and not notice the difference half as much," replied Mother, dropping her work, basket and all, on the floor, and leaning over Father's chair sealed his mouth with her crossed palms so that he could not answer and thus she had the last word.

I being at the very end of twenty, and allowed to go that night to the Seventh Regiment Fair alone with Evan, and even have supper there, quite agreed with Mother, and now being old I've never changed my mind.

XXII

ONE AND TWENTY—

Any other year in my life might have been lived again through imagination or make believe, but for me one and twenty stands alone. For me it was a year of reconstruction, for during it everything that had been or was to be, ended and was reborn. Late that autumn in the country, the dearest of the group we called the Aunties slipped away, so gently that we scarcely knew when, holding the while two of my tea-rose buds in her hand. Gatha decided that for her, the going should be followed by that which Aunt Harriet spent her eighty years of life in dispelling—gloom! Then Mother said to me, "This is your first year of free life, my daughter, make the most of it." So each one living by an individual light went her own way, which left me doubly Father's going-out companion.

Edwin Booth was in New York that season, playing at the Grand Opera House, his own venture of having a playhouse and being actor-manager having failed long since, so we saw him often. For me *Othello* and the *Merchant of Venice* were for the first time. For *Othello* he sent us a stage box, which we did not at all enjoy; it made us all self-conscious, Mother especially, and always afterward we had orchestra seats. It was during this season that it came to Mother and me at the same time, that plays of intense emotion affected Father precisely as did hurrying or going up many stairs, thus making another thing to watch and guard against.

Four parties there were that winter, all different

yet unforgettable, both for themselves and for the opposite viewpoints that they gave, mileposts for me to measure values in after years. The first was at Mr. R's, an elderly retired merchant who had a house on lower Fifth Avenue of the imposing brown-stone type, with a picture-gallery annex. Long a widower, he had recently married his third or fourth wife, I forget which, a stately, placid woman under forty, and the resultant baby boy may have been the cause of the great reception. Though it was not a christening party, the baby was exhibited in one of the upper rooms convenient to the ladies' dressing room, in a bassinet rich with point lace and ribbons. I suppose that the whole affair was really to show that the old man had started life anew and wished everyone to know it. The guests were of all ages and qualities; if one could not find someone congenial with whom to foregather, it was surely not the fault of the host. Yet it was a rather awkward sort of mixture for both host and guests, and proved the need of the entire separation of ages in entertaining that was a distinct mark of the eighties, so soon to come in. The people who desired to play whist found youngsters using the cosy corners for little flirtations; the couples who wished to dance in the picture gallery where the orchestra was stationed found serious-minded people critically examining the pictures without the least idea of hurrying. The only unoccupied spot that I saw when I came downstairs, having made my proper entrance as best I could—meanwhile losing sight of Father, who was a bit ahead of me in the crowd—was on the top step that led from one of the drawing-rooms down to the picture gallery, where between the velvet-covered handrail and the base of the arched entrance was a delightful nook from which I could see every one and everything.

The "Prodigal Son's Ball" were the words that

came into my head at the moment, without rhyme or reason, for moralizing never entered my head that winter, yet by that name I always think of this evening. Many flowers, music, warmth, lavish gowns and jewelry all combined and made an aroma, both mental and physical, a sort of exudation of humanity, that I cannot explain and yet was all pervading. I did not like its effect upon me. I was asked to dance, but I refused, I scarcely know why. I was fond of dancing itself, but I never came to like the parlor or house version of it. I suppose it was that the fine floor, wide space, freedom of motion and well-trained partners of Dodworth's dancing school had given me an impossible standard; even Evert Wendell with all his skill was not the same at a house dance, though under any circumstances it would be impossible to have imagined him either "breathy" or breathless like so many partners. Home dancing to me seemed very much the same as putting a girl who had known the horseback freedom of the country roads and open fields, to amble round and round the tanbark of a riding school.

Time passed quickly for me, nevertheless, and yet there was no special arrangement or focussing of events until supper was announced, silently, by the appearance of a procession of French waiters, this type now being seen quite as often as the genial colored men who once were thought indispensable. Some sort of lemonade compound had been served during the evening, but now the popping of champagne corks could be heard above the march music, for there was a partial attempt to follow the time honored custom of the Grand March to Supper, even though it no longer led down the basement stairs. Father found me and said I would best leave my nest to see the splendors of the table, which I did briefly. Beside the usual dishes, hot and cold, fried oysters, chicken salad, truffled boned turkey, there was terrapin over which the older men seemed to gloat. To me, who always had loved to have something to take home ever since the days of the ruffled mottoes at children's parties, the wonderful assortment displayed of what might be called food souvenirs seemed most entrancing. Not only was there a centerpiece of mammoth size made of little individual panniers of glacé fruits, held together by spun sugar that could be easily broken when the moment came, but there were silver épergnes of elaborately wrapped, cap and costume mottoes, with trifles in French jewelry attached, and imitation bric-a-brac made of nougat—such as paper weights, little boxes and the like.

"Could you get me any of those?" I begged Father as we left the table, and luckily I found my corner seat still unoccupied. Of course he could and did, moreover he shamelessly begged and brought to me the share of several other graybeards who had come alone and had no late-in-arriving young daughter who, on festive occasions, had always stayed awake to ask, "Father, have you anything in your pockets?"

I enjoyed the supper immensely, all but the terrapin which Judge Dudley Field insisted that I should try. The trouble was I did not know how to eat it and my mouth was filled with little bones, that might have been the claws of baby chickens. Then I paused for rest and leaning back in my nook, spread my best lace-edged handkerchief in my lap to sort and arrange my plunder. It was wonderful! If gathered up at the corners, the handkerchief would be full as an immigrant's bundle. I even meditated borrowing Father's unused one (Mother always saw that there were two fresh handkerchiefs in his side coat pocket before we left the house). One piece of nougat took my fancy particularly, it was a little book, the covers mottled to imitate marbled paper, the back being of dull green sugar. I would give that to Evan. Yes, we were very good friends, though he did treat me like a child. Sometimes we went to walk, after the organ music at Trinity of a Sunday afternoon, down to the sea wall at the Battery, to see the ships come in and the gulls dive for the wastage thrown from them. The last Sunday he had tucked a bunch of violets into my muff, so why not put this into his pocket as exchange? Friends could give and take flowers, or sweets, or books. Of course anything to wear or jewelry was different, quite different. Then I suddenly realized that the days were growing so short that these after-service walks must soon stop.

A new odor was filling the room; first I sniffed and then I saw. All about, especially up the sides of the stairs quite to my feet, were champagne bottles, some in napkin petticoats, some without, and more or less empty. As I was thinking of Gatha's one riotous song—"Champagne Charlie," not considered quite the thing even in private—something dark wrapped in a heavy garment swooped over me, and with a pair of green-gloved hands seized my handkerchief by the corners and whisked it and its contents away, saying, "You can give me these, for you are young and can get plenty more!" I must have exclaimed aloud, for Judge Dudley Field came quickly up the steps and seeing my flushed face asked, "What is it? Are you ill?"

"Oh! Judge, a woman in a black cloak and green gloves has just come through that door and taken all the things you gave me from off my very knees—they were in my new lace handkerchief and she took that too. She did ask me for them, but I could not speak. See, there she is over there, the one with that funny lopsided skirt. Oh, please, *please* stop her, she is going home, I think!"

The judge took one look and laughing, I then thought

heartlessly, said, "That is Mrs. ——" mentioning the wife of a distinguished American diplomat abroad. "I cannot stop her—nobody ever has been able to! I shouldn't be surprised to hear some day that she had rushed St. Peter, taken his keys, then pushed him out of the gate and locked it."

I really felt like crying, but then I remembered that grown women did not do it, at least at parties, besides I now was without a handkerchief. Shaking my skirt a bit, and making ready to go as I saw Father coming toward me, I felt something in a fold; the nougat book had escaped! At the worst I had something to exchange for a posy, and in three days it would be Sunday.

The next party was an "evening at home" at the Bottas' in Thirty-eighth Street. "Professor and Mrs. Vincenzo Botta at home, at eight o'clock, to meet Standing Bear, Bright Eyes and some members of the Indian Commission," so read the invitation written on a calling card. Could there have been a greater contrast than between the Prodigal Son Banquet and this gathering of generally informal and wholly interesting people? The rooms, the typical parlor, library and extension dining room of a house of usual width, were in a sense perhaps shabby, the floors covered only by Chinese matting rugs scattered here and there: a few bits of bronze, a head of Dante in marble, some pictures, a desk, not set in order for a party, and well-used books filling irregular shelves. Standing Bear, much over six feet in height, was a very good specimen of a picture-book Indian, well chosen by those who wished to interest us of the East in matters relating to justice for the Red men. He gave the usual talk about the Father at Washington, the Great Spirit and the White Brothers, which his wife translated, going so fast that it appeared she must have learned the little piece by heart. She was really pretty, and also the picture-book type both in face and clothing—a really possible and acceptable Minnehaha. It was not anything that they said that gave the gathering the decided atmosphere that it possessed; it was the lack of affectation and the interest in life in general that seemed to possess the guests. I, who always felt it difficult to begin a conversation or remember what I had meant to say when started, found myself talking volubly to a young Irish poet with red hair and a lovely buttery brogue, several minutes before Mr. Stedman introduced us at the moment when we were in the midst of a discussion as to what constituted a shamrock. I said that it was a clover, almost like the small, crisp-leaved white clover that in America follows where leaves have been burned. He said, "No, it is not like anything outside of Ireland." At this juncture Mr. Stedman beckoned to another young fellow, tall and with a sharply bent Adam's apple that acted as if it wished its owner would swallow it but he couldn't, and said "Here is a Scotch botanist, born in the United States and living in Canada, he can tell you"—which he proceeded to do, via precise dry details of order, genus and species, at the end leaving us where we started from our own a priori, both right and both wrong.

"Stupid, very!" does some one say? No, different, something to think of, and presently when the Indians had gone on to the next house where they were to speak, for they would not stay to take the usual party food, Professor Botta himself gave a charming reading from Dante's sonnets, first in English then in the unctuous Italian that comes the nearest to making Latin a live language.

Supper? There really was none, except dainty little ices and sponge cake, passed about by the hostess and the guests themselves. Also on the sideboard there was a coffee urn and some old Italian wine to which those who wished might help themselves. We were at home by eleven. And the next day the Irish poet sent me some clever little lines, via Mr. Stedman, "To the Irish Shamrock that grew in America."

Christmas came, Christmas, 1879—among other things I had eight lace or lace-edged handkerchiefs, all much better than the one Mrs. —— had waylaid. The story of my bewilderment and the lady's audacity had been spread and much enjoyed by those who knew her. These being old friends of Father's, they had attempted reparation. Evan sent me a set of Tennyson, an English edition bound in tree calf rather like Mr. Cook's, yet far finer than his copy. I looked to see if there was anything written on the fly leaf—yes—but only my name and the date.

"Ellen," said Father musingly, as he handled the volume as if looking for a particular poem, "if I remember rightly, the first book that I ever gave you was a Tennyson in two thin volumes bound in boards. A strange coincidence; how history repeats itself."

"A coincidence that merely goes to show that this generation holds Tennyson in the same esteem as did our own," replied Mother, for some reason rather crisply—suddenly the room seemed to grow strangely chilly, though there was a hearth fire.

The third party was in the afternoon, brief and called in my memory book, "The Tragedy of the Green Lemonade."

Much interest was being aroused at the time by a collection of Japanese bronzes that had been brought to New York by an expert who not only lectured upon them but upon Japanese manners, customs, beverages, etc., it being the vogue to have him at tea and informal receptions. To such a one at Mrs. Dinsmore's were we bidden. The atmosphere of Oriental art was rather unintelligible to me, though I could appreciate the lovely metal work shown, without interpretation, and being very thirsty, I found a seat in a quite empty side room where was a large punch bowl of translucent greenish lemonade, and some quite small glasses, presided over by a Japanese in picturesque garb. As soon as I entered he offered me a glass of lemonade on a curious tray, dragon's tails forming the handles. I sipped it—there was barely enough to call it drinking. It was delicious in spite of its odd color, smooth, almost oily, so I held out the glass for more, then a third time. Why were people who had everything to do with so stingy with mere lemonade? Then again seating myself I wished that the window could be opened a bit, for the beverage was the reverse of cooling. Suddenly there was an explosion of light somewhere, and my knees seemed to strike my forehead with great violence! Then a great ball like a gigantic soap bubble was whirling about, of which I was the centre! Through its rainbow hues I saw some people enter the small room, among them being Judge Dudley Field. He spoke to me, but I could not answer, my tongue seemed larger than my mouth and quite filled, but I must have looked toward the punch bowl pathetically.

"Have you been drinking that?" I nodded yes.

"How much?" I managed to raise three fingers.

"Good heavens, child, it isn't lemonade, but if I guess rightly a mixed punch they are using now, a combination of fermented cucumbers and rice, and devilish strong. Let me see, what can I do for you?" Realizing the source of the misery gave me control of my tongue, at least. "If you can, would you please navigate me back to Father?"

This the Judge did with due caution, pausing in the hallway to give me air, yet chuckling meanwhile.—"Here, Doctor," he said when Father was located, "is a girl who had enough sense left after drinking arrack and sake punch in mistake for lemonade to ask to be navigated to her father!" But I did not laugh—to me it was real tragedy.

Immediately after New Year's, promise of a fourth party arose over the edge of my horizon, pleasant as the full moon on a cloudless summer night: A theatre party, and it was to be for my birthday, the twenty-sixth of January. The first real party that I had ever had. Eight people—four girls, four men—two carriages, a box at the new Gilbert and Sullivan opera, *The Pirates of Penzance*, and to return home afterward for supper. This much was already planned, the make-up of the guests was left to me, not that the choice of real mustached men (not "Willie boys") was any too large. I was too much surprised to realize this party at first, then it began to dawn upon me that some one beside Mother and Father must have planned it. Sister Bea, of course—she was always thinking of some one's pleasure. Bea confessed to speaking of some festivity but her idea was not a theatre party. Then when the tickets came and Father put them in his desk I saw the business envelope they were in was Evan's!

With *the* day came flowers and candy, then candy and more flowers, the last of these being a wonderfully built-up bouquet of the new long-stemmed roses held by an inverted white satin petticoat, heavily fringed, while a shower of white jasmine sprays prevented any stiffness of effect. I groped among the blossoms for a card, but could find none, until examining them one by one, drinking in each separate perfume, I located a few sprays of wallflower and with them was Evan's card: "Best wishes for perfect happiness." Well, what more could be desired? Perfect happiness! Exactly what would perfect happiness be—anything that I had not already?

The party list was made up and every one accepted,

Helen, Jane, Edwina and I being the woman half; the men a physician, a publisher, a lieutenant in the navy who was at home on a furlough, and Evan. Eight people, two carriages; where was there room for the chaperone? Who was she to be? Sister Bea, of course. But mother and Bea decided that very morning that there need be no chaperone.

I have not the least remembrance of what we said or did at my birthday celebration, I who can remember with photographic clearness other happenings of trivial importance from the very dawning of memory. I do know that we all flirted in a very harmless way and tried to be at our several bests, that we enjoyed the *Pirates*, though *Pinafore* outshone them. That mother and Bea managed a delicious hot supper, and after it my health was drunk in tiny glasses of old port wine that had come down to Uncle Charles from his father Gideon Soule of Exeter. Also that the girls stayed at our house that night and of course we visited from room to room, chattered and did not go to sleep until early morning, yet breakfast was at eight the same as usual.

A few days later Evan happened in to tell about a painting that he had located which Father was anxious to see. Father had not yet come home though it was late afternoon, and as we went into the library together Evan drew a chair before the fire and an unwonted silence seemed to fall between us. To break it I brought out a set of books, *The Broadstone of Honor*, that had come from the binder that day, the manner of work and tooling having followed Evan's suggestion. In examining the workmanship with a professional eye and folding back the covers to see if the books opened easily as they should, a volume slipped almost to the floor; we both reached for it, I caught it, and at the same moment Evan's hand closed on mine—closed but did not at once relax its grasp. Ah! in that one single moment I knew what in life came next—the Fairy Prince and he was Evan! Father meant well by head's giving advice to heart but it was not a matter for advice. It simply *was!* Father came in and presently, having an engagement that prevented his taking dinner with us, Evan left. Did he also know? Had he no fairy godmother to tell him the tale of this Prince and whisper to him that I was the Princess-in-Disguise? Atop of this flashed back what months ago I had heard him say in general conversation, that he was planning different work and would likely go home the following summer to stay.

Where were my godmothers, Love o' Laughter, Love o' Nature, Love o' Home, that they did not help me? Must I doubt their power, or now having come of age, would they abandon me?

Quietly Love o' Home, coming behind, took me by the shoulders, turning me about very slowly so that I must look at every object in the room and looking thus remember for all time—Mother coming in freshened for the evening, wearing a lace fichu about her neck fastened by the cameo cherub pin, Father's gift after my birth and meaning me—Father putting aside the evening paper at sight of her. Then Love o' Home seated me gently in the armchair that Evan had drawn toward the fire, and pressing a strong hand on my shoulder, whispered, "Wait!"

XXIII

APRIL RAIN

GLOW of June weather followed Easter, even though it gave place over-night to the sharp, swift slants of April rain. It was on a Monday evening, well do I remember the day, as following a Sunday when Evan had neither come to renew, as we might, the sea-wall strolls, or made any sign whatsoever. One final festivity there was for me before the earlier going to the country that was planned on account of Bea's children. This was a great charity bazaar at the Madison Square Garden.

We had gathered in the library after dinner and I was experimenting with a costume to be worn at a booth where Helen, Jane and I were to appear in fancy dress. Mine, guided by the material available, was forced to be on Spanish lines. A crimson crepe shawl fringed and heavily embroidered, a black lace scarf and high comb of tortoise shell belonging to Grandmother Murdock, high-heeled black satin slippers, and a pair of castanets. I was posing and prancing about gaily while a discussion went on as to whether rouge was permissible as long as it was in character, for since I was naturally dark and with little color the vivid red of the shawl increased my pallor. Bea said yes, of course, no one would criticise me for using it in such a part. Suddenly Mother went forward to the parlor and opening the piano began the liveliest of tunes from memory, half country dance, half improvised tarantella.

Being in the mood I danced until I was quite breathless, and fell down exhausted on the rug at Father's feet.

"You might have been an actress, among other things," said he, smiling, as he fingered an artificial red rose that, with the comb, caught the lace about my head.

"Why, Father! Have you forgotten that I did want to act four years ago, even before I had given up wishing to be a surgeon, when I realized that I wouldn't allow any liable-to-be-fidgety-at-any-time woman to use a knife on me? Don't you remember? You let me ask Mr. Booth and he said that I had voice and go but that with my stocky frame I would never get beyond low comedy?"

"How about your 'one night stand' and the ragbag gypsy part that nearly made tragedy of a comedy?" asked Bea, who now lived only a block away and often came over after dinner. Then even Gatha laughed heartily with us. As for the "One night stand" it happened in this wise. When our group at school, who went to Number One together from various parts of Eleventh Street, were round about fifteeen, we were seized with the infectious plague of private theatricals then raging among our elder sisters, who had formed a really rather clever Comedy Club. Our scope for plays, as well as actors, was decidedly limited, but we picked out a very simple "for home use" gypsy play from *Our Young Folks* that only required four characters, and as for the chorus the play might be done either with or without. Ella M. was the gypsy mother, Constance B. (whom Boldini has since painted, giving her the real gypsy diablerie) was the tender-hearted daughter, Gertrude W. the kidnapped child, but who would be the wicked kidnapper, the gypsy man? He must, according to the directions, among other things wear "short ragged pants of some coarse material," and there was also a great deal of scowling, muttering and desperado near-swearing in the part. The girls would none of it, and the only "Willie boy" available was a blond and stuttered dreadfully when embarrassed. So I rashly said that I would be the gypsy.

Then it occurred to me how about the pants, of what could I make them? The big square store closet in the upper story of the house (once the hanger for hoopskirts) was always an inspiring sort of junk shop, so I retired there to look about. As I sat on a trunk the family ragbag caught my eye. It was full to the bursting point and as it swung from a bar opposite to me rather suggested a man on the gallows, for it was both black and long. Trousers! the very thing! Going downstairs very quietly I obtained scissors and sewing materials and locking the door set to work. First I emptied the rags in as compact a heap as possible and laying the bag flat on the floor planned out the pants. The bag was oblong and square at the four corners, and the string already there would hold it about the waist. Then cutting the bag across the bottom I split it up halfway in the middle to form legs—not realizing until I came to sew them that their shape was like that of a paper doll, with no room for sitting!

The garment was smuggled down and added to the other duffle that I had collected and I went over to the Mitchells' house to rehearse. Everything went extremely well, except that a musical finale, called "Home Again! All Their Weary Wanderings O'er," which we applied to the Jolly Brothers Galop, was keyed too high and ended in a squeak. But that was of small account and we might hit the key better on the final night.

The audience, to our astonishment, numbered about fifty adults besides the young people and as we peeped from behind the curtain, recently a bedspread, our excitement became intense. All went fairly smoothly even to the song, but as the outwitted bandit turned to stride off the stage with a final showing of teeth and growled "Ha! Ha!" the applause went wild. The actresses bowed, but the applause continued,—they wished the bandit, it seemed, so I returned, bowed properly and repeated my exit, when the applause was mixed with laughter and cheers. Then the unexpected reality of my character study of rags became evident, for owing to the lack of anatomic regard my sewing had given way in spots and my red flannel underskirt, which I had tucked up but not removed, was oozing with startling realism in several critical places.

. . . .

We sat a long time before the fire, we five, those that had been the family before sister Bea went away and breaks began to come. The April rain fell softly on the flat tin roof above the library, and then dashed in sudden capricious floods against the windows. The well-ordered books looked primly down at us and the newer furnishings grew more familiar and inviting. We babbled on familiarly about this thing and that, little bits of the past, and half hopes, half wishes with more ambition in them for the future. Bea said, "This room is 'the study' again tonight. Library, as we call it now, is the right word, of course, but the old study, with its old furniture and shabby books all tumbling about, seems more a part of our real selves."

"It will take a year or so to make me feel at home in the new environment in spite of my great satisfaction in it," said Father, looking about him and then at us, I thought a bit wistfully. "Do you know, Mother Bea, your eldest son regards my new desk as sanctuary and has chosen a little drawer in which he hides his treasures safe from the smaller children? His confidence is a great joy to me."

"If only you could have had this room and greater

leisure for your writing ten years ago," said Mother, who could never free herself from the thought that Father had delved so hard for a mere crumb of the loaf from which she had seen others cut thick, well-buttered slices with small exertion.

"Wife," replied Father, flashing quickly from his mood of revery, "no one should ever complain who has never had a wound through the affections," and as his eyes held hers, all rebellious and ambitious regrets faded from them; for it had never been for herself that she had wished for anything.

The talk about the old study bore us all back about the fireplace that was the centre of this Land of Memory. Those who had gathered there from time to time represented all creeds—from the Paulist Fathers Hecker (once of the Brook Farm cult), Baker, Hewit, Deshon, Father Bjerring of the Orthodox Greek Church—Julius Bing—Emma Lazarus the Hebrew poet of vision and charm and one or two mysterious Oriental gazers into the crystal ball and such. At first the fuel had been unblinking coke, hot, glowing but imperturbable, held in a high-barred grate, having no air of cordial invitation other than being warm and that the equally unsympathetic iron fender-bars made a convenient foot rest. Emotional Liverpool coal soon followed, then wood chunks led the way to the real hearth fire of wood in the new library.

Once when I was well under ten and had been allowed to sit up beyond my allotted time, Mr. Bryant had arrived, the first of the group that gathered weekly of evenings at our house. I stood in awe of Bryant in those days, yet not exactly that, but something half-way between awe and thinking from some of his ways that he might be kin of the "Old Father William" quoted in *Alice's Adventures;* for the story was still fresh in my mind about how one bitter cold winter night he had refused the hot oysters that Mother had cooked in a "blazer" (mid-century for chafing dish) and asked for an apple and a glass of water! In telling of it Mother said that the apple was so cold that the skin squeaked as he pared it, and Bea had remarked that if he enjoyed apples and water, next time we had better give him apple sauce and be done with it.

This evening he had been less aloof and more human, so that I had dared stand by his knee as he asked me what I liked best in the country home. I said birds and wild flowers, and also that I knew "Robert of Lincoln" by heart. He smiled as if pleased and began to repeat the poem, slowly and without inflection of any kind. "Why doesn't he speak quicker and make the bob'o'link fly faster?" was the thought that has always remained. He has ever been to me a poet of written thoughts without poetic personality.

Father said, "I knew Bryant as well as any man, he opened the Gate Beautiful of woods and fields and left it open for all to follow, but the poetry of Nature came slowly, the American Puritans spurned it—yet withal Bryant was a Puritan, a Puritan Greek. His letters were almost commercial in their directness, but once in a time affection and the poetic mood came to the surface. Do you remember this?"—turning to Mother as he ran his hand through a package of letters in his desk drawer and took out a small sheet covered with the familiar writing and read it aloud. "I think it would be difficult to find a note more spontaneous or subtly expressed."

Roslyn, Long Island, N. Y.
June 10, 1875.

Dear Osgood.

This is the holiday of the year, and I want to see you at Roslyn and hear some of the good talk which you always bring with you, such as Cicero heard from his friends at his villa of Tusculum, such as Cowley delighted in at his retreat at Chepstow and Milton celebrated in his elegy on Lycidas.

Next week the strawberries in my garden, already pouting and reddening, like offended babies, will have come to a better temper and will sue to be gathered, and the late genial rains promise an abundance of them. Any day after Tuesday. What day shall it be? Come for as long a time as you are able. The visit will not be half made if you do not stay two nights.

Very truly yours.—

W. C. Bryant

Though it was yet early Father presently started upstairs to bed and I, taking off my finery, made a pile of it on the couch end, when slipping down behind, it lay unseen. So after going to the door with sister Bea, when Brother George came for her, I went upstairs without returning to the study, quite forgetting the Spanish costume.

It must have been nearing daylight when Gatha called me. Father was very ill, in great pain in his chest and had difficulty in breathing. I must dress quickly and come down to be with Mother while Gatha with one of the maids, would go at once for Dr. Draper, who now had left Twelfth Street and lived up and across town. This was before the day of house telephones.

Could this be the same Father who had laughed and shared our half silly gayety only a few hours before? For a long time I held his head against me trying to ease his breathing by rubbing him gently between the shoulders, for Mother, usually so efficient, seemed paralyzed. Then the doctor came. It was, he said, congestion of the lungs from poor heart action. Half the day they worked, Dr. Kinnicut joining Dr. Draper. There were no trained nurses to be had then, only a willing, stupid woman who upset things; but we would rather be alone.

Father was yet conscious, and his eyes wandered about the room and fixed themselves first on Mother then on me, so speakingly that I wondered if he was thinking of that other day when he, Mother and the doctor had waited my coming in the selfsame place. A hearth fire burned as then, wood logs now replacing coal. The windows were open. "Fresh air and his body kept warm," was what the doctor wished.

"We are doing our best," said Dr. Draper gently in answer to Father's questioning glance, "but"—he hesitated—and the old-time sense of the responsibility of the physician to the patient asserted itself—"you are gravely ill." With a lovely smile Father said, quite clearly, "After God, ah! what it is to have faith in one's physician!" Then turning toward her he groped for Mother's hand.

There were many things to be done below stairs—dispatches to be sent—that I could do, stone bottles and jugs to be looked up to hold hot water to keep an even temperature within the bed. I could work but not sit still, and Dr. Draper's exquisite face, outlined against the window and now supremely sad, turned toward us and with merely a move of the eyes told us to go—that this was Mother's hour.

It was late afternoon, when being in the study replenishing the fire and trying to fix my mind on what I must get ready for the night, I heard Evan's quick light step come through the room; he put aside the separating curtain, stopped short at sight of me, and suddenly held me in his arms.

"Who—how did you know?" I half whispered.

"Know? Why, your telegram. I came as soon as I received it"—and he held the yellow paper toward me. "Surely you must have sent it."—"Father is dying, come."—Through the confusion of the past few hours it drifted back to me that in sending others I had done this almost unconsciously through the intensity, the bitterness of my need.

"I do not know exactly why I did it; I was sending some telegrams for Mother—and I—I really do not know—I had to see you."

"I know why it was sent. It was to give me the courage to say what I have not before dared—that I love you—though the words have been in my heart and on my lips these two years past. Now they are spoken once for all. Tell me what I can do today, and from now on—how best help you? How help your mother?"

Night came and the watch meant simply a shift of physicians; Gatha arranged their food and all through the night every half hour Evan went from the kitchen up the stairs with the refilled hot-water bottles which I took into Father's room. At four o'clock sister Bea returned and they forced me to go to my room and lie down. This I did without undressing.

It was gray morning light when I awoke and saw that Dr. Draper was holding my hand and smoothing my forehead very gently, that I need not wake too suddenly. He did not speak words but his face told me—Father, my friend, my chum, had slipped away with the dawn. For a moment all I heard was the soft insistent fall of April rain and then I realized. "What must I do?" I asked the doctor, who said that he was going to stay a while with Mother, for she was utterly spent.

"The next thing, now and ever,—there will be always much for you to do."

I stumbled half blindly down the stairs, dry-eyed, grim, unthinking, and as I reached the top of the lower flight I heard strange voices. Already people were coming and going in the hall. Through the widely open doors the sun's rays over the low house tops were scattering the gray clouds and showing the blue through the last slant of the rain. At the stair foot stood Evan, his face clear cut and very pale. He had been out evidently to breakfast—and to freshen from his night's watch. As he looked up and saw me, in his eyes there shone the light of that perfect understanding that alone is everlasting love. As I went down, the open door framed the wagon of a flower peddler banked with belated Easter lilies and great trays of pansies in flower. The moist air held and brought in the fragrance of violets? No, not violets, wallflowers—of which there were a few fresh sprays in Evan's coat.

Quickly he led me back into the study and motioned that I must lie down. Beyond the sofa's end were heaped the gay clothes I had worn two nights before. A lifetime lay between; I could not look at them—the things became so vivid and alive. Then as he prepared to go, and to come between me and what must be done, drawing the curtains again that I might not be disturbed, another panic seized me. "Soon you too must go away—home—you said—this summer."

"You are my home," he answered gently, and then the curtains fell behind him.

As a vision of healing it all revealed itself, and with it tears came. Father in going had not closed the door, but in passing held it open for the coming of another whom he trusted, that I might not be left alone.

XXIV

TOMORROW

AGAIN it is April. Today I have been in New York striving to piece together a patchwork of the city that I knew. It is forty-five years since that other April day and twenty years since we left the Rhinelander block. Downward from Forty-second Street the taxicab pushed its way slowly along Fifth Avenue.

At Thirty-fourth Street I asked the man to turn west to Herald Square, where, a score or so of years ago, one New Year's Eve Evan and I had gone forth from the cheerful Dutch Room of the National Arts Club on the street's north side, where the Gilders, Stedman and others were of the company, to mingle with the jovial throng gathered to hear midnight clanged forth by the hammerers of the bell upon the Herald Building, while the bright-eyed owls ranged above the coping winked and blinked after the fashion of electric lights, some wisely and some quite frivolously. Now shorn, despoiled of these ornaments, dismantled, dwarfed and shabby is that building; a hundred office signs of incoherent trades tell of the decadence of what, when the giant presses working in plain sight behind the polished plate glass windows, was one of New York's sights.

The Arts Club itself, a most informal meeting place, more evenly balanced between wielders of the pen and brush than now in its Gramercy Park home, frames pictures both grave and gay. I see Walter Damrosch seated at the grand piano playing the accompaniment to his newly composed music for Kipling's "Danny Deever," at once stirring and descriptive in the highest degree of the frightful emotions of the poem. Carleton's deep, rich voice enunciated the words that stabbed like bayonet thrusts. "Tremendous"—said a man's voice almost in my ear, as I clung trembling to the end of the piano, toward which the crowd had pressed me. I was much relieved at the finale to see that the speaker was Charles R. Miller, the well-seasoned editor of the New York *Times*, who stood wiping drops of sweat from his forehead, drawn forth by the music's power.

A shift of scene—a social afternoon to introduce one of the parents of the New England story of pent-up-morbidity, Mary E. Wilkins Freeman, now come via New York to live in New Jersey. Like many others I asked the inane question, "How do you like New York?" "Oh, pretty well," she replied, "but of course it's crude to Boston." Yes, these were her exact words, for I wrote them on a card before I had a chance to forget or inadvertently mend the sentence.

At Twenty-sixth Street we turned and skirted the north, east and south sides of Madison Square; complete obliteration of the landmarks. The Brunswick gone, the Garden where Evan and I had rubbed noses with the dogs at many a show and watched Howlet handle the reins over some perfect hackneys, were a mass of wreckage. The block of good old houses where was Number Seventeen spotted with trade, and Dr. Parkhurst's church, that long stood the overcrowding and squeezing process, many years gone. The great Barlow house on the north-east Twenty-third Street corner, once a place of wide hospitality, and where was housed the library Evan catalogued with love, coupled with personal regret at its disposal. Gone like the American Art Gallery on the street's south side, where it was sold. No doors of welcome hereabouts! The mid-street traffic gradually thinned, and at Twenty-third Street the sidewalk procession of the workers from the great loft manufactories overflowed the curb line, each side street swelling the tide. Men and women, often hatless, of many nationalities, either foreign born or so saturated by alien heredity that no trace of the smelting process was visible, pushed their way, though in no apparent hurry, gesticulating, aggressive, showing no courtesy to the women of their own breed that swarmed along the gutters, no kindness to the bearded and old that necessity forced among them. To get there first—to get all—was written on every face except those few whose dull stolidity seemed to make them progress only by being pushed.

Twenty-third Street. The Fifth Avenue Hotel, the place of one time respectable revelry and testimonial banquets—long time gone. Gone, too, the Hoffman House, where paintings considered of questionable taste added to the attraction of the famous bar, where Edward Stokes was once host, he whom the lure of Josie Mansfield led to shoot his rival, fat James Fisk, filling the newspapers, as did the Beecher-Tilton trial, with material that barred them from home reading. Now from the lack of novelty both affairs would slip by unreproved in censored movies, if such there are.

Maillard's, that used to nestle at the back of the hotel. A beau who gave Maillard's bonbons was a beau indeed, for the stamp of this shop was a guarantee that those who bought its wares were paying the greatest compliments in sweets that could be had outside of Paris. After a period at Thirty-fifth Street the name has gone altogether from the Avenue.

Down a bit in West Twenty-fifth Street; Trinity Chapel is there. Twenty-fourth Street: nothing familiar. Once the Madison Square Theatre was a stamping ground where for a few years the Mallories struggled with one of the periodical uplifts of the stage, and compromised as usual. *The Merry Widow* with, I think, Marie Jansen, was the last play that Evan and I saw there.

West Twenty-third Street—the Eden Musée—vanished. A raw but amusing edition of Mme. Tussaud's. Here in addition to the wax figures, automatic chess-player, etc., to be seen, the same half dollar gave admission to the concert hall, where one might see Hermann the great magician, or enjoy the half-wild music of the first Hungarian Gypsy Band, led by Muncksy Bela, which made a fame that took it into society where music of this class was a novelty and soon became a vogue, quite supplanting Lander. Altogether this is a street of strangeness; even the memorial tablet placed on the building where once Booth's Theatre stood was blotted out by a commerical sign. A Booth Theatre, a name only, is somewhere up Broadway.

Fifth Avenue again, where were clubs and private homes of generous entertainment. The Roberts House and picture gallery among others are all gone. At Eighteenth Street had stood Chickering Hall, a sociably small auditorium, where a fine concert might be heard for one dollar—Emma Thursby, it might be, reviving the old-time English ballads that had held their place in Mother's early youth; Wilhelmj with his singing violin, Reményi, or lovely Maud Morgan, in classic draperies playing the harp, making a picture of the world's springtime of music, her sturdy father at the organ stirring the depths of harmony in rich accompaniment. Or it might be a choral concert of the Church Music Society led by Dr. Pech, once choir master of Trinity. Here also in June, 1875, many citizens as well as Americans at large gathered to greet Bryant on his eightieth birthday, and give to him a splendid silver vase of classic form into which had been wrought after Whitehouse's design by the skillful hammer of the silversmith scenes from his poems suggested by Father—one of the first achievements of repousée silver work to be done in New York, and now in the Metropolitan Museum, even though the designer was English and the master workman, Soligny, French by birth. Also it was, as I recall it, and the fact brought forth much comment, through Father's sense of fraternal justice that both artist and artisan were on the stage at the presentation.

West Fourteenth Street. Did I ever bring carrots and greens in my little basket to feed the Van Beurens' cows in the pasture just west of the corner? Yes, a memory not a dream, for I yet have the basket!

Eleventh Street. The long remembered "Wicked Church" is there, an organ evidently having sanctified it, an organ too that makes its bid for public service via fine recitals; and at night cruciform lights send their rays above its doors. Should we cry out *too* loudly about the best belonging to the past? Yet I feel about the stoneless churchyard of tombs much as I did of yore. Even more grim, it seems, since I have lived wholly afield, to have one's clay bound down by city weight of the material things instead of making earth under the sweetening air of country skies and wild blown grasses.

Westward to Sixth Avenue. The Hebrew graveyard in its crooked corner stands firm and grim. The wooden gabled Grapevine—the quaint saloon of two stories with its gilded bunch of grapes has vanished, of course, and a block of high buildings begins there. I'm wondering if the branch of Minetta Brook is still trickling through the cellars of this block? Laughing as it slips through the pipeway they had to give it, when they rebuilt, because all the skill of engineers could not safely suppress its merriment.

Cross Sixth Avenue. Of the shops below Fourteenth Street where Evan and I had gone in and out familiarly, Rowland's the taxidermist and naturalist alone had not only stayed but bettered, crossing the avenue and doubling in size; a son was now in charge, but out of the back room came the father from whom years back we had bought the finely antlered head of a Virginia deer, so skillfully manipulated that it seems yet in the flesh. "Oh, yes," he said, when after puzzling for a moment he recalled me, "we are doing well. People get out of the city and go out of doors more than they did a piece back. They set more store by outdoor things. We can't mount song birds and such like any more, and it's a good thing, too. But fur rugs, game, fish panels and all the aquarium stuff more than make up." Another betterment.

West of Sixth Avenue, the Rhinelander Block is there, but how it has shrunk in comparison with its remembered importance! Broken and flapping porch screens and utensils on the upper piazzas give a hint of "light housekeeping" within. Paper slips are stuck here and there on doors or posts—the "Room to rent" badge of decadence. Once, once it all had seemed so big, almost *grand*, as children use the word. Can it be twenty years since a rat coming up the front stairs had given the hint that time was up? For to the thrifty housewife a rat on the stairs is like the sign to a sailor of rats leaving a ship—it is time to go—so we did! Mother, Evan and I.

Again westward in Eleventh Street. Then I had an

argument with the taxi driver. He could no longer follow the route as given because a "one-way street" rule called for the reverse. So we must walk a bit, Margaret and I, and meet him at Jefferson Market.

How pavements rebuff feet used to greensward or earth paths! Another building holding its own and much, much more. St. Vincent's Hospital is many times the size it was that red-letter day (I was meant to be a surgeon and physician, only my sex had played up to the part and street accidents seemed to be my only outlet) when, breaking bounds, I was waiting outside the enclosed hospital yard to see the ambulance enter or leave, and a sympathetic interne who must have watched my interest day by day offered to let me ride beside him across town to Bellevue Hospital, to which place a couple of hopelessly derelict drunks were to be transferred. All would have been well if Gatha had not spied me as we rounded the corner on the homeward trip. Mother was away and Gatha never forgave! Yet what did it really matter, that half day passed in bed? For I was tired out and spent by the excitement and it did not undo the ride, while the thrill of the adventure is with me still. It was a messy, jarring ambulance, those of today surely are a betterment.

What had become of Taffy John? The chubby little shop, I found, was not even a neighborhood memory. With the Brewery, it vanished completely. Now Seventh Avenue is cut through and a way runs bias to Jackson's Square. On a small triangle called Mulry Square a gorgeous petrol station outflavors the butterscotch, fresh cocoanut, blubber rubbers and beer sandwiches of memory.

I turned to look for Jackson's carpenter shop and wood yard where I used to gather up small blocks for playing at building in the days when there were no tractor toys. Alphabet blocks and Crandell's combinations of flat wooden slabs with deep grooves and tongued ends that might be fitted together according to one's ingenuity were all that could be bought. On the site of the yard stands the Sheridan Theatre, an outpost of that travesty of the open fields now called Greenwich Village.

Down a bit to the rear of the Court House, Jefferson Market and Engine Company Number Nine, where I was wont to go in on evening wanderings to feed apples or carrots to the splendid horses. Glittering motor engines stand in their stead, asking feeding and grooming but no petting, yet this too is doubtless a betterment—if only the last of those horses have found some rest pasture and no more of their race are ever forced to strain and slip on icy asphalt streets. We loved horses, so that I wish they might be banned from work in every city.

The mirrors in what was the Columbian Saloon opposite on Greenwich Avenue are dim and fly-spotted. Already reconstruction threatens it. The Y. M. C. A. uses it last, but strangely enough it was much cleaner and better kept under its old vocation, more alluring in every way. Here sometimes in going around to the market I had seen, more than once, a man having an unusually introspective type of face for such a calling, cleaning the brasses, the walk, or sometimes pausing to lean against the wall of the saloon, gazing skyward in a sort of sad-eyed revery, quite oblivious to his surroundings, or the short jacket and waiter's equipment hanging on his arm.

During the last year of the World War, at a reading far away from New York given by John Masefield, I was seated very near to him so that I looked into his face as, with eyes wet with emotion, he read from that strangling poem, *The Widow in the Bye Street.* Suddenly that street scene of Greenwich Avenue floated across between us, for an instant the two faces seemed to blend. Later as we took tea together I mentioned the incident. "Ah, yes," he said, "it was doubtless I, for I worked in that saloon for several months."

Inside Jefferson Market only one familiar name remained above a stall—that of Davis the fishmoner, evidently one of the third generation. The outside flower shop where John Morris, Ninth Ward politician, notary public, etc., held forth, a man of fiery socialistic speech and kindly deeds, who is to be remembered for having sold the freshest, sweetest, largest bunches of the long-stemmed violets to be had in the city for a quarter. The shop is there and I closed my eyes that I might see him standing at the door, but when I opened them he had gone.

To the Brevoort for luncheon. Here was a landmark left, for had not Cooper, Irving, Thackeray and Dickens, all in turn, been feasted there? The building, yes. But at the tables of the café there were but few of distinctly American lineaments, while a few females of cubist build, the new tradition, did most surely proclaim their nationality and rapid emancipation by the awkward way in which they blew out or sucked in the smoke of their cigarettes pushed far from their lips by awkward holders, much as we children used to "make believe" with the long, brown, beanlike pods of the catalpa. Women who smoke should do it as a grace, unconsciously, caressingly, there is no other excuse. Before you become expert, my sisters, you have very much to learn!

Down again past Number One Fifth Avenue, the School That Was. The one time stable alley, always unsavory, sometimes disreputable, where laborers from the streets gathered at the noon hour, rag pickers sorted their plunder and pushcart peddlers discarded unsalable bananas. From the standard of the etiquette of the large classroom that overlooked it, to be conscious that the place even existed was *oban*. Washington Mews: so reads the sign. The Alley, now a narrow open street cut through to University Place, is wind-cleaned and sunny. Improved? Assuredly; the stables, revamped, are trimmed with glazed tiles of pottery, and plant boxes decorate the windows of the miniature apartments, wherein those of real or fancied artistic temperament elect to dwell to get the "atmosphere," whatever that may be. I wonder? This is one of many places threading New York that make those who "have been" confess, that love the past as they may, some much praised things of "the good old days" were shibboleth!

The northwest corner of the Square. What had become of the great Rhinelander house, the house where William the first lived out his long life, keeping his health and pink-tinted cheeks by going, as he often told Father, even on the coldest winter mornings to an unheated bathroom in the basement for a cold plunge, something that at this period was seldom done even by youth. The house has been engulfed by a five-story apartment, another covering the back garden, where was the trellised stable with its arbor of wistaria vines, hung heavy with purple clusters to be annually raided by the "alley boys."

Round the corner to Macdougal Alley, from which O'Connell and his bull dog Hennessy's Mike, alias the Frog, came forth. Here the old stables had been transformed into studios of real sculptors and painters. A new order, a betterment in every way, yet not a part of my New York. Where might I find it? Had it no soul?

"Go to Trinity Church," I told the taxi man.

"Where's he?" he asked in a tone in no wise apologetic. Then I noticed that his features were of the Yiddish type and that his accent matched them.

"At the head of Wall Street, a large church," I said briefly.

"Vall Street, yas I know *him;* I find it." So he did, quite speedily, by zigzagging down the Bowery, past the Tombs and Five Points region, once the famous purlieu, coming into Broadway below City Hall Park and so down without more delay.

"This church? No?" he asked in doubt, as we reached Trinity.

"Yes," I said, preparing to pay him.

"You say *beeg* church, he little! Dose buildings all around, *dey* beeg!" And he sped away with an air of satisfaction at having corrected my description.

Silently Margaret and I went into the churchyard by the lower gate, passed Hamilton's tomb, crumbling in many places, and bound with bits of copper wire like many others of lesser importance. We paused a moment to honor Bradford, New York's first printer, then going back of the church and facing Broadway we paused before a flat slab in the grass not far from the fence palings. "Let us sit down a moment even if the grass is damp," I said, just as I had done when, at sixteen, Father had left me to read Grand-aunt Rowson's simple story of the girl buried there and through it, feel the deep roots of me and come in touch with romance, wrong and sorrow combined. Then the church dominated its surroundings, but now it is dominated and enclosed. Old Trinity *did* seem small. Almost crouched like a thing at bay, holding its own by sheer force of the spirit within.

Yet here was something unchanged—Charlotte's stone, upon which I placed my bunch of country pansies. Oftentimes they say flowers are brought there by those who read the story written one hundred and thirty years ago, but still printed and sold. The oblong hollow, where once a metal name plate had been, was worn smooth by years of weathering. Recent rain had made a little pool of it wherein two sparrows bathed and preened. Presently they flew toward the carved coping above a window across Broadway from which a few straws hung that told of nest making. Life and mating! Ah, poor Charlotte! All the surrounding commercial towers of stone have not obliterated your romance or frightened away the sparrows—who, like you, came from overseas.

. . . .

I am at home again. It is night. A softly cold night of April. The sunset glow lingered on and tinged the northern sky until the frost-pink fingers of a late Aurora picked it up. The hearthfire still smoulders.

The doors are locked and I go slowly up to bed. I am very tired and my limbs are heavy. The young beagle bounds upstairs, pausing at the top to be sure that I am coming, the old dog lagging after follows step by step. What is there left to the woman of forty married years, who must now lock the doors, put out the lights and go alone to bed? For her remains Faith, Love and Work—giving Patience, which is the bloom of Everlasting Hope.

Presently sitting by the window, I look cityward. Have I been there today? Yes, I close my eyes and see it pass before me. Not my New York, of small ways and happenings, but the New York of magic, the Wonder City of the World! Its masonry-walled buildings rising tier upon tier, as if to uphold the clouds, everywhere honeycombed by windows whose lights mingling with the stars at night, tell of unceasing toil. Ah! the stimulation and the suffocation of this city! The incentive and the despair! Good night, New York! *My New York, good-bye!*

Orion is fast stepping his springtime course down the western sky. The circling earth swings toward dawn linked by the endless chain of stars between. Have I slept? Perhaps, I am not sure, it may be only living ahead of time. Yet suddenly the air has the early morning freshness, Jupiter is signalling the sunrise, while a few robins on the wood edge break the night silence by their reveille. The dogs get up, flex their muscles, sniff the air and lie down again. The fragrance of wallflowers comes up from the little frame under the window, the same odor that greeted me at the stair foot that other April morning so many years ago. This poignant perfume is like the dreamed clasp of a dear hand.

Last night I was oh, so weary, but now the wings of my spirit seem freshly pinioned. Another day? A tomorrow? Dear God, there will *always* be a tomorrow—somewhere. Beloved—Good morning!

By

MABEL OSGOOD WRIGHT

THE FRIENDSHIP OF NATURE
BIRDCRAFT
TOMMY ANNE AND THE THREE HEARTS
WABENO THE MAGICIAN (SEQUEL)
CITIZEN BIRD——
FOURFOOTED AMERICANS (SEQUEL)
THE DREAM FOX STORY BOOK
FLOWERS AND FERNS IN THEIR HAUNTS
DOGTOWN
AUNT JIMMIE'S WILL
THE GARDEN OF A COMMUTER'S WIFE
PEOPLE OF THE WHIRLPOOL (SEQUEL)
THE WOMAN ERRANT
AT THE SIGN OF THE FOX
THE GARDEN, YOU AND I
PRINCESS FLOWER HAT
GRAY LADY AND THE BIRDS
THE OPEN WINDOW
POPPEA OF THE POST OFFICE
THE LOVE THAT LIVES
THE STRANGER AT THE GATE
STORIES OF EARTH AND AIR
STORIES OF SKY AND SEA FOR SCHOOLS

UNIVERSITY OF MICHIGAN
3 9015 02454 9068